D1499028

Urbanization and Urban Growth in the Caribbean

An Essay on Social Change in Dependent Societies

Urbanization in Developing Countries

edited by Kenneth Little

V. F. Costello: *Urbanization in the Middle East*
Josef Gugler and William G. Flanagan: *Urbanization and Social Change in West Africa*
Hal B. Levine and Marlene Wolfzahn Levine: *Urbanization in Papua New Guinea: A Study of Ambivalent Townsmen*

Urbanization and Urban Growth in the Caribbean

An Essay on Social Change in Dependent Societies

MALCOLM CROSS

Lecturer in Sociology, University of Surrey

CAMBRIDGE UNIVERSITY PRESS

Cambridge
London   New York   Melbourne

Published by the Syndics of the Cambridge University Press
The Pitt Building, Trumpington Street, Cambridge CB2 1RP
Bentley House, 200 Euston Road, London NW1 2DB
32 East 57th Street, New York, NY 10022, USA
296 Beaconsfield Parade, Middle Park, Melbourne 3206, Australia

First published 1979

Set, printed and bound in Great Britain by
Cox & Wyman Ltd, London, Fakenham and Reading

Library of Congress Cataloguing in Publication Data

Cross, Malcolm.
Urbanization and urban growth in the Caribbean.
(Urbanization in developing countries)
Includes bibliographical references and index.
1. Urbanization—Caribbean Area. I. Title.
HN192.5.C76   301.36'09182'1   78–67307

ISBN 0 521 22426 8 hard covers
ISBN 0 521 29491 6 paper back

One for Mo

Contents

Preface

A recent review of a four volume compendium on the West Indies (Comitas and Lowenthal, 1973) complained that by limiting its purview to the non-Hispanic Caribbean it suffered from an all too common myopia (Lewis, 1974a). While there can be no doubt that clarity of vision will be better served by meticulous comparison across the major linguistic and cultural divisions in the Caribbean, the need is more clearly expressed than achieved. Indeed the present essay poses the problem with far more acuity than it delivers solutions. However, if it encourages others to undertake the primary research that is still largely conspicuous by its absence then it will be of some value.

Urbanization and urban growth are Janus faced phenomena, bringing the material comforts and cultural concentration of modern living for some but housing squalor, unemployment and discontent for others. It is the thesis of this brief volume that whereas some parts of the world may have the autonomy of action necessary to control the process, the Caribbean has usually been denied this power and independence. It is an area of the world whose history has made it peculiarly vulnerable to the effects of decisions made elsewhere. For the most part these decisions have instigated forces conducive to urban growth and rural decline; forces that are both material and cultural in nature. People have been prised from the land by the impossibility of making an adequate income and weaned from it by an education that has effectively denigrated agricultural employment. The cities and towns have been the nuclei of prestigious values and ways of life but because they themselves have been the acolytes of metropolitan centres, they have often lacked the wealth to fulfil the promise of the urban ideal. This book outlines some aspects of these economic forces and provides an overview of the main features of urban population growth. It then considers the implications and consequences of these processes for Caribbean societies and concludes by examining the responses of policy makers and planners.

In ten years of research on the Caribbean it is hard to identify with accuracy the parentage of one's ideas. I can only say that I have benefited greatly from many conversations with fellow students of the area. In particular David Nicholls and Asher Tropp have always provided wise counsel on parts of the region with which I am less familiar. However, I

ix

can blame no one but myself for whatever errors and absurdities this book may contain.

The University of Surrey provided the funds for a visit to the Caribbean in 1975 to collect material for this book which I am pleased to acknowledge. The series editor, Professor Kenneth Little, has shown tolerance and understanding in the face of an inordinately delayed completion and provided me with perceptive and constructive comments on the first draft. It is a pleasure to thank Marie Elmer and Maureen Etherington for producing an elegant typescript from my spidery hand with speed and accuracy. Finally, while I could not imagine life with the Griselda that most male authors evidently prefer, writing this book has taken many hours that my wife and I could have enjoyed together and for which a dedication seems a meagre recompense.

M.C.

Leatherhead
September 1977

El hombre de tierra adentro
esta en un hoyo metido,
muerto sin haber nacido,
el hombre de tierra adentro.
Y el hombre de la cuidad,
ay Cuba, es un pordiosero;
anda hambriento y sin dinero,
pidiendo por caridad,
aunque se ponga sombrero
y baile en la sociedad.

(Nicolás Guillén, 1947;
see note p. 155)

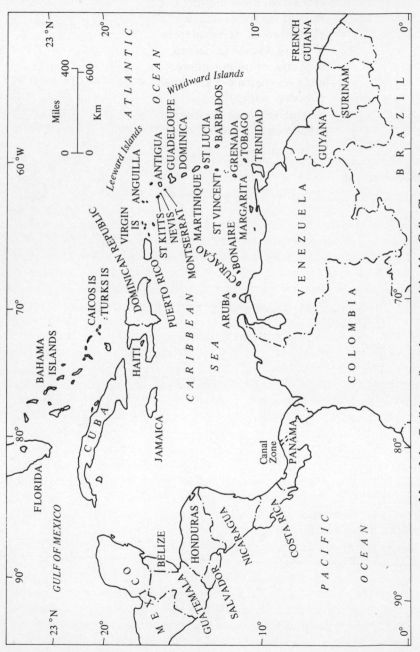

Map of the Caribbean (based on an original by Colin Clarke)

1 Introduction

The student of Caribbean societies is inevitably confronted with what at first appears a bewildering array of historical connections, cultural patterns and social forms. Almost every generalization has to be qualified, every feature tied to specific locations and every theory set within the tight constraints of individual circumstance. Inevitably this leads to problems in defining the area, and what usually emerges is a mixture of location and historical experience. In general I will adhere to this conventional solution but I will go further and argue that the area defined in this way does, with inevitable exceptions, possess a unity and consistency at the level of political economy. But first, in what ways does the region pose problems of ready definition and demarcation?

It is a truism to note that the Caribbean is a sea and not a land mass, but it is equally true that insular territories are central to a definition in terms of physical geography. In this case the 'Caribbean' consists of the islands within the Caribbean sea. This minimum definition includes the two great chains comprising the 'bow of Ulysses', as the English nineteenth century historian J. A. Froude called the Greater and Lesser Antilles. They bend, to use Patrick Leigh Fermor's (1950) graphic simile, from the *os coccyx* of Trinidad 'like the dislocated vertebrae of a spinal column' northward and westward to culminate in the massive island of Cuba only seventy miles (110 km) from the Florida Keys. In the south east lie the lava icebergs and coral accretions of the Leeward and Windward Islands; the former rising with unexpected drama from the sea, so that tiny Montserrat has a mountain almost as high as Snowdon, while in Martinique, Mont Pelée towers restlessly above St Pierre ready to repeat its quixotic destruction of 1902. Barbados on the other hand, is a flat, featureless plain comprising marine sediments on a coral base, while Trinidad, less than ten miles off the coast of Venezuela at its nearest point, is properly a part of that enormous land mass, with steaming, verdant hills hiding the flora and fauna of the Amazonian basin.

Beyond the 'Lilliputian' societies of the Leewards and Windwards, the Greater Antilles (Puerto Rico, Hispaniola, Jamaica and Cuba) are also mountain tops, but of a different order. They do not chart a fault line as in the south but comprise the summits of an extension to the great Western Cordillera which continues on the North American and South American mainlands. A few miles north of Puerto Rico the Atlantic plunges to a

1

depth of nearly six miles, while, within a sixty mile radius, *Pico Duarte* in the *Cordillera Central* of the Dominican Republic on Hispaniola rises to 10,300 feet, the highest point in the Caribbean. In contrast to British popular imagery, it is these four countries that dominate the islands of the Caribbean sea. They cover 90 per cent of the surface area and shelter 89 per cent of the insular population.

A solution to the problem of definition may be sought by extending the spatial boundary to include the circum-Caribbean countries of Central and South America. By this measure, the area includes the Yucatan province of Mexico, Honduras, Nicaragua, Costa Rica, Panama, Colombia and Venezuela. But now the geographical definition gives way under the weight of its own logic. These countries may border the Caribbean but most share little with the islands. Even though, like the Dominican Republic and Cuba, they may have had their indigenous cultures suffocated by the blanketing pressure of Spanish conquest, they are not truly Caribbean; their great land masses have shifted the centre of gravity inland so that few important centres of population lie on the Caribbean coast.

Consideration of historical connections highlights the problem of completely rejecting the wide geographical definition. The tiny population of Belize (formerly British Honduras) on the Caribbean coast of Central America must be an exception. After the exploitation of logwood and mahogany forests by slave owning Spanish and British settlers in the seventeenth and eighteenth centuries, Belize became a colony in 1862, having much in common with other British Crown Colonies in the West Indies. Similarly, Guyana (formerly British Guiana) is not only a mainland territory but the sea that washes its 270 miles (440 km) of shoreline is the Atlantic and not the Caribbean. Yet, despite the size of this country (83,000 sq. miles; 215,000 sq. km) it shares much in common with other West Indian territories, as do the other two Guianas – Surinam and French Guiana (Cayenne).

These mainland territories complete the most satisfactory definition of the Caribbean: the Greater and Lesser Antilles with the addition of the mainland territories of Central and South America which share more economic and historical features with the islands than they do with their Latin neighbours. This still leaves the problem of the 700 islands and 200 cays comprising the Bahamas archipelago. Although only twenty-nine of these are inhabited, the total land area at 5,300 square miles is greater than Jamaica and the largest island, Andros, is bigger than Trinidad and Tobago. However, the islands are spread over 700,000 square miles of sea and stretch 600 miles from a point just off the Florida coast to almost reach the northern shores of Hispaniola. Moreover, Andros only contains 9,000 people and, what is more important, the Bahamas have not really experienced the consequences of a similar economic structure to the rest of the Caribbean. Export agriculture has never been dominant because of the poor soil. Physical, historical and demographic considerations place the Bahamas in a marginal role as far as the Caribbean is concerned and, although occasional mention will be made of these islands, they will not constitute a central focus of this essay.

Three levels of diversity

Within the area defined there is astonishing diversity, that may be partially appreciated by considering it at three different levels. In the first place, there can be few regions on earth that have been so subject to the vagaries and vicissitudes of European fortunes, conflicts and ambitions. The societies of the present day intimately mirror this history. Cuba, Puerto Rico and the Dominican Republic are often omitted from surveys of the region yet they reflect more accurately than anywhere else the early period of Spanish hegemony which lasted from the closing years of the fifteenth century for more than 150 years.

The depopulation of the remaining Caribbean islands, as the Spanish scoured the area for indigenous Indians to enslave in the gold mines and sugar fields of Cuba and Hispaniola, permitted the relatively easy intrusion of French, English and Dutch colonizers in the seventeenth century. The British took Jamaica from the Spanish in 1655 although by then Barbados had been settled for thirty years. A number of Leeward Islands followed (St Kitts, Antigua, Nevis and Montserrat) while the French became established in Martinique and Guadeloupe as well as in Cayenne or French Guiana and other islands, such as Grenada and St Lucia, that were later to change hands at frequent intervals. The high point of French ambitions was confirmed by the occupation of Western Hispaniola in 1697 to become the famous colony of Saint-Domingue (Haiti). Meanwhile the Dutch had acquired Surinam in 1667 in return for New Amsterdam (New York) and Dutch traders were rapidly settling in the adjacent territories of Demerara and Berbice.

The eighteenth century was the period of greatest European interest occasioned by the wealth that flowed to France and Britain to provide such an important capital contribution to the Industrial Revolution. Sugar was by far the largest British import at the middle of the century and the slave trade one of the most profitable industries. The need to placate and encourage the West Indian plantocracy ensured that few, if any, voices were raised in opposition. The settlement following the Seven Years War in 1763 gave the Caribbean a relatively modern appearance with Cuba returned to Spain and Guadeloupe to France (in exchange for Canada). By the end of the American War of Independence twenty years later Britain had added Grenada, St Vincent and Dominica while France retained St Lucia and, much more important, still had control over Saint-Domingue, although the latter was to be lost as a direct result of France's approaching internal convulsions.

It is not simply that European struggles embroiled Caribbean societies in conflicts that provided them with so many unique and ready made histories. The islands themselves were hardly untouched by this process and even today demonstrate patterns of linguistic and cultural diversity that are astonishing. Moreover, the imposition of alien control on a people who are not themselves indigenes, must produce acculturation on both sides so that new forms of speech and communication spring from the coalescing of unrelated precursors. Thus the area does not only rely on the main languages of Europe, but has developed many new forms of uniquely creole communication, often rendering near neighbours incomprehensible to each other when they claim to be speaking the same language. The French occupation of St Lucia and Dominica has provided the vast majority of the population with a French patois, even though the official language is English. The Haitian élite still speak French, but the urban working class speak one variety of patois and the rural folk another. Dutch is the official language of Surinam and the Netherlands Antilles, but the rural population of the Dutch Windward islands speak English, while in Curacao they speak a tongue called Papiamento, which has Spanish roots, and in Surinam the working class of African descent communicate in English based Sranan.

On top of this, a third obvious and compelling level of diversity is provided by the origins of the populations themselves. These are immigrant societies often established for strategic advantage or to consolidate the quest for booty. In time they developed capitalist oriented agriculture on a massive scale, demanding in the process a continuous supply of quiescent labour. Slavery is the leitmotif of that history, but even that momentous series of events does not exhaust the Caribbean's experience as a recipient of non-indigenous peoples. The poor white servants, whose arrival predates African slavery, the Spanish speaking mestizos who paralleled it, and the Indians, Indonesians, Portugese, Chinese and others who followed have all left their indelible mark. Internal migration within the region, particularly during this century, has added Jamaicans to Cuba, Haitians to the Dominican Republic and Grenadians to Trinidad. The result is an area with wide disparities in the size and composition of constituent populations. Table 1.1 shows the degree to which size variations obtain, ranging from Cuba's population of more than 8,000,000 to the Turks and Caicos islands which together add only 5,000 souls to the total. In fact 77 per cent, or over 20,000,000 people, live in the four largest countries and in none of these is English the official language.

Another author, using earlier data but including some tiny islands omitted from this table, noted 'more than one half of all West Indians live in a society larger than 3,000,000, but the mean population per society is 366,000, while the mode is a society of only 7,000 persons' (Lowenthal, 1960: 788).

In the face of this complexity is it possible to identify any similarities, without which comparisons become meaningless and generalizations impossible? At the level of political economy the answer can be in the affirmative. Political debates today cover a wide range of unrelated issues, and economies reveal divergent structures, but all have had to, or still have to, come to terms with the uniquely New World experience of being dependent suppliers of tropical primary products for Western European or North American markets.

Plantation societies

The plantations of the New World were established in response to needs expressed in the Old. In this sense the plantations of the Caribbean soon became integrated into the burgeoning economies of Europe. As a result plantations must be seen as part of a capitalist system. However, they operated in circumstances that were, initially at least, highly unusual and as a result they acquired a number of pre-capitalist features – the most outstanding of which was slavery itself. Unlike the emerging factories of Europe in the eighteenth century, Caribbean planters could not call upon a reserve pool of labour power. Labour had to be imported, and that was expensive. Moreover, since the products of the plantations were destined for metropolitan markets there was no need to generate a local demand for goods or services and therefore no need to stimulate domestic consumption by paying wages. Again, sugar cultivation was highly profitable, and for most of the seventeenth and eighteenth centuries it must have seemed as if demand for the product would never fall. There was no need for a very flexible labour force; what was needed was a constant supply of labour power, not an elaborate labour market that could respond to a declining demand. Slavery was a system that met all these needs. It was a source of new labour which could be coerced rather than encouraged through remuneration. All the while demand for sugar remained strong, the inflexibility of the system did not matter and neither was it relevant that no local market was generated. If supplies were maintained then slaves could simply be worked until they dropped and little expenditure had to be undertaken for food, housing or medical care.

Conditions changed in the nineteenth century and sometimes, as in Haiti, the plantation system did not survive. More commonly it adapted from its essentially pre-capitalist form, based on slavery, to become much

TABLE 1.1   *Population of the Caribbean, 1970*

Commonwealth Caribbean (1970)	
Jamaica	1,848,512
Trinidad and Tobago	938,506
Guyana	701,718
Barbados	236,891
Belize	120,670
Leeward Islands	
Antigua	64,794
Montserrat	11,498
St Kitts/Nevis	45,327
Virgin Islands (British)	9,765
Windward Islands	
Dominica	70,214
Grenada	93,622
St Lucia	100,583
St Vincent	86,944
Bahamas	169,000
Cayman Islands	10,087
Turks and Caicos Islands	5,584
US Virgin Islands	71,000
Cuba	8,663,000
Dominican Republic (1970)	4,011,589
Haiti	4,856,000
Puerto Rico (1970)	2,712,033
French Antilles	
Martinique	352,000
Guadeloupe	339,000
Netherlands Antilles	220,000
Surinam	403,000
French Guiana	41,000
Total	26,182,337

Source: Commonwealth Caribbean, 1970; Dominican Republic, 1970; Puerto Rico, 1970; other estimates for 1970 from Davis, 1969.

more like a network of rural factories dependent upon wage labour. This new corporate style had implications for investment from overseas, which greatly increased, and with it the demand from metropolitan governments for a greater say in colonial issues. In 1865, for example, Crown Colony government was instituted in Jamaica after a bloody uprising, and in 1928 the old Dutch constitution was replaced in Guyana by indirect rule. The changed conditions that led first to the abolition of the slave trade and then slavery itself were three in number. Falling demand for sugar products in Europe after the Napoleonic Wars, together with alternative sources of supply, marked the end of the halcyon days for the West Indies. Plantations were abandoned and it was no longer possible to retain profitability with large amounts of fixed or overhead capital invested.[1] Wage labour was a much more adaptable and flexible system – especially if grants of land could be made to ensure that labourers did not move too far from the estates. Second, by this time there was no shortage of free labour, except in one or two places, such as Guyana or Trinidad, where large tracts of unused land were available far from the estates. Third, the emergence of a 'coloured' group, largely the offspring of white planters and slave mistresses and variously termed 'free coloureds', '*affranchis*', or '*gens de couleur*', brought a qualitative change to Caribbean communities. It had already been apparent that ports would grow to become cities of some size and substance and this new intermediate group acted as a catalyst for this process. But trading and services require customers and although many coloureds actually kept slaves, it became apparent that wages for some were income for others. Moreover, the surplus generated by slaves from subsistence lands allocated to them by plantations had, in societies like Jamaica, already established an island wide marketing system that spurred on mobility and initiated an invisible pressure towards a monetary system and cash economy (Mintz, 1974).

Although other considerations played their part, particularly opposition to the plantocracy by the newly powerful bourgeoisie of Europe and, of course, the agitation of liberal reformers and working class organizations, it was the tensions of a changed international economic system that brought the greatest pressure on the plantations to transform themselves. They did so in most parts of the region to become part of a modern capitalist system more centralized, more efficient and with greater separation between ownership and control. That is, they reflected changes occurring in other parts of the Western economic system in the second half of the nineteenth century.[2]

None of this is to say that wide variations did not occur in the plantations of the New World; indeed many have tried, with some success, to suggest typologies of plantation forms (cf. Pan American Union, 1959; Wolf and Mintz, 1957). However, even those parts of the region where influence was minimal owe aspects of their dependence to the same forces that brought the plantations into existence in the first place. For most, even where a peasantry evolved, the social relations of production were uniquely affected by the development of large-scale 'agri-businesses', based on a monoculture, with a small, often racially separate, minority controlling the lives and fortunes of a large mass. It is this fact that renders it possible to speak of 'plantation societies' and thus to impose some coherence of form on a region which otherwise denies categorization. Sidney Mintz has recently written with clarity on this theme. After noting that even common processes occurred at different times, that metropolitan powers differed greatly in culture and commitment to the area, that the islands and territories differed in ecology and physical structure and that the populations were often ethnically complex, he writes that the effects of plantation dominance 'were felt throughout the region, wherever men were brought together in large numbers, with more coercion or less, to plant, harvest, and process; such "factories in the field" go back to the sixteenth century in the islands, and have continuously affected not only the economy of the region, but also the character of its communities and the people in them' (Mintz, 1974: 257).

Urbanization and urban growth

'Urbanization' is a term used in many different senses and in widely varied contexts. It may be used to describe the greater emphasis on service industries within an emerging economy, or the prior change to mercantilism. It may be employed with a sociological focus to refer to the development of 'urban' social networks, or peculiar patterns of social interaction that are said to exist in urban life. Again, some will prefer a normative view and characterize urbanization as a set of values, attitudes and beliefs that comprise a 'modern' Western perspective on the world, while others will opt for stressing, in the manner of Herbert Spencer, that urbanization is a process characterized by increasing heterogeneity through increased structural complexity and concomitant differentiation of function. Demographers tend to prefer more prosaic definitions and are, for the most part, satisfied with defining the term as the process whereby the balance of a population shifts from residence in rural to urban locations. At its simplest, this says nothing about the increased complexity of life, the patterns of social relationships or changed attitudes and beliefs. Such transformations may *give rise* to these developments but the term 'urbanization' is not defined so as to entail them.

It is this latter definition that will be employed here, not out of any disregard for the other processes, but precisely to recognize their importance. The working definition of urbanization as a process producing a greater proportion of total population living in centres defined as 'urban' allows complete freedom in the exploration of causation and the monitoring of effect. It may well be, as we will actually argue, that a series of economic, political and social forces produce this change, and that in turn it affects the nature of life and culture in important ways. However, Charles Tilly is right to insist that we would 'be better off with a consistently demographic view of the process, treating changes in norms, social relations and economic activity as possible causes and effects of migration, natural increase and urban growth rather than parts of the package' (Tilly, 1967: 104). In this way the causal links and attributable effects are left open and subject to empirical investigation. Nothing that is related to this complex process is defined out as being beyond the limits of our interest, which encompasses both growth of the relative size of the urban sector through differentials in fertility and mortality rates, as well as patterns of migration.

In fact this simple definition commends itself in another important way for, in the sense that 'urbanization' connotes an intrusion of modern, Western values through the medium of the urban form, it may be said to be of little relevance for the Caribbean. This is not because of a lack of Western influence but rather because of its *total* dominance which has been felt in rural areas as much as urban. This point deserves some amplification for it directs our attention to one facet of Caribbean social and economic structure that is, perhaps, unique. The emergence of cities elsewhere obviously predates Western expansion. The sudden growth of Japanese cities following the Meiji Restoration of 1868, the earlier establishment of Indian cities or those of the western Sudanese kingdoms, had nothing to do with modern imperialism and in that sense they suggest an evolutionary linkage between rural and urban structures. Colonial expansion, on the other hand, tended to capture rural economies in a web whose centre was the mercantilist city oriented to Western economic needs. For example, it was markets and minerals that motivated West African colonialism and even in the nineteenth century, when political ambitions added an increased fervour to the demand for economic incorporation, land was largely symbolic of boundaries and not a crucial factor in active production (McNulty, 1976). Even the settler societies of the south and east never produced crops of comparable significance to sugar for Western economies and the colonial system was imposed on a complex pattern of dispersed homesteads. True in Kenya and the White Highlands area of East Africa colonial settlements dominated and distorted rural economies by channelling infrastructure developments into white owned areas, but nevertheless an indigenous rural economy did exist. The colonial presence, while not wholly urban, was superimposed on a traditional, native form (Soja and Weaver, 1976).

Caribbean societies, after the obliteration of their indigenous peoples, clearly fall into the second category, except for the critical difference that the web was first spun in the rural context. The result was that rural and urban life styles share the affinity with pre-colonial examples but do so in a form which is quintessentially colonial. Even though Caribbean cities were later to develop the characteristic features of colonial ports, it was the rural areas that were first enmeshed in European economies. The cities were not the spearheads of this intrusion even though they were later to become the bulwarks of the system it created. The fact is that there are no 'traditional' sectors to Caribbean societies. All are, or none are; a fact which throws into high relief the economic rather than the cultural causes and consequences of urban growth.

One result is that there is no equivalent to the integrative function performed by voluntary associations as we know to exist in West Africa (Little, 1965). These do, of course, have a role but the function of helping to overcome the disruptive consequences of wage labour, or of providing the new avenues of mobility in a world hitherto dominated by autocratic elders, is less critical when the transition is only between one wage system and another and when age in rural society confers no more authority than it does in the city. As the next chapter will argue, there are powerful theoretical arguments in favour of preferring an approach to colonial and postcolonial urbanization in terms of political economy rather than preserving the focus on patterns of acculturation and the diffusion of Western values. The Caribbean adds a peculiar fillip to this approach for the other must lose explanatory power when urban and rural areas are not divided by significant cultural difference. In one sense, therefore, a book on urban transformations in the Caribbean cannot be a book on 'urbanization' as it is commonly defined.

However, adhering to a simple demographic definition, the processes we observe are similar to elsewhere in the 'Third World'. Two summary tables, using data that will be explored in far more detail in later chapters, may help to make this clear. Table 1.2 shows the proportions of total population within the Caribbean (excluding Guyana, Belize, Surinam and French Guiana) who reside in rural areas and urban locations of varying sizes over three time periods. It is apparent from this crude aggregate estimate that the proportion who live in rural areas is still high but falling quite quickly. It is not surprising to find, in an area with so few cities approaching one million, that most of the growth in city dwellers appears to be taking place in medium sized cities of more than 500,000 but less than 1,000,000 people. By comparison, during the same period the rural population of West Africa fell from 89 per cent to 80 per cent of the total, while in tropical South America it plunged by twice as large a proportion to 47 per cent in 1970. A greater proportion of the population in South East Asia live in rural areas, but over the same period this fell by a slightly smaller amount than the Caribbean, from 86 per cent in 1950 to 80 per cent in 1970. Thus, in contrast to Western Europe where only a minority of the people live in country districts, the Caribbean still has over one half living outside towns and cities. When compared with poorer parts of the 'Third World', however, the population is more balanced between the country and the city.

In Table 1.3 the same basic estimates are examined in terms of rates of change of populations living in units of a given size at specified dates. For this purpose 'town' is defined as an 'urban' area of under 100,000 people

TABLE 1.2 *Proportion of Caribbean populations in rural areas and in four urban size classes, 1950, 1960 and 1970* (per cent)

Year	Rural	Urban				Total
		less than 100,000	100,000–499,000	500,000–999,000	1m or more	
1950	64.8	20.8	7.7	—	6.6	100
1960	61.5	21.1	7.0	2.7	7.6	100
1970	57.5	21.8	6.2	7.9	6.6	100

Source: Davis, 1969, Table C.

TABLE 1.3 *Annual growth rate of Caribbean populations, 1950 to 1960 and 1960 to 1970* (per cent)

Period	Total	Rural	Urban	Town	City
1950–60	2.2	1.7	3.1	2.3	4.2
1960–70	2.4	1.7	3.5	2.8	4.2

Source: Davis, 1969, Table D.

and 'cities' are units above that figure. The 'urban' rate is a combination of the two, while that for the 'rural' sector is based on the rates of change of proportions living in the residual category. The proportion living in urban areas is increasing at twice the rate of those living in rural areas, and this appears to be accelerating because of a greater concentration of population in smaller urban locations. Again, this is a function of the small population of the Caribbean region and the fact that there have in the past been so few cities of any size. However, the proportion living in cities has the highest average annual increase; a figure of 4.2 per cent per annum represents a doubling of the proportion of total population living in such locations every seventeen years. The 'urban' rate of change at around 3.5 per cent is lower than many other 'Third World' regions in the 1960–70 period (tropical South America, 4.6 per cent; South East Asia 4.7 per cent; Western Africa 6.2 per cent) but considerably higher than North America (2.2 per cent) and Northern Europe (1.0 per cent) (Davis, 1969, Table D).

It is clear that urban growth is not something that *necessarily* affects the balance of a population, but will only do so when such disparities between urban and rural growth rates obtains. Similarly, there is no reason why urbanization, or a change in that balance, should affect the culture of a society or the social relations that comprise it in any simple or direct manner. There is ample evidence to suggest that rural life styles and patterns of social interaction may be retained in an urban milieu. On the definitions used here, however, urbanization entails absolute or relative urban growth, normally consequent upon differential fertility or internal migration. Although it is perfectly possible to imagine progressive urbanization as a result of differential out-migration, the most common circumstance is one produced by internal population movement. Urbanization is therefore a demographic change which will be commonly associated with one or both of the following social processes. First, a changing balance of population will increase the probability that the social relations and culture of the city or urban centre will become more pervasive. Of course, urbanization may not be produced by relative *city* growth but by the expansion of smaller urban communities, and the archetypal social relations of the urban area need not permeate through to all urban residents, but the *probability* of a more pervasive urban life style must increase.

Second, where urbanization is a result of the physical movement of people, it will lead to some social changes in the lives of those people. The social division of labour, for example, is likely to alter, as is the manner in which income is earnt and resources expended. Family patterns may change, if only by the increased probability that many extended families will be divided by the migration of some of their members.

The second chapter of this book discusses the relevance of various theoretical orientations to the understanding of urbanization and urban growth in the Caribbean, concluding with the view that while many pressures towards urbanization may stem from processes found in other 'underdeveloped' contexts, the legacy of 'plantation dependence' has supplied a peculiar stamp in which the rural economy has become increasingly marginal to that in the urban sector for the majority of those dependent upon it. The latter is itself characterized by progressively higher levels of capital intensive investment and resultant unemployment.

The story of Caribbean urban growth and urbanization must start, here as elsewhere, with a consideration of economic factors. Chapter 3 examines the manner in which Caribbean rural economies have been uniquely fashioned by the legacy of plantation dependence, a phenomenon that cannot be ignored even when considering efforts at diversification and economic restructuring. In the last resort the changes in social structure must depend upon the interpretations by individuals of their economic and social circumstances and for this reason a main focus of this chapter is on the principal implications of economic organization for income equality and employment.

While income factors are of crucial significance they do not comprise the whole story. Equally important to the potential for real economic reward is the pressure of need, and this must mean the number of mouths that must be fed and the level of dependency that Caribbean populations have on their principal income generators. Chapter 4 considers the whole question of population growth and the subtle interplay of people and resources. It also examines the current efforts at control, made now more urgent by the restriction of external migration flows.

The following two chapters are intended to present an overview of social organizations and social stratification. The first is concerned with the main features of primary and secondary social groupings with particular reference to the implications of urban growth and progressive urbanization. This entails an examination of the peculiar features of Afro-Caribbean kinship and the concomitant household patterns. Social organization is not, of course, simply a reactive phenomenon and the chapter concludes with a discussion of the manner in which secondary groupings are both disseminators of urbanized culture as well as reflections of the tensions and frustrations that uncontrolled urban growth so frequently creates.

Consideration of structured inequality in the Caribbean context has to start with the reality of ranking by phenotype or ethnic origin. Chapter 6 provides some evidence on the background to the typical complexity of major territories but rejects the common assumption that racial and ethnic ranking can be considered apart from differential access to scarce economic rewards. Social classes have themselves to be understood in an evolutionary vein and the argument is advanced that changes consequent upon the growth of corporate plantations led both to the pre-eminence of urban centres and the emergence of an intermediary social group who are often as distinctive on racial as on socio-economic criteria. The permeability of Caribbean cultures to Western attitudes and beliefs is as true for the criteria of social ranking or deference as it is elsewhere. Inevitably these values and expectations are materialist by nature and urbanizing in impact. Educational systems are institutionalized projections of such beliefs and must therefore play their part in promoting urban drift, unless a self conscious, decisive step is taken to reverse this tendency.

It is no surprise to discover that an area of the world so complex in history and cultural connections should possess a wide variety of development strategies. Chapter 7 surveys this continuum and argues that, when coupled with the strength of creole identity, we are able to devise a simple classification for understanding how politicians and planners have reacted to the phenomena of urban growth and the extension of urban influence.

2 Theories of urbanization and dependence

The theoretical contributions to the study of urbanization have tended to be of two kinds; one fundamentally typological and the other 'processual' in character. The first seeks to characterize the essential features of the 'rural' and 'urban' locations. This may be done in a wide variety of ways but it concentrates less on the mechanisms whereby *change* occurs and more on clarifying the differences between one and the other. The second kind of contribution is more genuinely theoretical; that is it seeks to establish relationships between variables such that we may predict a particular outcome, or attribute an identified state of affairs, to a temporal sequence of causes. In the latter category, we would include those views sometimes referred to as 'functionalist', which aim to understand a social phenomenon by identifying its role in helping to maintain a predetermined pattern of mutual relationships.

The theoretical status of contributions on urbanization is not, of course, the only distinction we can make. We can identify a difference between those who perceive the problem as an instance of a more general transformation process from 'traditional' to 'modern' societies and those, by contrast, who regard the transition as one characterized by changes in the system of production and distribution. The former view has a typological tradition as well, readily exemplified by Robert Redfield's work on the 'folk' and the 'urban', while the processual aspect can be labelled the 'modernization' view (Redfield, 1947). On the other hand, the work which conceives urbanization as a concomitant and product of capitalism may be classified, for want of a better name, as Marxist theory. It is paralleled by a non-Marxist classification typified by writings on the 'dual' economy. A simple cross classification may help to clarify this attempt to structure our appreciation of this complex literature.

Figure 1 *Theoretical orientations on urbanization*

Theoretical level	Conception of rural-urban transformation	
	Tradition/modernity	Pre-capitalist/capitalist
Typology	Rural–urban continuum	Dual economy
Theory	Modernization	Marxist

These approaches have certain strengths and identifiable weaknesses when related to the Caribbean situation. In fact each will be rejected as a suitable perspective to adopt but, prior to this, it is important to understand a little more about all four kinds of orientation and the questions they raise for inquiry.

The rural–urban continuum

The first point about this simple device is that it is essentially descriptive and not explanatory. The object is to define the nature of 'rural' and 'urban' types (usually ideal types) of social relation or of culture. Devices such as this have a long and time-honoured history in sociology, ranging from Sir Henry Maine's legalistic distinctions between pastoral ties of 'status' and urban bonds of 'contract', to Emile Durkheim's separation of mechanical and organic forms of social solidarity or Ferdinand Toennies' famous classification of social relations dependent on either 'natural' or 'rational' will (*Gemeinschaft/Gessellschaft*) (cf. McKinney, 1966; Loomis and McKinney, 1963). It is hard to overestimate the degree to which these or similar classifications have infiltrated our thought; the very separation of pre-industrial from industrial society, or of modernity from traditionalism inevitably connotes ideal type forms or patterns of social relation.

In most cases the key differentiating factor, upon which changes in cultural or social relationships are thought to depend, is simply the demographic change resulting from concentration and increased density of population. Two examples may demonstrate this common view. For Durkheim the change towards a greater role for *organic* solidarity or social cohesion is dependent upon greater complexity and interdependence of the constituent parts of a social system, and this itself is a necessary consequence of numbers and the 'density' of social relations. As Durkheim wrote in the *Division of Labour in Society*: 'From the time that the number of individuals among whom social relations are established begins to increase, they can maintain themselves only by greater specialisation, harder work and intensification of their faculties' (Durkheim, 1964: 336–7). The style of life and pattern of interrelations is thus dependent upon the concentration of population. As Durkheim was at pains to point out, the pressures associated with the increased 'intensity' of life may produce patterns of development which we associate with the growth of cities and emergent civilization, but they often produce pathological reactions as well.

It is the way of thinking and acting that gave rise to these unwelcome concomitants of urban growth that Louis Wirth was later to label 'urbanism'. Wirth argued that three variables (numbers, density and heterogeneity) could 'explain the characteristics of urban life and ... account for the differences between cities of various sizes and types' (Wirth, 1938: 18). These characteristics were thought to be many, but included a distinct personality type, the primacy of secondary relationships, formal organizations, anonymity, greater social and spatial mobility and weakened bonds of kinship and neighbourhood. It is true that not all aspects of urbanism were perceived as regrettable, but the central thrust of this typology is upon the association between 'urbanism' and social problems, which are themselves conceived in a pathological vein.

The major difficulty with these kinds of approach is not that differences of culture and social relationships are described as they are, because it is useful to demarcate the characteristics of 'rural' and 'urban' living. The problem is that the only theory which is developed is one which suggests that 'urbanism' is the result of concentrated population. This is not a theory of *how* populations came to be concentrated, and thus it cannot be a theory of urbanization; it is a theory which is dependent upon correlations between social phenomena and spatial variables. Unfortunately, there does not appear to be any very powerful relationship between the two. It is quite possible to discover 'rural' kinds of primary or *gemein-schaft* relationship in city centres, while the 'country' may reveal many instances of 'urban' relationships. This is especially true of smaller societies with easier communications, like those that are the subject of this study, since here there may be even more opportunities for *urbs in rure*, to use Pahl's phrase (Pahl, 1965; Pahl, 1975).

It is probably true to maintain that there are features of urban life which are particularly important in the sociology of urban growth. As R. Dewey suggested there are structural features associated with greater complexities in the division of labour and peculiar forms of inequality that do demand our attention (Dewey, 1960). However, for understanding urbanization, it is the inequalitites and divisions *between* city and countryside that have to be understood. Concentrations of population are the effects of such relationships, not their cause. We can elaborate typologies of this kind as freely as we wish, and they may thereby be more useful in accurately identifying significant features of the variables we want to relate, but contrary to the views of some (see McGee, 1971: 47), they will not aid the main theoretical task.

Modernization theory

There are numerous theories of social change that could be bracketed together as 'theories of modernization'. Like the majority of rural–urban continua, they tend to focus the attention of the investigator on to patterns of social integration, where the urban or more modern sector of the society is perceived as the independent or explanatory variable. Modernization theories do have the advantage of stating a hypothetical relationship, but it is one which does not come to terms adequately with the colonial or postcolonial reality of Caribbean societies. The fundamental reason for this problem is that modernization is conceived as the transformation of 'Third World' societies into liberal capitalist democracies, and urbanization is seen as a concomitant of this process, since the city is the nucleus for the cultural penetration of the modernizing society.

An essential ingredient of the modernization approach is a 'culturalist' line of argument which maintains that social systems are organized and controlled in the last resort by the values, attitudes and beliefs of their social actors. It follows that if a society is attempting to undergo a social transformation from a 'traditional' to a 'modern' state then researchers should investigate these values and beliefs and, if they are required to give policy advice, they should suggest ways by which these may be replaced by others more conducive to change. Two examples may illustrate this perspective.

There is an extensive literature on the dimensions of value systems or 'value orientations' as they are sometimes termed. Most of the recent work originated with the contributions of Talcott Parsons and it is characterized by a functionalist approach to social change. One such study is that of J. A. Kahl on Mexico and Brazil who sought to measure 'modernism' by breaking this value component down into five variables. The 'modern' man was one who scored highly on a scale of 'activism' as opposed to 'fatalism', who betrayed a relatively low degree of integration with relatives but a high level of individualism, contact with the mass media and a pronounced interest in urban living. 'Modern' men also saw the occupational structure as open and regarded the sacrifices of occupational effort as worthwhile (Kahl, 1968: 18–22). The 'modern man' is stimulated by the city and urban life; 'he sees it as open to influence by ordinary citizens like himself'. Furthermore 'he sees life chances or career opportunities as open rather than closed; a man of humble origins has a chance to fulfil his dreams and rise within the system. He participates in urban life by actively availing himself of the mass media. He reads newspapers, listens to the radio, discusses civil affairs' (Kahl, 1968: 133). Not surprisingly, the thesis is advanced that the more modern one's men, the more likely a society is to develop and modernize, that is to converge towards the goal of 'development' reached by the United States. Another study illustrates the theoretical thinking that underpins this assumption.

An influential work by Bert Hoselitz suggests that the difference between an advanced economy (or the 'advanced' sector of an underdeveloped one) and others is that the former is characterized by:

(i) Universalistic norms in determining the selection process for the attainment of economically relevant roles.
(ii) Roles that are functionally highly specific.
(iii) Norms for selection to these roles that are based upon achievement.
(iv) Elites that are oriented towards 'social objects of economic significance'.

(Hoselitz, 1960: 41).

Since the underdeveloped society has a predominant value system exactly opposed to this pattern, the problem becomes one of understanding the mechanism by which a transformation may take place. One crucial mechanism is the city itself because cities 'exhibit a spirit different from that of the countryside. They are the main force and the chief locus for the introduction of new ideas and new ways of doing things' (Hoselitz, 1960: 163).

The development problem is how to promote the natural 'diffusion' effect of the city so that it overcomes the 'resistance' of rural areas occasioned by their attachment to traditional or 'folk' ways of life. The cities have a cultural effect on the rest of society and by so doing they are able to provide a set of values and principles more conducive to the rationalism inherent in the modern business ethic, and thus to economic development. Hoselitz grants that, in the colonial context, a city or urban centre may have had a 'parasitic' effect on its hinterland, but this he regards as a short run phenomenon. In time, 'factors of change developed in and around the city which had the effect of turning the parasitic character of the city into a generative one' (Hoselitz, 1960: 193).

Hoselitz is aware of the fact that migrant patterns to urban centres differ in the underdeveloped society from the analogous processes in the West, in that the latter were accompanied by industrialization. Migration here is seen as a response to the attractions of the city, not through employment but through 'the relatively strong pull of superior consumption patterns' (Hoselitz, 1960: 202), coupled with a decline of opportunities in rural areas. Again, the theory of urbanization is dependent upon the effects of diffusion; as more and more people develop, or are socialized into, Western values, they will naturally migrate to that centre of these values – the city.

There are three main areas of weakness to the modernization approach to urbanization which seriously limit its application in the context of understanding Caribbean societies. First, all approaches, to a greater or lesser degree, betray strong ideological elements which manifest themselves most clearly in a rather blatant ethnocentrism. The 'modern man' discussed by Kahl is a well known figure, an individualized version of the

American Dream. There is every reason to oppose a thesis of simple convergence based upon technological determinism. There is no reason to suppose that technology and industrialization will mould advanced societies in the same fashion, let alone assume that the developments of capitalist societies in the West will be emulated by 'developing' countries. The very existence of the advanced societies is one of the crucial reasons why this will not take place. Second, the argument is based upon a 'culturalist' premise which inevitably produces two false, or at least partial, assumptions. One is that it is 'culture' which determines, rather than being itself fashioned by and responsive to other forces, and the other, which is closely related, is that social control through culture is more important than, say, constraint through differential access to scarce resources. It is often Max Weber's writing on the relevance of an individualized ethos, stressing the ascetic commitment to worldly success, that is advanced as support for the culturalist position, but Weber was insistent on defining the city as founded upon a 'market settlement'. He went on to qualify the definition by pointing to the difference between production and consumption cities, and those that subsequently developed major administrative or garrison functions, but it was the relationships of trade and exchange that separated the 'city' from other forms of settlement (Weber, 1958: 65–75).

The third ground for opposition to the modernization perspective is that it perceives the process of change between the urban centre and the rural hinterland as one of *diffusion*. In fact this is a two stage process; the Western nation diffused the culture of modernity to the 'developing' country or colony where it becomes concentrated in the city. The city then extends its influence throughout the land. If the previous criticism is granted some worth, then the process of diffusion of cultural traits as a theoretical perspective for understanding colonization processes loses some of its explanatory power. It must be based upon the premise that only cultural forces are important in structural change. However, there are other limitations. Diffusion is also an 'integrationist' approach because it can only throw light upon how the rural sector becomes more like the urban, and thus, perhaps, on why it is that rural dwellers are attracted to city living even when economic returns are not obvious. However, what if the relationship between the two appears to be one of growing inequalities and possibly incipient conflicts? One can certainly discuss *obstacles* to diffusion of 'modern' values but hardly understand the tensions and conflicts engendered by a growing impoverishment of rural economies. And yet, as we shall see, that is the *leitmotif* of Caribbean rural economy. The diffusionist thesis, therefore, is not an adequate theoretical perspective; it has the virtue of focussing attention on *relationships* between sectors of society, or between one society and another, but in common with all 'modernization' approaches it presumes an autonomous determining role for 'culture' and is wedded to assumptions of gradual, consensual change which hardly tally with the poverty and burgeoning inequalities that are characteristic of the processes we seek to understand.

It must be stressed that no one is attempting to deny the differences that exist between city and rural life or culture, nor indeed that reciprocal influences of one upon the other will be important in appreciating patterns of change. What is being argued is that urban culture is more properly viewed in the context of the relationship between metropolitan society and satellite, and that relationships between the urban 'core' and the rural 'periphery' within the dependent society must also be viewed in terms of what will later be termed 'plantation' economies. Before developing the main strands of that position, however, it is necessary to examine the two kinds of approaches to the urban–rural relationship that do indeed stress economic distinctions.

The dual economy thesis

The dual economy thesis is associated with the Dutch economic historian J. H. Boeke (Boeke, 1953). It is a 'theory' generated by the colonial experience, and is primarily concerned to show that colonial economies are typically made up of a less sophisticated, pre-industrial agriculture sector and a technologically advanced and sophisticated urban sector. For Boeke these do not inter-relate or inter-penetrate – except to a minimal degree – and for this reason the approach is less of a theory of the *relationship* between the urban and rural sectors, than one actually suggesting that each occupies a separate economic world.[1] Moreover, in clear distinction from the previous approaches, this separation is independent of culture. As Boeke puts it:

'It may well happen that members of economically divergent groups are linked by the strongest and most intimate ties of some other nature – ties of religion, of nationality, of local patriotism, of artistic feelings, of language. It may also be that 'economically' related persons lack every vestige of mutual loyalty; they may be distinctly hostile – rivals, distrusting and shunning one another [Boeke, 1953: 19–20].'

Since Boeke tends to focus on the imposition of an alien economic order, he adds to our understanding of the colonial situation. What is missing, however, at least in the dual economy thesis, is any appreciation of the effects that the colonial city may have on the rural sector or, indeed, the repercussions of particular forms of rural agricultural development on the spatial and social form that colonial cities take. His contemporary,

J. S. Furnivall, who also wrote extensively on Dutch and British colonial practice in South East Asia, was far less limited. For him, the 'working of economic forces makes for tension between groups with competing or conflicting interests; between town and country, industry and agriculture, capital and labour' (Furnivall, 1948: 311). What is particularly interesting is that the peculiar heterogeneity of ethnic allegiance commonly found in colonial contexts exacerbates these conflicts, since the ameliorating forces of nationalism or a common language or religion are often absent. It is this situation that he referred to as the 'plural society' (cf. Cross, 1971). This is an important contribution that helps us understand the continuing relevance of ethnic and racial identity in the Caribbean; a theme to which we will return in a later chapter.

The dual economy thesis has, therefore, to be rejected precisely because it cannot pretend to be a theory of *urbanization*. What it does do, however, is focus our attention on the crucial significance of the colonial relationship and the significance of economic or materialist forces. The social implications of these forces are developed and elaborated in Furnivall's contributions.

Marxist theory

Marx himself did not assume that urban development was determined only by capitalist means of production, but the peculiar form that concentrations of labour power took had to be seen within the context of the generalized need to extract surplus value from proletarian labour power. All societies have a 'social' division of labour characterized by an urban–rural distinction; this takes on the features associated with capitalist development because of the latter's peculiar economic division of labour. An economic system dependent upon the power of a class employing private capital will increase urbanization to lower costs of production and speed up the circulation of capital. As a Marxist author recently put it: 'The city ... appeared as the direct effect of the need to reduce indirect costs of production, and costs of circulation and consumption in order to speed up the rate of rotation of capital and thus increase the period during which capital was used productively' (Lojkine, 1976: 127). When it comes to understanding the same kinds of process in underdeveloped contexts, Marx is suggestive but less precise. He was in no doubt that the rural sector could not be considered aside from the urban development which arose as capital accumulation occurred in Europe. As he put it: 'The first presupposition of [large industry] is to draw the land in all its expanse into the production not of use values but of exchange values' (Marx, 1973: 511). That is, land is a part of the capitalist system. The problem is that colonies do not develop large industries in themselves.

They *supply* large industries overseas and this is why attention is concentrated on the relationship between colony and metropole. As for the plantations in the New World, which he described as 'anomalies within a world market based on free labour', they had to be considered capitalist after the abolition of slavery but Marx never devoted any time to considering the *internal* relationships between groups within a colony (Marx, 1973: 513).

In fact, of course, one of the classic problems with applying Marxist analysis within the colonial world is that the economic system, since it was not based on domestic capital accumulation but rather on the export of capital overseas, never gave rise to the groups that were conceived as the dynamic elements of Western development. Colonies typically lack a bourgeoisie, although they developed consumption orientated middle classes based on what Max Weber would have called status groups (*stände*), and they also lacked an urban proletariat greater than, say, 10–15 per cent of the labour force. Groups which have emerged as significant, as we shall see, have tended to be the peasantry or the lumpenproletariat, both of which were regarded by Marx as of either negative or marginal importance to economic and social change.

The most interesting and important developments in classical Marxism for the purposes of this book, have been those associated with the name of Gunder Frank and other internationalist oriented Marxists of the *New Left Review*. These contributions are sufficiently well known not to need elaboration here. Suffice it just to note that although Frank is adamant that urbanization in the underdeveloped world has to be seen within the context of the integration of colonies into networks of international capitalist ties (hence his staunch rejection of the separatist elements in Boeke's approach) (Frank, 1969: 221) this has done little to develop our understanding of the role that plantations play *within* the colonial context. And yet that is the key question. It really is not very helpful to redefine peasants and lumpenproletariat as the 'real proletariat' in order to pretend that underdeveloped countries are *simply* capitalist. It is more complex than that (cf. Frank, 1969: 360).[2] As a recent hostile critic pointed out there is a real danger in Frank's approach of substituting 'the clarity of dogma for the complexity of truth' (Blakemore, 1975: 76). That said, a framework for analysing the ties of dependency is the only tenable approach to understanding the patterns of change within the contemporary Caribbean. Despite the myriad variations in historical circumstance it is the one common feature. That is not to say that different forms have not existed, but the cornerstone of most Caribbean societies has been, and is, the plantation. And the plantation is the creation *par excellence* of the dependent economy. It is to a statement of the central features of plantation dependence that we now turn, after a brief comment on the 'colonial context' in which these relationships have been traditionally located.

The colonial context

The precise role that capital accumulated through the imperial control of the tropics played in the development of Western capitalism is the object of considerable debate amongst economic historians. Whatever the true picture, there is little doubt that this was a *prime* consideration for both Britain and France, the major European imperial powers in the nineteenth century. The following statements illustrate the arguments well; the first is from Benjamin Kidd, the well known opponent of Marxist analyses, writing approvingly of imperialism at the close of the nineteenth century, and the second is by Sidney Oliver, onetime Governor of Jamaica, in an important volume whose main purpose was to explore the implications of the relationship between 'white capital' and 'coloured labour':

'With the filling up of the temperate regions and the continued development of industrialism throughout the civilised world the rivalry and struggle for the trade of the tropics will, beyond doubt, be the permanent underlying fact in the foreign relations of the Western nations in the twentieth century. This anticipation must be based in the first place, on the fact of the enormous extent to which our civilisation already rests on the productions of the tropics, and, in the second place, on the fact that the principle, underlying all trade – that exchange of products between regions and peoples of different capacities tends to be naturally profitable – finds in commerce between ourselves and these regions its most natural expression [Benjamin Kidd, 1898 quoted in Curtin, 1971: 34].'

'when the European colonises or annexes tropical countries the force that actually sets him in motion is a desire for his own commercial or industrial profit to secure some position necessary for the defence of Imperial communication or other national advantage, and not a desire to benefit coloured people [Oliver, 1929: 113–14].'

It is colonialism, or the attempt to control overseas territories for the expansion of trade and the transfer of surplus to the metropolitan country, that was in turn a major consideration in imperialism, or the political domination of such territories. Of course, as the Caribbean illustrates so well, colonial questions survived long after imperial control, and this is not simply a recent phenomenon with the 'independence' of Commonwealth Caribbean countries. For example, in the case of Haiti, the imperial period ended with the advent of formal independence after the French Revolution (January 1804). However, as Nicholls (1974) reminds us, 'the question of the foreign ownership of land remained a live issue throughout the nineteenth century' (Nicholls, 1974: 14). As early as the 1860s, Edmond Paul had propounded a theory of economic autarchy, based partly on the continuation of legislation against white land ownership, in an unsuccessful attempt to prevent foreign penetration of the country's economy.

The 'colonial context' is defined as a system of external domination or economic control over a subject population or the structural and cultural legacy of that control. That is, the term is extended to include a situation where the direct political control may have passed as long as the previous structure is still identifiable. Fundamentally, it is a system founded upon economic exploitation, or the attempt to extract capital and profit by the monopolistic control of market relations, but political and cultural dimensions are also important in understanding the various forms that colonialism has taken in the Caribbean. Urbanization and urban growth are social processes whose understanding is intimately linked with the history of colonial domination and the attitudes, practices and assumptions that it engendered.

Many attempts have been made to provide more sophisticated definitions and classifications of colonialism, but none with great success (see Ribeiro, 1970; Horvath, 1972). What is more useful is George Balandier's characterization of the colonial situation as one likely to be riven with crises and conflict (Balandier, 1970: 21–56) where, to begin with, the foreign owned economic sector seeks to grow by horizontal and vertical integration. It needs to control the supply of labour, which is a key issue since the labour intensive nature of the original investment is a characteristic feature. The work force itself is deeply divided by economic reward. This situation inevitably produces conflict with traditional (e.g. craft) occupations and, even more fundamentally, with the everyday economic needs of the masses, since unemployment remains high and wages low.

On the political front, the colonial situation transforms numerical majorities into sociological minorities by institutionalizing élite positions on ascriptive criteria. While the ultimate political sanction, force, may be used initially to quell opposition or organize the labour force, its use will be less obvious in later years as legitimacy for power differentials is sought through other means. Over time, as all begin to share a common culture, the sanction of brute force becomes even less easy to apply since one of its justifying elements, ethnic difference, is less available. When this happens other distinctions, sometimes more subtle – such as religion, or sometimes cruder – such as race, will be employed.

In terms of social structure, the colonial experience tends to destroy the original culture or traditional ways of behaving, and education and religion are used as mechanisms of re-socialization into acceptance of the status quo. The family will possibly be affected by this process as well as by the insecurity of employment which is a prime mechanism for inducing labour passivity. Economic, political and social hierarchies tend to coalesce in the ideal type colonial context and this superimposition provides enormous resilience to change. It also affects traditional alliances or possibilities of political mobilization. For example, when race becomes overlaid on economic and political distinctions, those of mixed background, who would naturally seek to indentify with élites in order to improve their competitive position, will be less likely to seek any kind of alliance with the working masses. Typically too, the concentration and lack of divergence between social, economic and political hierarchies produces a remoteness and inaccessibility which generates and propagates stereotypical images of constituent groups.

From the particular context of urbanization we may identify three levels of the colonial situation. In the first place there is the relationship between metropole and colony which colours all internal developments. This is not to say that the process is a simple one of economic determinism, for although the ties of imperialism are powerful, economic experiences vary from one context to another, largely on account of political and cultural features. For example, French colonial policy has always been 'assimilationist' whereas the British specifically evolved 'indirect rule' to preserve the economic ties while reducing the administrative and bureaucratic burden. Also, individual colonies may well develop strategies of resistance to metropolitan control. This is not simply truc in the case of the old plantocracies before the rise of aggressive colonialism in the nineteenth century, it is also possible under other conditions. Blakemore, for example, provides impressive historical evidence of one such case in Chilean history (Blakemore, 1975).

Second, the relationship between metropole and colony becomes translated into an 'internal' situation in the urban/rural divide of the colony. As we shall see, this takes on peculiar and important properties in the New World context, but the crucial point is that the urban centre acts, and reacts, as the 'core' to the 'rural' periphery. A complex web of economic and political relationships emerges where, in the New World at least, the typical control by the urban centre is counterbalanced by the reciprocal force of the rural trade link. The city can be seen in terms of a bridgehead for the processing and passage of the produce from the colonial monoculture. Third, the core/periphery relationship narrows to the urban context itself within the very structure of the city. The urban centre is not a homogenous mass; the inequalities engendered by the exploitation of the rural periphery are paralled by the unequal sectors of the underdeveloped city. Unemployment and poverty at the periphery contrast with the affluence of the commercial and trading élite in their privileged neighbourhoods.

These processes are characteristic of colonial or post-colonial contexts. What we must now do is examine how they take on a peculiar form in plantation systems before concluding by translating these generalizations into guidelines for subsequent and specific investigation.

Plantation dependence

Plantations may be defined as labour intensive organizations established for the cultivation of a single agricultural product for export. Moreover, the fact that they are normally located in the tropics, are commonly associated with foreign ownership and have historically been dependent upon the forced participation of unskilled alien labour, has identified their activities with racial oppression and a rigidly maintained gap between labourers and management (see Beckford, 1972: 53–83; Thompson, 1959: 26–36; Mintz, 1959: 42–9). They are capitalistic in nature, to a degree seldom found elsewhere in Third World agriculture.

The colonial relationship is one which leads naturally to burgeoning inequalities of both a social and spatial kind. Resources concentrate with controlling groups and in those parts of the peripheral territory that maintain the relationship with the metropolitan country. Rather than urbanization being the consequence of industrialization in the urban centres as it was in the West, it is the outcome of policies in the rural regions and industrialization overseas which promote the concentration of population and by so doing help to supply markets for the imported manufactures from the colonial country.

It is important to realize, however, that such situations are not in themselves non-expansionist. It may be true to say that this 'internal' aspect to colonialism typically produces: 'certain intra-national forms of patterned socio-economic inequality directly traceable to the exploitative practices through which national and international institutions are linked in the interests of surplus extraction and capital accumulation' (Walton, 1975: 35). But colonies can in theory, at least after they gain political independence, seek to do two things to alter the balance in their favour. As Mandle (1972) has recently reminded us, they can seek to break the monopoly of the colonial power by buying imports elsewhere or by substituting internally produced alternatives, and they may also seek to alter the monopsony of the metropole by selling their produce on other world markets. Mandle is only interested in the internal/external dimension of this situation, but he is right to stress that:

'Whether or not resources are drained from one country to another depends upon the relative market power of the traders which, in turn, reflects the development of the productive forces of each. Whether a metropolitan country is able to act as a monopolist, and hence drain resources, depends upon the extent to which the hinterland country is successful in searching for alternate market outlets and widening its structure of production [Mandle, 1972: 54].'

The crucial point is that in societies where plantations, owned and operated by metropolitan concerns, have a significant stake, 'widening of market opportunities' will not occur. It is this which makes it possible to speak of 'plantation societies'.

The internal structure of a society is, therefore, highly relevant in determining the outcome of a particular set of trading relationships. Also, a political dimension is added to the forces that influence this outcome. What is particularly interesting, although not discussed by Mandle, is that the domination of an economy by plantations also has internal effects on the relationship between the city and rural regions for similar reasons. Thus, just as the political influence to determine external trading relationships is crucial, so too is the capacity to influence the free operations of the labour market.

A standard definition of 'plantations' points out that: 'They differ from other kinds of forms in the way in which the factors of production, primarily management and labour, are combined' (Jones, 1968: 154). Basically this is a reference to the fact that plantations are typically labour intensive. They employ large numbers of unskilled workers. The discipline of skill is replaced by coercion, which is made more necessary by the incipient shortage of labour. Such artificial means of labour control have been progressively slavery, indentureship or political controls over the alternative options for work. These elements account for the traditional fact that labour returns on plantations show a poor correlation with productivity. In turn, we are not saying that all Caribbean economies are so dominated by plantations, or even by agriculture of any description, that there is nothing happening within them which is uninfluenced by this fact. What we are saying, on a theoretical plane, is that none are feudal, none are simply capitalist and few only have a peasant base. Most, however, have a history where plantations have played a dramatic economic, political and social role, which is particularly significant in interpreting the sources and patterns of the shifting balance from rural to urban living. The 'neo-colonial' or colonial relationship has internal and external effects. Just as the price paid for manufactures has been high because of the monopoly position of the metropolitan supplier, so too has the price of land, the cost of credit or the charges for marketing been high for the rural dweller seeking non-estate work because of the dominant position of the plantations. Just as the earnings derived from the export of primary products have been relatively low, because of the monopsonist position of the metropolitan buyer, so too have the wages paid to plantation workers been low because of the control plantations have had over employment prospects in the rural regions. The resultant poverty and unemployment contained within the colony as a whole promotes a tendency to migrate to the urban centres of the metropolitan countries. The poverty and underemployment of the countryside produces a parallel tendency to migrate to the colonial city.

Universal trends towards capital intensification – made possible by locally generated surpluses, which are themselves the product of the artificial control over the labour market, promote this tendency, which may be exacerbated by increased labour demands derived from improved organization. The cities, or more likely the primate city, lacking an industrial base, provide opportunities for service workers and a clerical staff but not for the unskilled worker. Rural migrants do not necessarily fare badly in comparison with city dwellers in the process, but the end result may still be a rising sector of unemployed, particularly amongst the young. These problems have their effects upon the spatial organization of the city as the middle class and commercial sectors concentrate to avoid the burgeoning lumpenproletariat. Meanwhile, as before, investment is channelled into three areas; facilities for export and import, facilities for middle class consumption and facilities for promoting the circulation of capital. Thus palatial banks, concentrated in a commercial sector, help to speed capital into new factories for the assembly of cars and household appliances while still maintaining their funding to the export and import industries. Public funds are typically channelled, in this simplified scenario, towards improving the infrastructure for each of these sectors. If planning exists it will mainly be concerned with the integration of and facilities for commercial institutions; if roads are built they will connect middle class residential areas with urban centres, or possibly provide better communications for new service industries such as tourism. If major projects are commenced they are likely to be concentrated in the provision of deep water harbours, improved dock facilities or international airports and not in improving housing, health or education.

On this basis, what would a theory of plantation dependence predict on the topic of urban growth and urbanization? At the most basic level it would suggest the retention of traditional monocultures becoming less labour intensive as progressive mechanization was dictated by external competition. This would act as a spur to urban drift, as would the absence of extensive land reform policies. The retention of relatively inefficient production techniques and the domination of rural employment by a few concerns would tend to keep incomes down and thus contribute to the depression of the rural economy. A concomitant of this expectation would be a worsening of the relationship between population and rural resources because it would not be in the interests of those with power and influence to promote either effective contraception or successful rural reforms that would raise per capita returns. Moreover, the relative depression of rural economies would militate against the natural tendency for population growth rates to fall as real incomes rise. We would expect high rates of urban growth, particularly concentrated on certain sectors of major ports, coupled with continuing high rates of unemployment and a growing proportion of the population dependent on the declining wealth creators.

It would be surprising indeed if these conditions did not have repercussions in terms of social organization and social structure and, notwithstanding the important contribution of cultural determinants, economic marginality and an imbalance between population and resources could be expected to produce disruptive consequences in primary group structures. At the secondary level, organizations and associations – historically located in a colonial tradition – might be expected to have evolved a role supportive of the status quo and conducive to the hegemony of urban values. In terms of structured inequality the expectation would be that previous divisions and their legitimating ideologies would have been retained, not necessarily as powerfully as before, but it would be unlikely that racial ascription, for example, would be removed unless fundamental alterations had been made to the class structure. Moreover, educational services would be also likely to serve the purpose of promoting a value system that was largely externally oriented and thus profoundly urban in its implications.

Politically the expectations attaching to a simple model of plantation dependency are less clear. This is because political institutions are so profoundly influenced by the particular nature of the colonial connections. The precise degree of autonomy permitted under colonialism, the length of political independence and the assumptions regarding popular involvement in political processes, may all be expected to constrain and determine the political experience of Caribbean territories and thus necessarily the policies on urbanization that a particular government has pursued.

What we need to do now is to measure these sets of expectations against the actual situation. Do Caribbean economics actually approximate to the 'plantation model' and if so, does this have the postulated effect on migration patterns? What of the cities? How have they developed and what happens to the rural migrants? After examining these processes, we may go on to investigate in more detail the major features of Caribbean social structure. The plantation societies have rightly been called a 'culture sphere' since the particular forms of relationship associated with their peculiar past have provided features in common, although the richness and diversity of these structures and processes shake any theoretical ideas to their foundations. Yet, of course, it is precisely the complexity of the problem that makes theoretical explorations so necessary.

3 The economic order

Advanced industrial societies of the world typically reveal patterns of economic activity that include the cultivation of food crops to feed their populations, the export of manufactures, the provision of international services to provide foreign reserves and maintain the value of their currencies, and the capacity to determine growth by investing resources derived from savings and profits. As the oil crisis of 1974 showed so clearly, they are not *independent* in the sense of being autarkic, or economically self sufficient, and many, including the UK, are enmeshed in a complex web of trading relations. However, as much as they are subject to influence from other quarters, in the last resort they are free to determine economic policy. Constraints may be, and increasingly are, set by treaty obligations, such as with the EEC, but within these, policies to increase investment or demand, or to transform the economic structure, may be implemented by national political decisions and by manipulating any of the fiscal or monetary levers now at the command of most governments.

Dependent economies of the so called 'Third World' do not have this capacity. Major decisions are made beyond their shores which may affect employment and economic growth. Sometimes multi-national companies are able to command resources greater than the government revenue of the dependent economy. They have the power to export commodities in a raw state for manufacture or use elsewhere. They can determine prices by cartel agreements with no reference to the fortunes of the work force or governments dependent on the industry. They are able to transfer their operations altogether to more lucrative locations. In effect the 'Third World' economy becomes enmeshed as a subordinate partner in an economic system whose locus of control lies at the heart of the industrial economy. In economists' terms this lack of control is manifest by an absence of the usual relationships between, say, wage costs and employment levels, which means that the normal practice of wage restraint to limit production costs and prices, and therefore sustain demand and employment levels, is denied to dependent economies (see Brewster, 1973). Contrary to Gunder Frank's position, this does not mean that all economic expansion is impossible while the relationship with the metropolitan economy exists, but it does mean that economic planning is largely futile (cf. Booth, 1975: 75).

Plantation dependency is different in kind and in degree. It is the most extreme form of dependency, often maintained and legitimated by centuries of colonial rule. The power to sell produce elsewhere or obtain manufactures from other sources or transform economic relations is not, however, necessarily absent. The intensity of dependence in plantation economies can only be gauged by the extraordinary degree to which opportunities for change, even where they do exist, will be overlooked. Plantation dependency is not simply extreme because of the inequalities of power between the metropolis and the satellite, but because such inequalities are perceived as legitimate by those who suffer from them.

Plantation dependency is different in kind from other forms of dependent relationship because the origins of plantations are essentially pre-industrial and because its influence is as near to totally pervasive as any one economic institution can be. The history and geography of the Caribbean have provided plantations with a role that is unique in both a temporal and spatial sense. The plantation dominated the economic effort of most of these societies when agriculture was the only form of production and, unlike the rest of Central or South America, it was able to impose its unique form of social and economic relations on populations which were imported especially for plantation production.

Caribbean rural economy

The last few years have seen vigorous attempts on the part of many Caribbean governments to break the hold of export agriculture in order to diversify into food production for domestic use or build up an industrial sector of importance. Agriculture contributed 10 per cent to the GDPs of twelve Caribbean Common Market (CARICOM) countries in 1972(UN: 1974).[1] As Table 3.1 shows, however, there is a wide variation between the Leeward and Windward Islands, where 18 per cent of GDP came from agriculture, and at least three of the larger four Commonwealth Caribbean countries (Trinidad and Tobago, Barbados, Jamaica and Guyana). If anything the economies of the French Antilles and the poorer countries of the Dominican Republic and Haiti are more dependent on agriculture. In most cases the dependence is falling, sometimes quite drastically; for example, in Barbados, agriculture, forestry and fishing fell from a quarter of GDP in 1966 to an eighth in 1972. In the latter case increases in tourist revenues, manufacturing output and higher levels of public expenditure have produced this change, which mainly derives from a shift away from the traditional dependence on sugar for export. Thus the sugar industry of Barbados contributed over 21 per cent to GDP in 1960 and only 7.7 per cent in 1972 (Barbados, 1973: 1–8). This case is unusual, however, for in the majority of instances agriculture, and in particular export agriculture, comprises the most important economic sector.

The key role of agriculture is even more obvious if a breakdown is made of the labour force, since agriculture is more labour intensive than any other industry. Thus in the case of Barbados 17.7 per cent of the labour force was involved in agriculture, a fall from 26 per cent in 1960. Although there are a number of exceptions, the proportion of the labour force in the agriculture sector is usually much higher than this, as the table shows. The figures are a little out of date but there is no reason to suppose that the pattern has changed in the intervening years.

TABLE 3.1 *Contribution of agricultural sector to employment and GDP in selected Caribbean countries*

	GDP %		Labour force %	
Dominican Republic	24	1972	60	1972
St Kitts Nevis/Anguilla	24	1971	45	1960
Jamaica	9	1972	38	1960
Antigua	3	1971	31	1960
St Lucia	23	1971	53	1960
Dominica	29	1971	52	1960
Barbados	12	1972	26	1960
Trinidad	5	1972	20	1960
St Vincent	25	1971	43	1960
Montserrat	17	1971	47	1960
Grenada	30	1971	43	1960
Guyana	20	1972	37	1960
Puerto Rico	10	1964	19	1964
Haiti	45	1973	80	1970
Martinique	27	1961		
Guadeloupe	33	1961		

Sources: Commonwealth Caribbean Population Census 1960: Dominican Republic 1970; CHISS, 1971; United Nations, 1974.

The export picture too, shows up rather differently to the crude breakdown of GDP. In the less developed countries of CARICOM a distinction may be drawn between the Leeward Islands (Antigua, Nevis and St Kitts, Montserrat, Anguilla) which are still largely dependent upon sugar, and the Windwards (Dominica, St Lucia, St Vincent, Grenada) which now produce bananas, citrus or spices as their agricultural staples. In St Kitts, 80 per cent of export revenue is derived from sugar, but the last few years have seen the collapse of this industry in Antigua, where most of what remains of the agricultural labour force hope to make a living from the development of a sea island cotton industry. In Dominica, the banana industry now provides about 75 per cent of export revenue but the quantity and value of this produce has been declining in recent years, as it has in St Lucia which is almost equally dependent on this commodity for export revenue.

In the case of the larger CARICOM countries the pattern is somewhat different due to the far greater importance of the mining and extractive industries. Jamaica has tried to reorganize the agricultural sector with a new project called 'Land Lease' which is designed to try and improve the use of idle land, most of which is owned by the plantations. In the past sugar and bananas have constituted around 15 per cent of export revenue. The high price for sugar in 1975 increased this proportion to 25 per cent, although the tonnage of cane actually dropped to 361,000 tons. Bananas have declined in importance against stiff African competition and now only constitute 2.4 per cent of export revenue. In Trinidad the sugar industry dominates the agricultural sector but only constitutes 3.3 per cent of export revenue (1973). However, if one excludes the revenue from oil the sugar industry constitutes 26 per cent by value of the balance. In Guyana, sugar again dominates the agricultural sector although constituting a declining proportion of export revenue. In 1973, when production at 266,000 tons fell well below the expected yield, the industry provided 30 per cent of export revenue, although when the very important rice industry was added this rose to 39 per cent of the total. With the exception of Puerto Rico, which has been more successful than any other Caribbean territory in developing a manufacturing export sector, the other territories largely emulate this position. There are exceptions, of course, as in the Netherlands Antilles which has no agricultural industry of any significance, but on the whole the rural economy is of major importance.

The degree to which this sector is dominated by the plantations is shown in Table 3.2. This reveals that although the peasantry own the vast majority of farms, and these are typically less than five acres, they do not own most of the land. It is the relatively few plantations that control the larger proportion of farm land. In fact the position is considerably more pronounced than that shown in this table, since it provides no information of the *quality* of land. In fact the plantations own the best land in all areas since, whatever their political power today, they were able to gain this control at a time when their influence was paramount. The dominance of the plantations is not, of course, true in all regions. Even within the Commonwealth Caribbean, there is considerable variability. Barbados and St Kitts approximate to what has been termed the 'pure' plantation model while St Vincent and Dominica have never experienced the same degree of domination (Best, 1968; Levitt and Best, 1975).

Even though this variability exists, and even though some societies,

TABLE 3.2   *Plantation and peasant land holdings in the*
Commonwealth Caribbean 1960

	Plantations (>500 acres)		Peasants (<5 acres)	
	Farm land %	All farms %	Farm land %	All farms %
St Kitts	57	0.4	15	95
Jamaica	45	0.2	15	79
Antigua	42	0.3	27	91
St Lucia	34	0.2	18	82
Dominica	32	0.3	13	75
Barbados	31	0.2	13	98
Trinidad	31	0.3	7	46
St Vincent	24	0.1	27	89
Montserrat		0.7		93
Grenada	15	0.1	24	90

Source: Beckford, 1975: 87.

such as Cuba and Haiti, do not have recognizable plantation forms, it is still possible to speak of the Caribbean region as one key sector of 'Plantation American' (Wagley, 1960). In the early years of the colonial experience the plantations would have been greater in number. Now, they have become concentrated in the hands of large, foreign owned corporations. For example, in Guyana in 1909 (then British Guiana) there were forty-four estates owned by thirty-three individuals or companies. By 1935 this total had declined to thirty estates owned by four companies and two families or individuals. In 1967, there were only eighteen estates and eleven factories, nine of which were run by the firm of Booker Sugar Estates, part of the giant Booker Bros., McConnell Ltd based in London.[2] The same kind of concentration has occurred elsewhere. In Trinidad, Caroni Ltd., which the Trinidad government has now nationalized, dominated the industry and was itself a subsidary company of Tate and Lyle.

It is important to notice that plantations often produce inefficient resource allocation. There are a large number of reasons for this but among them is the fact that most of the controlling companies have aimed for vertical integration. Plant and equipment for processing, export and transport of one staple product cannot easily be switched elsewhere as market opportunities change (Beckford, 1969: 339). Diversification into other profitable areas, such as importing firms, may produce a lessening interest in the efficient organization of agriculture, while early penetration often entailed land holdings far in excess of production requirements. For example, in Jamaica it is estimated that plantation land holdings exceed 200,000 acres while only 80,000 acres are cultivated (Girvan and Jefferson, 1971: 61). Moreover, in addition to imposing inefficiency and inflexibility in the use of resources, the multinational nature of the plantations may produce *national* economic consequences which are quite opposed to market forces. For example, if political decisions dictate the wisdom of such a policy, it is quite possible for plantations to reduce production in one country in the face of rising prices but expand output of the same staple elsewhere. A greater demand for domestic decision making in the Caribbean sugar industry has produced precisely this effect as multinational companies divert their energies to catching the profits of a buoyant market by expanding their sugar beet production within the EEC.

In those societies where non-estate land *was* available for manumitted slaves or freemen, or where marginal land was successfully settled, we can see the peasantry adopting a more crucial role. Some examples of this process are important for understanding the reason why the rural exodus to the towns has been exacerbated by the structure of the rural economy.

The Caribbean peasantry

The system of household production based on small land holdings in the Caribbean context owed its existence to the plantations, which needed large inputs of seasonal labour. In order to hold this labour as a rural proletariat, estates would encourage land settlement on plots sufficiently small and unproductive to ensure that wage labour was the only means of sustaining a household unit. It is this peculiar form of relationship that has led some to question whether the designation 'peasant' or rural 'proletariat' is appropriate. Richard Frucht, for example, pointed out in a study of Nevis that although the communities he investigated gained their living from the land, and had therefore a peasant *means of production*, they lacked the conventional *relations of production* of that class, precisely because of their existence on the periphery of the plantation system (Frucht, 1967). This might take the form of wage labour or a share cropping relationship to the plantations. Alternatively the gap between land production and subsistence may be made up by the remittances of urban or overseas migrants.

In other societies, where more land was available, the peasantry become 'reconstituted' after emancipation. Sidney Mintz, who coined this term, has stressed, however, that such consequences may mean the retention of direct ties with the plantations, as in Jamaica, or it may give rise to the steady decline in smallholders as the land becomes dominated by farmers of larger acreages, which has been the case in Puerto Rico

(Mintz, 1959; Mintz, 1974). Land was also available in Trinidad and in Guyana, but here the pattern was complicated by the arrival of the so-called 'East Indians' to replace the African labour on the plantations. In both societies, they came to dominate the rural economy and in both too they established an existence on lands released from plantation use or sold under Crown Land settlement schemes.

The interesting difference is that in Trinidad the peasantry remained with sugar production while in Guyana they seized the opportunity to develop an alternative staple and founded the rice industry, which now has such an important place in supplying the Caribbean and in boosting the agricultural exports of that country. In neither case are the holdings that small. For example, in the case of the Guyanese rice industry 229,300 acres were planted in 1973 to bring support to 45,000 people. On the basis that these family plots supported an average of six people, this would give average holdings of about thirty acres. However, other estimates put the average holdings at much less than this (Hanley, 1975: 145; R. T. Smith, 1957: 503). Twenty years ago, ninety per cent of holdings were under sixteen acres and over one half under four acres, but in 1957 there were only 152,400 acres under rice. It seems likely that holdings have expanded considerably, particularly with the support given to the industry before 1964, but the expansion has not necessarily been accompanied by greater productivity or efficiency.

Even where integration into the plantation economy appears to be minimal, the drive to mechanize and extend acreages may do no more than maintain pre-existing levels of subsistence. Hanley has pointed out that over a period of sixteen years the acreage planted in a West Demerara rice growing community had risen by only 8 per cent, while the number of tractors had gone up from seven to seventy-three (Hanley, 1975: 144). In a later paper the same author calculates that without even considering the costs of paying for this equipment (which have risen with worsening terms of trade) the surplus in money terms from an acre of local paddy had fallen from G\$142.62 (US\$71.31) to G\$113.16 (US\$56.58), a fall of over 20 per cent (Hanley, 1976: 21). Over the period since 1956, the Guyana Rural Consumer Price Index rose on all items by 35 per cent, which means that the fall in surplus was actually of the order of 48 per cent (Guyana, 1973: 75). In these circumstances, and with a rapidly expanding rural population, it is hardly any wonder that the lure of the urban centre is attractive or that in the past year or two, notwithstanding the introduction of more profitable varieties, a decreasing acreage has been cultivated.

Hanley attributes this overall pattern to mechanization and, although the situation is complex, it is undoubtedly true that the 'development' of the rural economy has lessened its attraction to peasant agriculture. Can it be said, however, that this example has any relationship to the plantation economy thesis that was developed earlier? The answer is, yes, but indirectly, for reasons that are both general and specific. In a general sense the rural rice growing community is bound up in a way of thinking that equates mechanization with modernity. It is a reflection of the materialist culture which pervades all areas of Caribbean life. Second, the sugar plantation giant, Booker Brothers, McConnell and Co. was the supplier of most of the machinery and equipment bought by the peasants. The vertical integration of these companies has effects upon the rural community even when the formal relationship of wage dependence is absent.

The Trinidad case is also instructive, although in a different sense. Here it has traditionally been the case that sugar cane farmers have supplied about a third or more of all cane crushed. These farmers range from small peasants with plots of under two acres to those with farms of many hundreds of acres. All, however, are intimately connected to the plantation system, since the sugar factories used for grinding the cane are owned and operated by the plantations. The latter benefit from this arrangement in two crucial ways. First, they retain their labour supplies, since few cane farmers can afford to work only their own land and, second, they have a ready supply of cheap cane because they are able to buy the farmer's produce at levels below their own cost of production.

It would be quite wrong to conclude that the Caribbean peasantry occupies a similar position in all societies. As a generalization, however, we can say that all have been influenced in one way or another by the prior or continued existence of plantations. When the peasant village is dominated by the plantations, the peasantry assumes a marginal, dependent status, subject to the vagaries of decisions made many miles away. In recent years this has meant a greatly increased expenditure, from locally generated surpluses, on mechanization. In all Caribbean countries with extant plantations, the labour component of production has steadily fallen with the inevitable consequence of higher levels of rural unemployment. This situation has been exacerbated by the inexorable rise in populations as overseas migration possibilities tail off while birth rates remain high. The inevitable result is further pressure from the rural periphery on to the urban periphery as more families crowd into destitution in the slums of Kingston, San Juan or Port of Spain.

The alternative pattern is where peasant villages have emerged with a more separate existence. These tend to more accurately parallel peasant settlements in other parts of the world with a stable social and economic structure. However, as the author of an anthropological study of one such settlement in Martinique put it, even where there is expansion 'it is large-scale agriculture which is expanding at the expense of the small producers' (Horowitz, 1967: 106). Meanwhile, patterns of inheritance within large families fragment the ever declining land holdings and population pressure again exacerbates the problem. In Moyne-Paysan, Martinique, the same process, repeated in countless villages, is experienced: 'Over the years the village was able to hold its own by exporting surplus population to the cities and overseas. But the capacity of the city to sustain an increasing population is severely limited and has probably already been reached' (Horowitz, 1967: 106). Moreover, the relationship of dependence reveals itself at two levels. With Martinique's incorporation as a *département* of the French state, the peasants have to compete with foodstuffs imported from the metropole. Furthermore, at the domestic level, the emerging affluent middle class buy up rural properties as weekend or vacation retreats and thus force up prices, change land usages and generally drive the peasantry into a new state of marginality.

In sum the rural economies of the Caribbean territories provide ample evidence that pressures to migrate to the towns and cities, or overseas, are powerful. It was precisely because of the inflexibility and intractability of problems in the rural economy, that most governments opted for a policy of industrialization in the period after the Second World War. It is to that we must now turn, after a brief comment on the other developments in the primary sector.

The extractive industries

The mining and petroleum industries are of crucial importance in some Caribbean countries. Jamaica, Guyana, Surinam, Haiti and the Dominican Republic produce over 40 per cent of the world's output of bauxite, the ore of aluminium. The Jamaican economy, for example, is now totally dependent on bauxite and alumina (13.8 per cent and 45.8 per cent respectively of Jamaica's exports in 1975). In Guyana, the nationalized bauxite companies (Guybau and Bermine) have expanded considerably since the takeover from Alcan in 1971 and Reynolds in 1975. It is now estimated that bauxite contributes 17 per cent to GDP and a far higher proportion of total exports, although following nationalization the industry was beset by a whole series of difficulties, from which it is only just recovering. In Surinam, the bauxite produced comprises 30 per cent of GDP and elaborate plans exist for the exploitation of huge deposits in the western part of the country.

The other major mining commodity deserving of mention is ferronickel. After sugar it is Cuba's most important export, while exports from the Dominican Republic almost doubled in 1973 from the previous year's total as the Falconbridge plant (financed by Canadian money) came into full production. Other minerals and ores are mined in relatively small quantities, but the oil industries in Aruba, Curaçao, Puerto Rico and Trinidad are of major significance. In the past each of these islands has refined imported crude oil (mainly from Venezuela) for re-export but the discovery of large off-shore deposits in Trinidad, together with the sudden rise in oil prices, has had dramatic effects on that country's economy. For example, the value of exports of mineral fuels increased by 245 per cent in the second quarter of 1974 over the same period in the previous year.

The pattern of ownership of these industries has changed considerably with the growth of vocal opposition to continued domination by foreign capital. In addition to Guyana's total control of the bauxite operations, the Jamaican government took a 51 per cent equity interest in the Kaiser Bauxite Company in November 1974, while the Trinidad government has taken over the refinery previously owned by Shell at Point Fortin. However, in addition to the problems of acquiring investment capital and securing markets, these important industries remain capital intensive. It is unlikely that the whole Caribbean bauxite industry employs more than 20,000 people. This means a negligible contribution to solving employment problems while at the same time producing a clear labour aristocracy who join the middle classes at the core of the urban economy and help to establish claims for levels of consumption that reverberate throughout the urban periphery.

Manufacturing industries

Caribbean manufacturing industries have been spurred on by the failure of agriculture to provide growth and employment potential. Inevitably the larger islands have benefited, since they can offer a more highly developed infrastructure, higher education levels and larger markets. In the 1950s the governments of the larger Commonwealth Caribbean countries all developed a policy of 'industrialization by invitation' characterized by duty free concessions on imported capital equipment and periods of remission from normal income and profits taxes. To some extent these developments have been successful, and the typical pattern is one where the contribution to GDP from manufacturing has grown considerably in the last decade or two. Seldom, however, has this growth been accompanied by concomitant expansion of employment possibilities as fledgling industries seek greater productivity and efficiency by following the Graal of increased mechanization. Thus the contribution to national income in the most industrialized economy, Puerto Rico, rose from 14.5 per cent in 1950 to 23.2 per cent in 1964, while employment actually fell over the same period from 18.4 per cent to 17.8 per cent of the labour force (Gonzalez, 1971: 94). Trinidad established an Aid to Pioneer Industries Ordinance in 1950 with the intention of emulating the Puerto Rican precedent. By 1963, although the labour force had risen by 100,000, these new industries had contributed under 7,000 new jobs, due to the high level of mechanization involved (Carrington, 1971b).

Not only are many of these new industries capital intensive, they are also often relatively short term. It is commonly the case that when a five or ten year incentive plan expires, a company, owned by North American or European investors, will move to another locale. Thus both Haiti and the Dominican Republic have expanded their manufacturing industries recently with firms migrating from Puerto Rico where increased labour costs and expiring agreements have served as a disincentive to con-solidated growth. The problem is that peripatetic industry is no way to build a manufacturing base to diversify a static economy.

Additional problems are created by the effects of expansion in the mining and petroleum industries. Instead of manufacturing possibilities being created from these industries, the logic of their organization has tended to prevent this occurrence as raw materials are exported for processing overseas. Furthermore, the presence of a relatively affluent mining or petroleum sector, able and willing to pay high wages because of the higher ratio of capital to labour, stimulates wages in manufacturing and in service industries. This has the effect of raising costs and reducing the ability of the local industry to compete with imports. It also promotes the mechanization of manufacturing and thus has deleterious effects on employment (Girvan, 1975: 120–1).

Tourism

If there is one single industry that has been heralded as the pathway from economic servitude to certain progress, it is tourism. In some cases, it has become the greatest generator of foreign exchange. Barbados, for example, earned 34 per cent of GDP from tourism in 1972 from over 200,000 visitors. Tourism is the major employer in the Netherlands Antilles and in the Bahamas and it has a major role in a number of Leeward and Windward Islands. However, the islands which are more firmly within the orbit of the United States dominate the tourist industry – particularly Puerto Rico, the US Virgin Islands and Jamaica. Even so, there have been problems with the tourist industry in the last few years. For example, from a high point of 517,000 tourists in 1973, visitors to Jamaica fell to 395,809 in 1975. Foreign exchange earnings fell too and occupancy rates are now below 50 per cent.

There are two senses in which tourist development is dependent upon external decisions. In the first place, tourism is notoriously responsive to recessions elsewhere since holidays are the first victims of belt tightening cutbacks in consumer spending. This occurred in North America in 1973–76. At the best of times the industry is seasonal, with grave consequences for employment during the low season, April to September. Second, the Caribbean tourist industry was developed for a particularly affluent sector of middle and upper class America which normally demands standards in accommodation and food that can only feasibly be met by importing supplies and utilizing capital investment from international hotel chains. The result is an external leakage effect produced by the diseconomies of increased import bills and little domestic control over the industry. A recent critic argues that tourism is in fact an instrument of underdevelopment: 'The large import component necessary to support tourism in the West Indies serves at once to sustain metropolitan economic growth and foreign imports while reinforcing underdevelopment; imported materials, foods prepared abroad, and expatriate staffs make up the "invisible" support system accompanying the traveller to the region' (Peréz, 1973–74: 475; cf. Talbot, 1974–75). Whether this is so or not remains to be seen, but there is no doubt that in the face of other domestic problems, tourism, particularly by those whose colour and culture identifies them as alien and possibly exploitative, underlines and exaggerates inequalities. If later research does indeed substantiate the estimate that seventy-seven cents out of every tourist dollar finds its way back to the metropolis as some contend, then the Caribbean islands will only have replaced one form of dependent monoculture with another.

Already there is evidence of a strong reaction against tourists. This has been shown in Jamaica and, more particularly, in Antigua, which is more dependent on the industry than any other of the Leeward Islands. However, other countries, notably Haiti, the Dominican Republic and recently Cuba, look upon tourism as a major area of future expansion.

Trade and development

While very many Caribbean economies have expanded in the last decade, with growth rates of 3 or 4 per cent in real, per capita terms, this has not necessarily led to a favourable trade balance. On the contrary, imports have tended to rise faster than exports, partly to provide machinery and capital equipment to expand production or increase efficiency, but partly too to satiate the greatly increased demand for consumer goods and manufactures. Thus, Jamaica, which has had a high growth rate for many years has also experienced chronic patterns of imbalance, exacerbated by very high levels of inflation in Western industrial economies. The tendency to import other people's inflation is a common feature of economies dependent upon imported manufactures, and it inevitably leads to even more reliance on foreign loans and aid.

In terms of trading links, the Caribbean is becoming more and more integrated into the Latin American pattern of relationship with North America. That is, the direction of trade has progressively shifted from Europe to North America and the typical pattern is one of deficit, except where the export of primary produce to the United States has provided a surplus with that country. The CARICOM countries, for example, increased their deficit with trading partners from EC$ 346.3m in 1967 to EC$ 1,204.4m in 1972 and this pattern is exactly paralleled in Latin America as a whole.

The President of the Inter-American Development Bank (IDB), which already includes five important Caribbean countries among its members (Barbados, Dominican Republic, Haiti, Jamaica and Trinidad and Tobago) and to which three more have applied for membership (Bahamas, Grenada and Guyana), recently recorded the extent of the trade links with the developed countries of Europe and North America. Thus in the period 1965–75 imports to Latin America from OECD countries quadrupled at constant prices while: 'Over the past six years United States exports to Latin America more than tripled, while during 1973–74, when the United States was experiencing a serious economic recession, its exports to Latin America recorded an extraordinary expansion averaging 50 per cent a year' (Ortiz Ména, 1976: 7). It would be folly to declare that there was a *direct* causal relationship between this and other elements of the economic relationship with the US, but this pattern of trade was accompanied by an increase in private capital investment, which, in Latin America and the Caribbean, has been growing at 12 per cent an annum for the last fifteen years. Most of this comes from the United States, which in 1974 held private investments of US$19,600m in Latin American and Caribbean members of the Inter-American Development Bank, well over double her holdings in other 'developing' parts of the world. What this means is that Latin America has to make massive interest payments on investments, largely to North America. For the five Caribbean members of Inter-American Development Bank these rose in real terms over the four year period 1970–73 from US$189m to US$248.3m per annum.

Income and employment

The economic structure of a society provides a framework within which social and political life can continue. In the Caribbean a characteristic set of economic relationships obtains which permits some generalization about the pressures and opportunities that face individuals and families.

But personal decision making, whether it be about where to work or where to live, does not bear much relationship to macroeconomic fortunes. It has to do with employment possibilities and returns from one's labour, both in absolute and in relative terms. For that reason we need to translate the characteristics of plantation societies into the constraints and experiences of everyday life. Urbanization is a set of social processes leading to transformed societies. But it has economic, demographic and social causes and consequences, among the most important of which are the patterns of income and employment.

Income

Overall levels of income for a country give a very crude measure of development. Per capita incomes for the Caribbean are recorded in Table 3.3, which shows that the richest group of islands had an average income per head forty-five times that of the poorest. There is hardly any difference between the per capita income of the US Virgin Islands and the United States herself, that is 93 per cent above the UK level in the same year. The Caribbean contains territories which in no real sense can be labelled 'Third World'; indeed the pattern appears to mirror that in the rest of the world since the rich appear to be growing richer. In 1970, the top income per capita was thirty-seven times the bottom and only three of the top eleven countries had average growth in per capita incomes less than that in the UK, whereas seven of the bottom eleven did so.

The World Bank estimates that these countries contained 20,000,000 people in 1973, but 80 per cent of them lived in areas with average per capita incomes of less than US$1,000. So although there are relatively rich territories, the majority of Caribbean people are poor, their countries qualifying for the label 'underdeveloped'. In fact 21 per cent lived in countries with average per capita incomes less than half this figure. It is also apparent that those areas which were or still are British colonies fare very badly in comparison with the rest. Of the twelve countries which had or continue to have this connection, ten have incomes less than US$1,000, and of the eight territories with per capita incomes less than US$500, seven have at one time in the recent past been controlled by Britain. Although the statistical liberties are obvious, it is interesting to compare the relative positions of the Dutch, French and British Caribbean. The French lead with average per capita incomes in their territories of US$1,207, followed by the Dutch at US$1,123 and then the British at US$956. A possibly fairer comparison is simply to take the Associated States; then the British Caribbean per capita income falls to well under half that of the others at US$466 per annum.

Growth in per capita incomes depends as much on limiting additions to

TABLE 3.3 *GNP per capita and growth rates for population and GNP per capita in Caribbean countries 1960–73 and 1965–73*

Country	GNP per capita 1973 (Market prices, US dollars)	Average annual growth rates (%) Population (1960–73)	(1965–73)	GNP per capita (1960–73)	(1965–73)
US Virgin Islands	5,910	6.1	4.5	9.6	11.1
Bahamas	2,320	4.0	3.6	2.2	−1.1
Puerto Rico	2,180	1.6	1.6	5.7	5.2
Netherlands Antilles	1,530	1.5	1.5	−0.4	0.7
French Guiana	1,360	3.8	3.2	3.8	7.1
Martinique	1,330	1.5	0.8	4.8	4.8
Trinidad and Tobago	1,310	1.7	0.9	2.1	2.2
Guadeloupe	1,050	1.6	0.9	4.3	4.9
Barbados	1,000	0.2	0.3	5.5	5.8
Jamaica	990	1.6	1.4	3.6	4.8
Surinam	870	2.5	2.2	4.2	2.4
Belize	660	2.8	2.9	2.0	1.9
Cuba	540	2.0	1.8	−1.0	−0.7
Dominican Republic	520	2.9	2.9	2.7	5.1
St Lucia	480	1.6	1.6	5.5	2.8
Antigua	480	1.9	1.9	3.5	−0.8
St Kitts–Nevis– Anguilla	450	−1.0	−0.9	2.4	−0.1
Guyana	410	2.4	2.4	1.5	1.1
Dominica	360	1.6	1.6	1.3	−0.8
Grenada	330	1.2	0.6	3.1	3.7
St Vincent	300	0.9	0.9	1.4	3.2
Haiti	130	1.7	1.6	−0.3	0.7
United States	6,200	1.2	1.0	3.1	2.5
United Kingdom	3,060	0.5	0.4	2.4	2.3

Source: World Bank, 1975.

the population as it does on economic expansion. Past performance is not that encouraging since much of the wealth generated by growth in the economies has either filtered overseas or has had to feed and support more people. However, those areas with very close ties of dependence have tended to do better, particularly where emigration possibilities have lessened population growth or where paternalistic support to integrated colonies has obtained. However, there is no general pattern of causation since such disparate islands as the Bahamas, Cuba, Antigua, St Kitts–Nevis and Dominica have actually experienced declines in real per capita income over the 1965–73 time period. Of course, none of these data say anything about the way incomes are distributed within each country.

Information on the distribution of income within the Caribbean is difficult to obtain. In the most detailed study so far available, the declining importance of agriculture and increasing industrialization, together with greater government intervention, led Fuat Andic to predict greater equality of family incomes in Puerto Rico (Andic, 1964). His data bear out this conclusion, since whereas the poorest fifth of families shared 3.5 per cent of family income in 1946/47, this had risen to 5 per cent in 1955. However the top 5 per cent still shared between them almost a quarter of family income at the later date (Andic, 1964: 113). Further data from the 1960 Census illustrate the same general trend, which is accompanied by an increasing proportion of national income being paid to labour.

Rural migration tends to have two opposed influences upon the distribution of personal or family incomes. On the one hand, urban wages are higher and the more families are supported in this manner the greater redistribution effect there is. However, there may be a greater risk of unemployment which has the opposite effect. The dramatic implications of living in such conditions in Puerto Rico have been illustrated by Oscar Lewis and, more recently, by Helen Safa. In the latter's study, almost 72 per cent of a shantytown or *barrio* sample were born in rural areas and most had worked on the land. When they came to the city the rural migrants were less likely to be unemployed than a comparable group on a government housing project and less likely to have family incomes under $1,000 a year (24 per cent and 35 per cent respectively). Of course this provides a powerful reason for migrating, even though it was less likely that wages were simply higher than that the wife of the householder was able to work (Safa, 1974: 26–9).

A study by Ahiram (1965) also looked at household incomes of Jamaica and Trinidad and Tobago and provided the following data on the Gini measure, which is a coefficient of concentration such that 0 is perfect equality and 1 perfect inequality.[3]

Puerto Rico (1953)	0.38
Trinidad and Tobago (1957/58)	0.39
Jamaica (1958)	0.53

These data would appear to indicate that the distribution of household income in Jamaica is considerably less equal than either Puerto Rico or Trinidad. However, more recent evidence on a survey of households in Trinidad produced a Gini coefficient of 0.51 (Trinidad and Tobago, 1974a: 143). Since this is unlikely to have been caused by greater inequality in recent years, this figure throws doubt on Ahiram's original survey.

What is of much greater significance is the relative distribution of incomes between urban and rural areas. Evidence of gross inequalities and widening differences could be a powerful reason for migration. This is a particularly crucial point, for decisions to migrate are not necessarily taken by comparing the current position of one's family with its earlier prosperity or opportunities, but by comparing how well one is doing now against how well one might do (on the basis of perceptions of other people's wealth) in the city. Ahiram also looked at this question in Trinidad and Jamaica and showed that within the rural regions of Jamaica, income inequality was greater than in comparable parts of Trinidad. This might show the greater dominance of the plantations in Jamaica but it does not help us compare the urban and rural sectors themselves within each country.

Again the problem of adequate data is paramount and Ahiram was forced to employ a much poorer technique for estimating these differences. On the basis of the contribution of industrial sectors to GDP compared to the employment offered in each sector, he showed that agricultural GDP per worker was only 35 per cent of average GDP per worker for the country as a whole. In Trinidad, agricultural work provided 70 per cent of the average GDP per worker, indicating greater equality between the sectors (Ahiram, 1965: 10). Even with all the deficiencies that these figures possess, they are worthy of further exploration.

Trinidad and Tobago is a useful example since, as we shall see, it does have a massive internal migration problem compared to some other territories and is blessed with excellent statistics, largely derived from a continuous survey of households and the labour force. A recent survey showed patterns of household income and expenditure and revealed median monthly figures by county as shown in Table 3.4.

TABLE 3.4 *Median monthly household incomes and expenditures by county in Trinidad and Tobago 1971/72*

	Income ($TT)	Expenditure ($TT)
Port of Spain	321	363
San Fernando	346	385
St George	357	423
Caroni	217	324
Nariva/Mayaro	158	163
St Andrew/St David	186	246
Victoria	252	309
St Patrick	261	266
Tobago	228	257

Source: Trinidad and Tobago, 1974a.

These data, obtained from a survey of over 2,700 households reveal two points of interest, in addition to the well known phenomenon that surveys of this type always show expenditure in excess of monthly income.

The first three regions encompass the genuinely urban areas of Trinidad containing the only three towns of any size – Port of Spain, San Fernando and Arima (St George). These three together have a mean household income per month of TT $350 while the remaining counties have a mean of only TT $232, or two thirds as much. While it may be true that rural residents make up more of their income in kind, through home grown produce, the survey did take account of this fact. Moreover, if we compare the degree to which expenditure exceeds income, there is a proportionately higher gap in the rural counties where expenditure exceeds income by 22 per cent compared to 17 per cent in the urban parts of the country. We may conclude that the pressures of making ends meet in this society are harder for rural residents. This is particularly true for a country like Trinidad where small size, high standards of literacy and good communications produce levels of aspiration and life style that minimize the cultural separation between country and city.[4]

In trying to gauge the increasing attraction of urban life, it is important to make an estimate of the income effect over time. We may do this in two ways: either by examining rural incomes in relation to those of the country as a whole over time or by using Ahiram's method and comparing the ratio of GDP by sector to labour force by sector. Trinidad data are again instructive in the first case, but comparative information from Barbados will be used for the second.[5]

The Censuses of 1960 and 1970, together with a sample survey in 1965 provide us with a three point comparison, although for the last census some figures are not yet available. Table 3.5 compares the returns from

TABLE 3.5   *Trinidad and Tobago: Median monthly income (gross) of male agricultural workers (self-employed or employees) compared with median monthly income for all workers 1960, 1965, 1970*

	Median monthly income (TT$)						
	Agricultural workers		All workers		Ratios		
	Self-employed	Employee	Self-employed	Employee			
Year	(1)	(2)	(3)	(4)	(1:3)	(1:4)	2:4)
1960	45.50	49.50	70.00	95.50	0.65	0.48	0.52
1965	41.00	70.50	86.50	146.50	0.47	0.28	0.48
1970	n.a.	94.50	n.a.	170.50	—	—	0.55

Source: See Note 5. N.B. For all three years TT$1.00 = £0.21 or US$0.50.

agricultural work to those obtained for all employment in Trinidad. It can be readily seen that the tendency has been for agricultural workers to lose ground in relation to all workers, except in the case of employees from 1965–70. The reason for this, together with the comparatively small fall in relative returns in the previous period, is almost certainly because of union organization. An important element in internal migration through-out the Caribbean consists of peasant farmers moving to wage employ-ment in the city. The Trinidad case illustrates why this might occur. Whereas in 1960 the median gross receipts accruing to self employed rural workers were just under a half those for all employees, by 1965 they were only just over a quarter. The temptation must be strong in those circumstances to move into the urban areas, or at least to move out of peasant production.

The method of comparing the contribution to total GDP between sectors is not as useful as looking directly at personal or family income but it does have the advantage, when viewed over time, of indicating areas or sectors of comparative growth. By dividing the GDP for each sector by the labour force employed in that sector we get an estimate of the per capita product, which is not, of course, the product due to labour. The following Table gives this information for Barbados in 1966/67 and 1970, and for Trinidad in 1968, 1971 and 1973. The important point is that in both countries the product contributed by agriculture has increased, but it

TABLE 3.6 *Sector GDP per capita for Barbados and Trinidad (current prices)*

| | Year | | Growth rate (%) | | |
	1966/67	1970	1966/67–1970		
	Barbados (EC$)				
Agriculture	1,988	2,719	36.8		
Manufacturing	2,113	2,794	32.2		
Construction	2,157	1,630	−24.4		
Government	2,804	4,320	54.1		
Other services	1,638	2,833	72.9		
	Trinidad and Tobago (TT$)				
	1968	1971	1973	1968–71	1971–73
Agriculture	1,764	1,810	2,108	2.6	16.5
Mining and manufacture	11,279	10,656	14,945	−5.5	40.2
Other	4,243	5,193	6,316	22.4	21.6

Sources: UN, 1974: 47, 164; *Barbados Development Plan, 1973–77*; Trinidad and Tobago, *Quarterly Economic Reports*, Oct.–Dec. 1969 Jul.–Sep. 1974

has done so less than the product in other key areas of the economy, most of which entail urban employment. Thus in Barbados in 1966/67 the per capita product from the government sector was 41 per cent higher than agriculture, but by 1970 it was 50 per cent higher. Similarly in Trinidad the mining and manufacturing sector, which has such a high per capita GDP because of its capital intensity, recorded a figure 539 per cent higher than agriculture in 1968 and 609 per cent higher in 1973.

What this exercise has sought to show is that whether we look at the incomes accruing to households or to individuals, or whether we look at the contribution rural employment makes to the national economy, the picture is clear: life in the rural sector is likely to be harder financially than life in the city and, on the basis of data from two relatively wealthy Caribbean countries, it appears to be becoming more so. This does not mean that those who migrate will necessarily be employed but this is another issue which may have independent effects upon both internal and external migration.

Employment

It has been noted already that the pattern of employment has changed markedly in the last generation as the extractive industries, manufacturing and service industries assume a greater importance. In 1960, 68 per cent of the labour force of the Dominican Republic was in agriculture but by 1970 this had fallen to 43 per cent. In Barbados, where tourism has become so important the decline was less, from a quarter to 17 per cent in 1970, but the prospect is that it will fall to under 11 per cent by 1977 (Barbados, 1973: 4–10).

The fact that few people are being employed in rural sectors, which can be amply demonstrated in many Caribbean societies, does not in itself indicate whether this change is due to few jobs being available or whether it is the case that people are *unwilling* to work in those industries. The little evidence we do have suggests that the position varies from one country to another. J. Harewood, for example, attributes about half the decline in the labour force working in the agricultural sector during the intercensal period 1946–60 to falling demand for labour in export agriculture while the remainder is largely accounted for by an apparent unwillingness to continue peasant holdings. Nearly all the parallel decline in Guyana is attributable to mechanization in the sugar industry, while in Barbados, the proportion of the decline due to this factor is given as two thirds (Harewood, 1972: 51).

There is, however, a very widespread view that agricultural work is poorly valued. It is often suggested that the stigma of slavery or the miseducation provided by an inappropriate emphasis in schools are the main reasons for this phenomenon. As to the first, the direct connection appears tenuous and unlikely. We have seen, however, that the dominance of plantations forces rural workers into dependence upon seasonal employment with increasingly poor returns and the threat of redundancy. That itself is enough to account for a pressure away from the land. The influence of education and the wider cultural status of farming is a factor that starts from the pinnacle of society and permeates throughout. It deserves more detailed treatment and will be considered in a later chapter. What is clear is that rural economies are in a relative decline in many areas of the Caribbean. The only major exception is Cuba where a dominant theme of development has been the promotion of the peasantry and the state farms and collectives. In this society alone has a conscious attempt been made to reverse the growing inequalities between town and country and here it has taken on the fervour of a religious crusade or demanded the zeal of a military offensive from all Cubans. As Hugh Thomas writes, however: 'The large investment which the Revolution has made in agriculture could certainly assure Cuba of being one of the most modern and prosperous agricultural countries in the world by 1975–80' (Thomas, 1971: 1,441). While this prophecy has not been fulfilled, in recent years, Cuba has been investing more than 25 per cent of GNP in agriculture and organizations like the Che Guevara Trailblazers Brigade have mobilized young people from Havana into remote regions to clear land for cane cultivation in order to obtain the elusive sugar harvest of 10,000,000 tons (Castro, 1968: 155). A popular centralized government pursuing socialist goals stands a much better chance of reversing or stemming the rising tide of urbanization, but even here the outcome is unpredictable. It may well be that income distribution and a massive emphasis upon the 'heroic' nature of agricultural work can lessen the power of other forces; Cuba, however, is still wedded to sugar production by mechanical means and, as elsewhere in the Caribbean, the proportion of the labour force engaged in export agriculture is expected to decline. Whether or not the expansion of food production, so vital to feed a burgeoning population, will absorb this labour is another matter.

Unemployment

A situation which is clear in other parts of the Caribbean is the maintenance of very high levels of unemployment. The Jamaican case, although worse and more persistent than some of the other Commonwealth Caribbean countries, is instructive. In 1943, the Census recorded that over 25 per cent of the labour force was unemployed which fell to 17.6 per cent if one excluded those seeking their first jobs. By the time Maunder (1960) came to undertake his survey of Kingston in the late 1950s, he found that 19 per cent of his sample of male wage earners was not working, of whom 14 per cent was classified as 'unemployed' (the remainder not seeking work) (Maunder, 1960: 138). The official rate for 1972 in Jamaica was 14.4 per cent of the male labour force and 13.4 per cent in 1973. The downturn in the economy in the last year or two, consequent upon the world oil crisis and a drought in 1975, which increased agricultural unemployment, led to an official overall estimate of 21.2 per cent in October of that year.

The 1970 Census of the Commonwealth Caribbean suggested that for the smaller islands unemployment ranged between 2.5 per cent of the active labour force in the tiny and prosperous Cayman Islands to 12.5 per cent in the less tiny and decidedly less prosperous island of St Vincent. These figures are almost certainly underestimates because of the problem of deciding who is in the work force and what constitutes unemployment, which are particularly intractable problems in islands without an organized work force. Official sources repeatedly estimate the unemployment in the Associated States at 15–25 per cent of the labour force. The unemployed in Barbados in 1970 were given as 9 per cent of the work force, while in Trinidad the total unemployed rose to 15 per cent in 1968, fell to a low of 12 per cent in 1970 and climbed again to 17 per cent in 1973. The Trinidad survey data permit a more refined understanding of the problem since, if the proportion is expressed as those without jobs who are actually seeking work as a proportion of those with jobs or wanting them, then the figure for the 1973 survey round falls to 11 per cent, and 10 per cent if women are excluded.

It is always difficult to gauge the extent of rural unemployment because it is much harder to do no work in the country where family plots of land have to be tended and livestock fed. The absence of a clear dividing line, such as receipt of wages, is another problem, as is the fact that so much of the rural employment is seasonal. However the Trinidad survey data point to unemployment being concentrated in construction, mining and manufacturing rather than in agricultural employment.[6] It is also apparent that unemployment is higher in urban rather than rural regions of the country, in fact almost twice as high. Similarly an International Labour Organization (ILO) report on the Dominican Republic in 1972 reported unemployment in Santa Domingo and Santiago to be 20 per cent, which is higher than for the country as a whole.

A characteristic feature of this urban unemployment (and possibly unemployment in general) is that it has disproportionate effects among the young. The ILO survey in the Dominican Republic, for example, showed that amongst the heads of households the unemployment rate was only 6 per cent indicating much higher rates among young people. In Trinidad a third of the male labour force between the ages of 15–19 was unemployed in 1973 while in Jamaica an official survey in 1972 put the unemployed proportion of the male 14–24 year old age band at 30 per cent. In fact it is possible to abstract detailed unemployment rates from the 1970 Census which show that for Trinidad and Tobago the situation was if anything worse in that year. Table 3.7 compares those unemployed but wanting work with the total working or looking for work in various age groups. Two features, sustaining the argument of this section, are immediately striking. The overall rate of just under 13 per cent hides a complex reality where youth and urban residence conspire to produce extraordinary unemployment rates. More than a half of the young men in the 15–19 age group in the urban areas are unemployed and wanting work and it is not until after their thirtieth birthday that the chances of them being unemployed fall below one in ten. It is equally striking that rural rates follow precisely the same pattern but are far less severe.

TABLE 3.7   *Males in Trinidad and Tobago unemployed and seeking work as a proportion of those with work or seeking work by age group and area of residence in 1970*

	Unemployment rates (%)		
Age group	Urban	Rural	All
14 years	76.7	35.0	61.0
15–19	53.0	22.4	42.0
20–4	27.6	10.3	20.5
25–9	15.6	5.9	11.0
30–4	9.8	5.0	7.4
35–9	7.6	4.3	5.9
40–4	6.8	3.8	5.2
45–9	7.1	3.4	5.2
50–4	6.7	3.2	4.9
55–9	7.6	3.3	5.4
60–4	8.2	2.6	5.3
65 and over	9.4	3.6	6.4
Total	18.3	6.6	12.8

Source: Commonwealth Caribbean, 1970.

The Barbados Development Plan 1973–77 also suggests that young people are not only more likely to be unemployed but also that they dominate the ranks of the jobless. Thus: 'In 1970 approximately 70 per cent of the male job seekers were under the age of 25 years and 80 per cent of the female job seekers were under age 25' (Barbados, 1973: 1–5). In Trinidad the proportion for males was 70 per cent in the same year and 90 per cent for females (Trinidad and Tobago, 1972: 10). The problem of unemployment is therefore one that faces the young, particularly in the years after leaving school. It has been estimated in Jamaica that only a quarter of the 40,000 school leavers are successful in obtaining jobs in any one year, and only about a fifth of the 10,000 school leavers in Guyana (Commonwealth Secretariat, 1970: 132). It should not be assumed that this phenomenon is short term or that it affects young people for only a brief period of their lives. The Trinidad labour force surveys showed that while 50 per cent of the men who were unemployed and seeking work in 1968 had not worked for up to three months, a quarter had either never worked or been unemployed for over a year. In the survey round at the end of 1973 the position had slightly worsened; 49 per cent had worked in the previous three months but 28 per cent had not found work at all or been out of work for more than a year.

Advances in educational attainment between generations naturally mean that the unemployed tend to be better educated than the employed. For example, in Trinidad in 1973 only 3 per cent of those with no education were actually unemployed, compared with 12 per cent for those who had attained standards 6–7 at the primary level. Unfortunately the survey figures do not control this cross tabulation for age so that it is impossible to see whether education is itself increasing the probability of unemployment. In addition, it has to be remembered that many who are recorded as working are only doing so on a seasonal or part-time basis. As Kuper reports, a labour survey of Jamaica in 1968 showed that only 55 per cent of the male labour force had worked forty hours or more during the week of the survey, while 41 per cent of the total labour force had been in work for less than ten months in the year preceding the interview (Kuper, 1976: 33). In the same year the Trinidad survey rounds revealed that 19 per cent of those in work had been working for less than thirty-three hours in the survey week.

The disturbing fact about the chronic problems of unemployment and underemployment as they affect the young in both rural and urban locations is that they do not appear to be on the way to solution as industrialization progresses. The figures for the comparatively indus-trialized country of Trinidad and Tobago have been given: in Puerto Rico, the most highly industrialized country in the Caribbean, unem-ployment rates have only fallen from 13 per cent in 1950 to 12 per cent in 1971, despite the fact that over the same period the number of workers in manufacturing doubled. Jamaica, too, has experienced unprecedented economic growth and still has the worst employment situation in the Commonwealth Caribbean.

The best analysis of the reason for this situation has come from Dudley Seers (1969), using Trinidad as a case study. What he calls 'structural unemployment' is produced through using techniques of production suited to high labour cost economies and through being geographically and culturally located in a region which ensures the importation of materialist consumption preferences. Over time, the situation may well deteriorate, for three fundamental reasons. In the first place there is rapid growth in the labour force, produced through population increase unrestrained by emigration as readily as in the immediate past. This problem is common to all countries, regardless of whether, like Guyana or Belize, they have low densities of population and vast tracts of underdeveloped land. The other two factors tend to be of increasing importance in precisely those countries that are better off or rapidly growing. The first is a rise in the import coefficient, or the propensity to import, which rises rapidly with every increase in income above a certain level. At low income levels, a sudden, even dramatic, rise will not produce this effect since consumers simply expand their consumption of locally produced food or housing. Particularly in countries with close contacts with the West, when a middle class emerges it will have Western consumption patterns which can only be satiated by imported luxury items. The mass media and the adoption of Western advertising practices may exacerbate this phenomenom by producing a demonstration effect on the country as a whole. As comparative affluence extends to other groups, such as a labour aristocracy dependent on the wealth generated by a capital intensive mineral industry, this effect becomes more pronounced. Seers is able to show that the import coefficient is positively related to both inequalities in the distribution of income and unemployment. That is, with greater inequalities of income, the stronger will be the influence of the élite upon imports, and this in turn has a negative effect on employment.

Last, contact with the West or with advanced industrial societies, whatever form that contact takes, will increase the likelihood that technical progress will raise the 'productivity coefficient', thereby producing unemployment through the expanded utilization of capital intensive techniques. As Seers expresses it: 'employment will tend to lag behind the rise in the labour force, and chronic unemployment to grow, in a country which is economically well behind the industrial leaders, especially if it is in close enough contact to be subject to their influence in many ways' (Seers, 1969: 231). Local governments who seek to try and prevent expensively trained or recruited employees from leaving the country have every reason to promote rather than prevent a high income sector in the economy. Foreign companies set international salary levels for their staff without considering the possible implications of their actions. By focussing their attention on the areas of easiest success, trade unions force up wages in capital intensive industries and create groups whose position cannot but exacerbate frustrations and divide the working class against itself. All these factors, and more besides, increase the probability of unemployment. The Caribbean is unique in the degree of external penetration, which extends so much further than even economic dependence. As Seers affirms: 'Underlying many of these obstacles is a set of tastes and attitudes, largely imported from abroad, which means that a large section of the population would rather, in the last resort, face a continuation of chronic unemployment than a reduction in their consumption of imports' (Seers, 1969: 240). In precisely the same way, migrants would sooner face the probability of urban unemployment, which has the promise of a better job and a taste of the consumer way of life so stridently promoted through the media, than continue the struggle in the increasingly marginal world of the rural economy.

4 Population structure and change

The progressive urbanization of a society is not necessarily dependent upon the size, structure or composition of its population. It is quite feasible to imagine a static population with dynamic urbanization or, on the other hand, the kind of situation towards which Cuba appears to be moving – rapid population growth accompanied by de-urbanization, or at least no change in the relative balance of countryside and city. However, we have sought to stress that the whole question of urbanization can only be approached and its social significance comprehended within the context of resource allocation. Population growth affects this allocation by tending to diminish per capita returns. It follows that the migration component of urbanization may be one response to the pressure on resources exerted by this process. In addition, population movement is seldom uniform in nature and must therefore affect the social organization of both urban and rural communities. Although urbanization may be a process most readily apprehended by using demographic criteria, these can never be used to gauge its social or political significance. But that is no reason for ignoring population change or the complex relationships between people and their habitat.

This chapter considers first recent changes in Caribbean populations and then examines the non-economic strategies that they may adopt when faced with pressure on their resources. It concludes by looking at overall patterns of urbanization and the effects these have had on urban centres. We begin by examining the evidence on population growth and changes in population structure.

Population growth

The evidence presented in Table 3.3 reveals that average population growth rates differ markedly for different territories. In the vast majority of the cases the increases are smaller for the second period than the first and the overall annual growth is now probably just below an average of 2 per cent. However, natural increases are considerably higher, being reduced by net emigration. Aaron Segal recently summarized the position as follows: 'Overall, the rate of population increase from 1950 to 1970 was approximately 3 per cent per annum for the Caribbean as a whole, and this is only slightly less than the Central American rate, which

57

is considered to be the fastest in the world' (Segal, 1975: 8). Haiti and the Dominican Republic have the highest birth rates but their rates of natural increases are mitigated by relatively high death rates. For example, infant mortality rates for most of the Caribbean are very low, often averaging forty per 1,000 live-births or less, but in Haiti the rate in 1970 was over 140. As table 4.1 shows, it is the higher death rates that reduce levels of natural increase in Hispaniola, even though the overall growth of population in the Dominican Republic is almost 3 per cent or enough to double the population in twenty-four years. It is the reduction in infant mortality accompanied by longevity and high birth rates that has produced the population explosion of the past twenty years (cf. Logan, 1968).

The general pattern of fertility has been that crude birth rates were high during the nineteenth century but fell off up to the Second World War. After this they rose dramatically but in most places have begun to decline in the past decade (Byrne, 1972). Jamaica is a good case in point; the crude birth rate fell to a low of thirty in 1945 but then rose steadily to over forty in 1960. It then stayed high for some years before dropping to a level comparable with the immediate post-war rate. Trinidad and Tobago is another example of recent major decline. The rate rose after the war to reach a high point of almost forty-two in 1954 and by 1960 it was still over thirty-nine per 1,000. An amazing decrease then ensued and by 1970 the rate had fallen to 24.5 which represents an actual decline in live births of

TABLE 4.1   *Crude birth rates, death rates and life expectancy for selected Caribbean countries (1973 estimates)*

Country	Births	Deaths	Natural increase	Life expectancy at birth Male	Female
Barbados	22.1	8.5	13.6	66.7	71.6
Cuba	25.4	5.8	19.6	68.1	71.5
Dominican Republic	46.0	13.0	33.0	55.9	59.7
Haiti (1970)	43.9	19.7	24.2	49.0	51.0
Jamaica	30.6	7.2	23.4	67.9	71.2
Puerto Rico	23.3	6.5	16.8	69.7	74.7
Trinidad and Tobago	26.5	6.7	19.8	67.9	71.2

Source: Nortman, 1975: Table 3.

23 per cent (Mandle, 1973). In some cases age specific changes in birth rates appear to be linked to social and political changes other than those

induced by the cessation of hostilities in 1945. In Cuba, for example, population had grown with the expansion of the sugar industry during the eighteenth and nineteenth centuries, partly by the importation of slaves but also by natural increase. However, the transition to lower fertility started early and by the 1930s the rate had fallen by 10–15 points to a figure in the low 30s. After the war it went on falling to reach 26.8 per 1,000 in 1958, just before the Revolution. The immediate effects of the Revolution on employment, health and general optimism pushed the rate up within a few years and it has only recently declined to its pre-revolutionary position.

Much more understanding of fertility patterns is possible by examining age specific fertility for other changes can be induced through alterations in the age structure of the populations, an event which has been widespread because of external migration. In fact, it is this latter phenomenon in Jamaica which is mainly responsible for the fall in crude birth rate; patterns of migration throughout the 1960s had a disproportionate effect on the number of women in child bearing years (Sinclair, 1974b:128). On the other hand, changes in fertility rate in Trinidad were produced through an entirely different process. Here, where emigration has never been a major source of population change, the decline was produced by falls in age specific fertility (live births per 1,000 women in specified age bands). As Mandle (1973) effectively demonstrates, it was a change initiated by younger age groups of women but emulated later by others. He was also able to show that this change was particularly marked with younger women in non-legal or 'common-law' marriages, but later affected older women who were in married unions more than those who were not (Mandle, 1973: 13).

A factor of relevance and importance in this discussion of fertility is the difference between urban and rural rates. There are many measurement problems here for it may be that rural women travel to urban centres to give birth, thus narrowing the well known differential between urban and rural fertility. However, in the first place, as Sinclair reports from Jamaica, there is normally a higher proportion of childless women in urban areas (Sinclair, 1974b). The actual proportion of such women has declined for all the age groups she examinied between 1943 and 1970 and had fallen most of all for the urban areas. For example, whereas in 1943 two thirds of women 20–24 in Kingston had no children, by 1970 this had fallen to under a third. Moreover, the traditional differential between the urban and rural areas had substantially narrowed. Sinclair suggests that this, and the more general narrowing of fertility differentials between urban and rural areas in Jamaica, may be the direct result of urbanization, as patterns of higher fertility found among rural women are transposed to the city (Sinclair, 1974b:168).

It would not be fair to conclude, however, that traditionally higher rates of fertility in rural regions have been completely eroded. Data on the average number of births to all women drawn from elsewhere in the Caribbean (Table 4.2) clearly show a remarkably consistent pattern between urban and rural sectors of two vastly different societies. This must obviously mean that the pressure on resources produced by increases in population is greater in rural regions, but it is not to say that such pressure will be as readily contained in urban areas for, as we have seen, unemployment is even more chronic in the towns. Even with levels of rural fertility lower than in the urban areas, we could still see substantial urban migration if rural resources were simply inadequate. As it is, high rates overall, and still higher levels in the rural areas with no major difference in death rates, must stretch rural resources even further.

Population structure

Another feature of importance is the effect that high fertility has on the age structure of Caribbean populations. It is an effect which is further exacerbated by urban–rural differentials. In all populations that have been subject to recent heavy additions through natural increase, there is a pronounced tendency for a high proportion to be below working age. This

TABLE 4.2 *Average number of live births to women in the Dominican Republic and in Trinidad and Tobago by age group and urban rural residence, 1970*

Age group	Urban	Rural	Both
	Dominican Republic		
15–44	2.36	3.10	2.76
45–64	5.05	6.29	5.74
	Trinidad and Tobago		
15–44	2.21	2.93	2.59
45–64	4.03	5.03	4.52

Sources: *Comentarios Sobre Los Resultados Definitivos del V Censo Nacional de Poblacion* (Santa Domingo, Oficina Nacional de Estadistica, 1972): Cuadro 15; *Trinidad and Tobago Census Bulletin No 3 – Fertility* (Port of Spain, CSO, 1974): Table 2A.

is amply demonstrated for the whole Caribbean in Table 4.3 which reveals that only in Barbados, Cuba and Puerto Rico does the proportion of under fifteen year olds fall beneath 40 per cent. In some of the Windward and Leeward Islands it actually rises to a half, which indicates an extraordinary burden on the working segment of the population. In

TABLE 4.3 *Distribution of Caribbean populations by age 1970 (or 1975 estimates) (%)*

Country	Under 15	15–64	65 and over	Total	Dependency ratio*
Antigua	44.0	50.7	5.3	100.0	97
Barbados	37.1	54.6	8.3	100.0	83
Belize	49.3	46.4	4.3	100.0	116
Cuba (1975)	38.0	56.0	6.0	100.0	79
Dominica	49.1	45.0	5.9	100.0	122
Dominican Republic (1975)	48.0	49.0	3.0	100.0	102
Grenada	47.1	47.0	5.9	100.0	113
Guyana	47.1	49.3	3.6	100.0	103
Haiti (1975)	40.0	56.0	4.0	100.0	80
Jamaica	46.1	48.4	5.5	100.0	107
Puerto Rico (1975)	34.0	59.0	7.0	100.0	68
St Kitts–Nevis–Anguilla	48.7	44.2	7.1	100.0	126
St Lucia	49.6	45.1	5.3	100.0	122
St Vincent	51.2	43.9	4.9	100.0	128
Trinidad and Tobago	42.1	53.5	4.4	100.0	87

Source: Commonwealth Caribbean, 1970. Nortman, 1975: Table 3

* The 'dependency ratio' is formed by dividing the age group from which the economically active are drawn into the remaining population. It will rise to 100 when there is one 'dependent' for every adult member of the population below 65 years of age.

most cases too, the proportion over retirement age is high and increasing. This can be readily appreciated by noting that Barbados, Cuba and Puerto Rico are well on the way to achieving a retired section of their population comparable to the 11 per cent in the United States or the 14 per cent in the UK. As we shall see, Cuba has continually eschewed a policy of attempting direct population control but even here there is a realization of the problems created by population growth and structure. In a speech in 1968, Fidel Castro pointed out that with an annual rate of population growth of 2.3 per cent and with almost 40 per cent of her population under fifteen years of age, Cuba had to invest 12 per cent of GNP just to compensate for population growth. Moreover: 'to develop the economy at a rate of no less than five per cent of the gross per capita product annually, 30 per cent of the available gross national product must be invested. And this effort must be primarily made by half the population, excluding children and persons over sixty' (Castro, 1968: 255). The dependency ratios in the table, which are simply the total dependent population divided by the 15–64 age group, show that Cuba is by no means in a bad position when Caribbean comparisons are made. The United States, Canada and Britain have dependency ratios of 55, 55 and 60 respectively and, although Cuba's ratio at 79 is much higher, it is healthier than the Dominican Republic, Jamaica or some of the smaller islands. It is worth pointing out too that limitations to population growth by emigration may have many advantages but improving this ratio is not one of them, since most migrants fall into the younger half of the productive age band (although where the children of such migrants accompany their parents they reduce the dependent population).

The burden imposed by dependent populations is also increased by educational developments since at higher levels this takes a greater proportion of the over fifteen year olds out of productive labour. The growth of population and longevity, however, are the main reasons why the situation is changing. This can readily be seen by realizing that in Jamaica the ratio was 69 in 1943, 83 in 1960 and 107 in 1970. Furthermore, a more accurate assessment of this situation may be gained by appreciating that not all in the 15–64 age category are also in the labour force, and by no means are all of those who are, actually working. In fact Jamaica again provides an instructive example; the number of persons dependent on every 100 *working* people increased by almost ninety per cent between 1943 and 1970 from 152 to 288 (Boland, 1974: 73).

What may not always be appreciated is that the burden of dependency is heavier in rural populations. This can be seen by looking at the age structure of rural and urban populations in the two cases shown in Table 4.4, Jamaica and Trinidad, with figures that are derived from the 1970 Census.

TABLE 4.4   *Population of Jamaica and Trinidad and Tobago by age group, sex and region of residence 1970 (%)*

| | Jamaica | | | | | | Trinidad and Tobago | | | | | |
| | Urban | | | Rural | | | Urban | | | Rural | | |
Age group	Male	Fem.	Both	Male	Fem.	Both	Male	Fem.	Both	Male	Fem.	Both
Under 15	45	40	42	49	47	48	40	37	39	45	45	45
15–64	52	55	54	45	45	46	56	57	56	51	51	51
65 and over	3	5	4	6	6	6	4	6	5	4	4	4
Total	100	100	100	100	100	100	100	100	100	100	100	100

Source: Commonwealth Caribbean, 1970.

From this we can see that the dependency ratios are as follows:

	Jamaica	Trinidad and Tobago
Urban	85	76
Rural	117	97
All	107	87

In other words the aggregate figures for both countries conceal the fact that in Jamaican rural areas there are 38 per cent more people dependent on every 100 persons in the working age group than is the case in the urban sector, while in Trinidad the parallel figure is 28 per cent. Although it is true that the relative impact of this situation is lessened by the greater proportion of the rural labour force actually reporting that they had worked, it is none the less true that demographic features such as these must in some áreas at least constitute a relentless pressure on available resources. When coupled with declining relative incomes, inadequate land areas and direct or indirect pressure from plantations, it is not surprising that the drift to the towns should constitute one avenue of release. But it is not the only option and we need to examine more closely the relationship between population and rural resources.

Population density and resources

It is by no means the case that what constitutes an intolerable pressure on rural resources in one socicty will also do so in another or, indeed, that within one society the capacity of rural economies to support a given population will be the same. The differential application of technology may produce more intensive farming or a judicious choice of crops may raise returns. Cultivation practices, the capacity for sustained labour or an ability to use land hitherto judged as unsuitable or infertile may have similar effects, as may supportive legal, administrative and political arrangements for the holding of land, the provision of services or the marketing of produce.

Table 4.5 amply demonstrates that there is a very wide difference indeed between the population densities of Caribbean states and dependencies. Barbados is among the most densely populated societies on earth, while the vast empty hinterlands of Guyana and Surinam have densities below any other country in Latin America and more redolent of Australia or the desert countries of the Middle East. The same differences are, of course, maintained if we discount the urban populations and divide the total land area by those who mainly gain their living from it. Of course, this is a very crude measure since we are taking no account of the amount of total land area that is fertile or economically usable. Much of the land area of Surinam and Guyana, for example, consists of the infertile sands lying behind the populous coastal and riverain regions or the barely penetrable jungles of the Amazonian basin. We really need a measure of the usable land, which is very hard to obtain because it is largely a question of culture and technological sophistication whether a piece of marginal land is deemed usable or not. Some light may be shed on this problem by defining the usable land area as the total farming area. In the case of Barbados, for example, the actual density of population per square kilometre in 1970 was 547 (this differs from the figure in Table 4.5 which is based on projection from the population in 1960). But the area under cultivation in farms was 80 per cent of the total land area so that the

TABLE 4.5   *Area, average density and 'approximate rural density'* for Caribbean territories 1950, 1960 and 1970*

Territory and area (sq. km, 000s)		Overall density			'Rural density'		
		1950	1960	1970	1950	1960	1970
Bahamas	11	7	10	14	4	6	6
Barbados	0.4	491	540	588	316	322	323
Belize	23	3	4	5	2	2	3
Cuba	115	48	60	76	21	25	31
Dominican Republic	49	44	62	89	33	43	56
Guadeloupe	1.8	116	153	191	99	125	146
Guyana	215	2	3	3	1	2	2
Haiti	28	112	144	175	98	123	144
Jamaica	11	125	149	184	96	105	118
Leeward Islands	1.1	110	124	130	84	89	86
Martinique	1.1	201	259	319	143	157	162
Netherlands Antilles	1.0	169	197	229	100	99	96
Puerto Rico	8.9	249	264	321	148	148	168
Surinam	143	1	2	3	1	1	2
Trinidad and Tobago	5.1	123	161	216	91	98	101
US Virgin Islands	0.3	78	93	206	32	41	78
Windward Islands	2.1	128	154	184	108	127	149

Source: Davis, 1969: Table H.

*The 'approximate rural density' index is formed by dividing the total area of the territory into the rural population. Although it is a crude measure, which says very little about pressure on resources, it is justified because 'urban' populations occupy relatively small areas of land and because it is the 'rural' population who use the land as their major resource.

density per square kilometre of farm land only rose to 688. Many of the smaller islands with volcanic, mountainous terrain are not as well placed. We can illustrate this by looking at the Windward and Leeward Islands in more detail. As Table 4.6 shows, the population densities on farm land in Grenada, St Vincent and Antigua are higher than their overall densities would suggest, because they have a relatively small proportion of their land under farm cultivation. If other things were equal the 'farm land density of population' would be a better gauge of the degree to which population pressure on resources was providing an important spur to rural migration.

TABLE 4.6 *Population densities in the Windward and Leeward Islands 1970* (per sq. km)

	Overall density	Farm land* as per cent total	'Farm land density'
Windward Islands	167	50	332
Dominica	94	41	227
Grenada	272	68	401
St Lucia	163	57	284
St Vincent	224	41	544
Leeward Islands	138	47	295
Antigua	147	31	470
Montserrat	138	85	163
St Kitts/Nevis	126	57	222

Source: Commonwealth Caribbean, 1970; West Indies Census of Agriculture, 1961.
*'Farm land' is not the same as arable land but should constitute at least four fifths of it.

As population geographers are quick to point out, all other things are by no means equal. For example, Alan Eyre (1972) is able to compute the population that can be supported on land utilized in different ways. His analysis of the complex variables involved on different assumptions produces estimates of the following potential densities of population that can be supported on land used for various crops (Eyre, 1972: 149). As his

	Potential population density per sq. km
Pasture	36–70
Bananas (good yield)	96–174
Sugarcane (small farms)	116–348
Sugarcane (estates)	186–695
Wet rice	2,107–2,663

case studies graphically reveal, a series of other factors will determine how much of this potential is actually realized. In addition to regional variations in edaphic and climatic circumstances, legal, social and political constraints will also determine whether potential productivity is perceived and obtained.

What is also striking in this important study is that these same factors will influence the strategy pursued by a rural community when it is faced with population pressure on resources. Eyre demonstrates how options are limited by showing that if per capita income is to remain at a stable level then one or other of three economic strategies must be adopted. First, the land may be farmed more productively by working harder, by increasing mechanization, by improving crop yields through superior strains, or increased use of fertilizers, or by changing to more lucrative crops. Second, the stock of land may be increased. Virgin land may be cleared or underutilized land brought back into cultivation. Third, the rural community may adopt the urban wealth creating solution and incorporate non-primary economic activity such as light industry or tourism. All of these are possibilities and, as Eyre shows, all have been adopted by some Jamaican rural areas faced with population growth.

Such economic solutions are vital but, as we have tried to show already, there is much in the economic order of many Caribbean societies that militates against an easy and ready solution along these lines. Despite public mythology to the contrary, there is little solid evidence that agricultural productivity can be greatly enhanced by harder effort. Crop yields can certainly be raised and there is every reason for supposing that the plantation history of the Caribbean has produced an inflexible attitude towards non-export crops (as the Cuban case vividly demonstrates) but change in these areas requires imaginative political leadership and investment in agricultural research and development. As to the first, the record is not encouraging, for, as we shall see, Caribbean politicians have too often associated development with industrialization and the emulation of Western urban sophistication. What non-primary investment there has been, has been totally urban in its location and usually lacking the involvement of so called 'intermediate technology' that would make it a viable possibility for a rural workforce. Furthermore, whereas Cuba has been able to extend arable land by thousands of acres, the continued rural hegemony of the plantations elsewhere, coupled with the lack of leadership from the urban core, has usually meant a relatively small increment to arable land stocks in recent years.

There are only two other solutions to population pressure on rural resources if per capita income is not to fall; the long-term strategy of population control or the short-term solution of migration, and it is to these that we now turn.

Policies of population control

The history of the Caribbean is one of almost continual involvement of governments in population policies. For most of the eighteenth and nineteenth centuries the object of these initiatives was to increase the labour supply to the clamouring plantations. When natural growth and declining labour demand produced the familiar crisis of recent decades, the solution has been emigration. Only in the very recent past, as one after another door has been closed, have Caribbean governments adopted specific population policies. Although there are varying degrees of commitment to these policies, it is possible to discern two rather different strategies. The first, characteristic of the Commonwealth Caribbean and Puerto Rico, is to establish a network of contraceptive outlets and to seek by persuasion to convince couples of the wisdom of birth limitation. The other strategy is largely confined to Cuba and it is to reorganize social and economic life so that motivation to reduce fertility is awakened as a by-product of greater affluence, optimism and sexual equality.

The first strategy owes its origins to a number of converging influences among which, for the West Indies, the Moyne Commission of 1938 was particularly influential. The report of this inquiry held back until after the war because of the fear that its critical tone could be used for anti-British propaganda, argued that a reduction of the birth rate was 'in one sense the most pressing need of the West Indian colonies' (West India Royal Commission, 1945: 245). The report did not provide concrete recommendations but did suggest that 'West Indian public opinion should recognise the vital importance of the population problem' (West India Royal Commission, 1945: 440). In Puerto Rico, the interest in family planning dates back to the 1920s, but, in common with many Roman Catholic countries, the idea has only gained acceptance as a way of ameliorating poverty or ill health rather than as a development strategy or as a way of controlling fertility. The first clinic was opened in Ponce in 1925 by Dr José Rolon but the following forty years saw mounting Church hostility, reaching a peak in the 1960s. Only after the publication of the encyclical *Humane Vitae* in 1968 did the Church move to a neutral position, which enabled the government to embrace a national programme of family planning in 1970 with the aim of reducing the birth rate to 15.2 per thousand by 1985 (Segal, 1975: 159–70).

In the Commonwealth Caribbean as well, national population control programmes have been built upon voluntary bodies, often with the assistance of international agencies like the International Planned Parenthood Federation (IPPF) or, more recently, the United Nations Fund for Population Activities (UNFPA). For example, the Jamaican Family Planning Association has its origins in a movement founded in 1939 but it was not until mass emigration was curtailed by the UK Commonwealth Immigration Act of 1962 that government interest was aroused, culminating in the National Family Planning Programme, which was launched in 1966 with the goal of reducing the crude birth rate to 25 by 1977/78. By 1974, there were 161 clinics in operation, but only 17 of them ran daily sessions for dispensing contraceptives or medical advice. A recent commentator has lamented the lack of clear direction in the official approach and advocated a 'radical incentive programme for birth prevention' which includes the proposal that '$1,000 should be given each woman in a sex union for each calendar year in which she did not give birth to a child' (Ebanks, 1975: 70). Such a policy, aside from being inordinately costly and administratively complex, would soon ensure that few women were outside a sexual union!

The policies pursued by the governments and voluntary movements in Trinidad and Barbados are of considerable interest because, although both are similar to the Jamaican case, these two countries have recently witnessed remarkable downturns of fertility. In the case of Barbados, government support for the Family Planning Association goes back twenty years and this organization now runs nine clinics, all of them in urban areas. Although net emigration has been the major avenue of population control in Barbados and has undoubtedly affected fertility by having a more significant effect upon those in the main child bearing years, it is reckoned that the activities of the family planning movement is the chief factor responsible for the halving of the rate of natural increase from 2.4 per cent in 1960 to 1.2 per cent in 1970 (Ebanks, 1975: 41).

The National Family Planning Programme in Trinidad was launched in 1968, seven years after the local Family Planning Association. By the end of 1975 there were seventy-two government sponsored clinics many of them integrated with child health and maternal services, and five non-integrated clinics run by the FPA. There is evidence that fertility decline has taken place but the problem here, as in Barbados, is to judge the independent influence of the population control policies. Clinics in both societies are well used and although both programmes suffer from high rates of 'drop-out', it would be remarkable if the distribution of so many contraceptive devices had not had a marked affect on fertility. But that is not the same thing as arguing that these programmes provided the *motivation* to use contraceptives. This could easily have stemmed more from increased prosperity and optimism than from efforts at education and persuasion by propaganda.

It is this point which characterizes the Cuban population policy. There is as much ease of access to contraception in Cuba as there is anywhere in the Caribbean, and Cuba is the only Caribbean society to legitimize abortion simply as a way of avoiding unwanted pregnancies. Landstreet records that estimates of 43–56 abortions per hundred live births have been made for Havana province in 1971 (Landstreet, 1975: 145). A recent statement by the Ministry of Public Health firmly locates family planning advice in the overall health programme and states: 'The health organization, among its activities in protecting the health of women, locates the mechanisms which under certain conditions permit the prevention of an undesired birth, as well as overcoming undesired sterility. This is done without including among its activities any which would directly stimulate an increase or decrease in fertility' (quoted by Landstreet, 1975: 144). There is plenty of evidence that the Cubans are concerned about population growth and, unlike the governments of relatively underpopulated (but still poor) Belize and Guyana, they have not pursued pro-natalist policies. The difference is that Cuban socialism is founded upon the belief that the prime concern is to liberate the inherent productive capacity of the labour force by reorganizing the relations of production. In the sense that this economic solution is an effective strategy for relieving the pressure of population on resources it could be seen as 'the functional equivalent of an anti-natalist policy' (Landstreet, 1975:148). More important, it may actually prove in the long run a more effective anti-natalist policy by providing the motivation for family limitation that appears to have been the major reason for fertility declines in industrial countries.

External migration

Family planning programmes have been visible and tangible population policies in the last decade, but it is unlikely whether they have been anywhere near as significant for Caribbean societies as external migration. Intra-Caribbean movements have a long history and Segal (1975: 9) reports that Cuba imported 230,000 contract labourers from Haiti and Jamaica between 1912 and 1924 to harvest sugar cane in Oriente Province. Trinidad has usually been a net importer of labour from Grenada or other Windward Islands and, although restrictions are now in force, the recent profitability of the oil industry has probably stimulated further illegal migration. It is illegal movement which characterizes most of the continuing movement from Haiti to the Dominican Republic.

The watershed in the recent history of migration outside the Caribbean was the British Commonwealth Immigration Act of 1962 which brought to a close a period of massive unrestricted migration that had built up after the Second World War. Segal estimates that from 1950 close on 3,000,000 people migrated overseas and that in no society was net immigration less than 5 per cent of total population (Segal, 1975: 17; cf.

Segal and Earnhardt, 1969). He writes: 'Between 1947 and 1962 ... approximately 10 per cent of the total population of the Caribbean emigrated outside the area. The major movements consisted of Barbadians and Jamaicans to England, and Puerto Ricans to the United States, but there were substantive movements of Cubans, Dominicans and Haitians to the United States' (Segal, 1975: 10). The estimated movements and their destinations are given in Table 4.7.

TABLE 4.7   *Caribbean net emigration 1950—72* (000s)

Country		Destination
Puerto Rico	810–60	US
Cuba	620	US
Jamaica	169	UK
	110–200	US
	30–5	Canada
Dominican Republic	155–250	US
Haiti	51–200	US
	10–15	Canada
	4	France
Trinidad and Tobago	41–65	US
	35–40	Canada
	24	UK
Leeward and Windward Islands	22–45	US
	59	UK
	8–10	Canada
Barbados	28	UK
	14–30	US
	7–10	Canada
Guyana	28	UK
	15–18	Canada
	12–15	US
Martinique	55	France
Guadeloupe	45	France
Surinam	30	Netherlands
Netherlands Antilles	10	Netherlands

Source: Segal, 1975: 219.

These estimates are necessarily crude, especially since they often depend upon settlement figures overseas which take no account of illegal immigration. For example, the Trinidad Government puts its own loss through net emigration over the same period at 62,107 which is well below Segal's figure but may include an element of illegal immigration.

What is more certain than the exact number of external or internal migrants is that this major population change has had profound demographic and economic effects on the Caribbean. It may, of course, be seen as a form of urbanization and we would then expect the migrants to be largely drawn from the rural periphery. Segal writes, for example, that: 'The emigrants, whether Puerto Ricans or West Indians, have come predominantly from the 20 to 35 age group, from rural areas, and from those with primary rather than secondary education' (Segal, 1975: 10). Moreover, in a discussion of the Jamaican labour force, Barbara Boland has suggested that external movement has 'affected most heavily rural parishes during the decade 1960–70' (Boland, 1974: 61).

The situation prior to 1962 is not quite as clear as this. Migrants have certainly tended to be young but there is some evidence to suggest that those going to Britain were disproportionately skilled and had been living in urban areas prior to their departure (Peach, 1968: 30). It appears to be the case that a two-stage process is at work. Rural migrants move first to the city with the intention of permanent settlement. After experiencing the intense problems faced there they then push on further overseas in the hope of finding better opportunities of employment and a steady income. O. C. Francis, for example, in a sample survey of passport applicants in Jamaica during 1962, found that rates of external migration from more isolated rural parishes were considerably lower than those nearer to the urban areas, while the urban areas themselves had still higher rates (Francis, 1965: 94). If we rework these figures, we can show the following approximate rates of external migration per thousand residents during that year.[1]

Urban	3.9
Semi-urban	2.4
Rural	1.4

Furthermore, although the vast majority of rural migrants were born in these areas, 64 per cent of those migrating from the urban sector had not been born there. This is certainly higher than the 1960 figure for Kingston, which has been estimated at about 50 per cent (Clarke, 1975: 99). Support for Francis' estimates of rates of migration came from a later division of total external migration by parish over the period 1960–70 (Hewitt, 1974: 27). A reworking of these data to make them comparable with those above (assuming migration to be equally divided in each year of the decade) gives rates of 3.4, 1.5 and 1.1 for every thousand members of the population in 1960. This suggests what we know already from other sources, that migration fell in the late 1960s. However, it adds to the theory that external migration is a disproportionately urban phenomenon.

It is always unwise to assume a direct relationship between population pressure on resources and migration. For example, Eyre found that those who were often in the most dire economic circumstances sometimes lacked the money and morale to migrate to the city and others have shown that there is no clear cut relationship between unemployment and external migration (Peach, 1968). The model proposed here would not lead one to assume that pressure of either an economic or demographic kind was the only criterion for understanding migration. Indeed, viewing the rural periphery, local urban core and overseas urban centre as a complex series of inter-relationships avoids the simplistic assumption that either 'push' or 'pull' factors are of overriding significance. The relationships are those of inequalities, which will have profound effects upon the allocation of human resources, but in the last resort it is the perception of those inequalities and assessments of relative interest which will determine the precise rearrangements that take place within economic and demographic parameters.

There is no doubting the importance of external migration on Caribbean societies. The loss of young people in the main child bearing years has reduced overall growth rates by at least 1 per cent per annum in the past two decades. Disproportionate effects have also been established by the greater loss of males, although this appears to be of much less significance than in earlier migration movements (Sinclair and Boland, 1974: 13). It remains the case, however, that there are marked differences in the sex ratio (number of men per 1,000 women) between urban and rural sectors with a higher ratio of men in rural areas at each age group. Table 4.8 illustrates this phenomenon and lends some limited support to the proposition that urban areas may disproportionately contribute to external movement. There are fewer men in proportion to women in urban areas for all age groups, although this could equally be the result of disproportionate female migration into urban areas (Hewitt, 1974: 32).

The pattern of external migration is gradually changing. In the first place there is a pronounced tendency for the traditional destinations to change as restrictive legislation comes into force. While the Dutch, French and US territories have unrestricted movement, there has been a replacement of Britain as a destination for Commonwealth Caribbean migrants by Canada which now rivals the United States as a host society.[2] As far as Britain is concerned almost all long stay migration from the Caribbean is restricted to dependents of those already in the UK. As this process is completed one of the major indirect benefits from emigration will cease, the remittances of migrants to their dependents. It is striking that in 1962 these payments, together with repayments on loans taken out to finance passages, covered 40 per cent of Jamaica's visible trade deficit (Levitt and McIntyre, 1967: 89), whereas in 1973 net private transfer payments in total only covered 19 per cent of that year's trade deficit.

TABLE 4.8   *Sex ratios in Jamaica and Trinidad and Tobago by region of residence and age 1970*

	Jamaica			Trinidad and Tobago		
	Urban	Rural	Both	Urban	Rural	Both
Under 15	973	1025	1011	1002	1012	1008
15–64	808	970	915	933	1000	967
65 and over	587	857	791	619	936	771
All	863	988	951	941	1002	974

Source: Commonwealth Caribbean, 1970.

External migrants tend to have slightly higher educational attainments than the general population, but the Caribbean has always been prone to the loss of much more highly educated people overseas. These have formed only a tiny proportion of total migrants in the past but their significance lies in their much needed and expensively trained talent. The tragedy of the 'brain drain' is that, with the exception of Cuba, recent restrictions on migration have been made entirely by the receiving societies, who have devised regulations which specifically exclude from restriction the very people the Caribbean can least afford to lose. Thus the Canadian government has a points system that operates to select skilled migrants and the 1971 Immigration Act in the UK excludes from restriction those with 'needed skills'. The precise extent of this problem has not been adequately surveyed but expert opinion is united in affirming its importance. In 1970, following the disturbances in Trinidad and Tobago, the Prime Minister, Dr Eric Williams, recorded that from 1965 to 1969 696 nurses had been trained but that 586 had resigned and emigrated. On that basis each additional nurse was costing the country six times more than the actual cost of her training.

Internal migration

There is no doubt that internal migration is the primary cause of urbanization in the Caribbean, if we mean by this the increasing proportion of total population in urban areas. Table 4.9 summarizes the position with estimates produced by the World Urbanization project at the University of California. Despite all the difficulties of definition and estimation there is no better source, even though subsequent censuses reveal quite extensive errors in overall totals. The picture on the relative balance is still very valuable and has been expressed in three ways. First, the pace of urbanization over the two decades can be seen from the 'growth rates'. These show that the populations defined as 'urban' at each time period almost invariably have higher annual growth rates than those areas defined as 'rural'. Between country differences are quite considerable both in terms of the absolute size of the rates and also in the difference between both sectors. The latter tends to be narrowing slightly as for many countries the rate of growth declines. The 'urban absorption rate' simply reveals the extent of overall population increases that can be attributed to urban growth. There is a slight tendency for this to be higher in populations that are already heavily urban but this is by no means invariably true. It is important to note that urban areas are absorbing more and more of overall population growth. In eight out of the eighteen cases cited the urban proportion of the population has risen by six per cent or more over the decade 1960–70.

The urbanization process achieved by shifts of population from the rural periphery to the urban core is in fact two processes in one, for within the urbanized area there is a major transfer of human resources from the centre of the city to the urban fringe. This process of suburbanization tends to institutionalize urban inequalities as the middle classes and more affluent groups retreat from the squalor of the city itself to the comparative prosperity of the suburbs. By so doing they will often 'leapfrog' the rural migrants in the slums on the rim of the commercial core or by-pass them as the latter are forced into clearly demarcated areas of the suburbs. The nature and extent of this process can be illustrated with some examples.

The Jamaican case clearly reveals processes that are at work in many major cities. Between 1960 and 1970 the population of Jamaica rose by 238,700 and the city of Kingston and the surrounding parish of St Andrew itself actually received 47 per cent of this total. But St Andrew itself actually received 53 per cent of the increase and the reason is simply that for the first time the population of Kingston fell in absolute terms – although declines in growth had been evident from the 1921–43 period. Whereas the city itself fell by 11 per cent, the suburban parish of St Andrew increased its population by the startling proportion of 42 per cent to 421,700. Had it not been for an estimated loss of 106,000 through external migration, the intercensal growth through natural increase (45 per cent) and internal migration (33 per cent) would have been 78 per cent (Hewitt, 1974: 27). As we have implied already this growth potential is not the result of industrial development or what Clarke calls an 'aimless drift to the towns'; rather it is an urgent attempt to escape from rural poverty (Clarke, 1975: 79).

Despite the obvious dominance of the Kingston Metropolitan Area in the urban life of Jamaica, other urbanization has also taken place. Roberts reports that the population of the small towns increased by 71 per cent between 1943–60, which is only slightly less than the expansion

TABLE 4.9 *Patterns of Caribbean Urbanization 1950–70*

Country	Annual growth rates* (%)				Urban absorption rate† (%)		Proportion of population urban		
	1950–60 Rural	Urban	1960–70 Rural	Urban	1950–60 (%)	1960–70 (%)	1960 (%)	1970 (%)	Change
Bahamas	2.7	6.0	1.3	4.4	64	76	47	54	+7
Barbados	0.2	2.2	0.1	2.0	90	95	40	45	+5
Belize	3.0	3.0	3.2	3.3	35	38	37	37	0
Cuba	1.9	2.3	2.2	2.6	61	62	57	58	+1
Dominican Republic	2.7	6.1	2.6	5.7	46	53	30	37	+7
Guadeloupe	2.3	5.4	1.6	4.5	31	42	19	23	+4
Guyana	2.7	3.2	2.6	3.2	32	33	29	30	+1
Haiti	2.3	4.6	1.6	3.8	24	31	15	18	+3
Jamaica	0.9	4.3	1.2	4.3	62	64	29	36	+7
Leeward Islands	0.5	3.5	−0.3	2.2	73	150	28	34	+6
Martinique	1.0	5.6	0.3	4.4	75	91	39	49	+10
Netherlands Antilles	−0.1	3.6	−0.3	3.1	104	110	50	58	+8
Puerto Rico	−0.0	1.5	1.3	2.8	102	64	44	48	+4
Surinam	2.4	3.2	3.7	4.5	42	42	36	38	+2
Trinidad and Tobago	0.7	7.2	0.3	6.0	84	94	40	53	+13
US Virgin Islands	2.4	1.4	6.7	9.3	40	67	56	62	+6
Windward Islands	1.7	2.7	1.6	2.6	24	37	17	19	+2
All Caribbean	1.7	3.0	1.7	3.3	51	56	38	42	+4

Source: Davis, 1969: Tables A and D.

* These are not strictly speaking 'growth rates' since the areas defined as 'rural' or 'urban' change over time. They are annual rates of change of population so defined at each period.
† The 'urban absorption rate' is the proportion of total growth attributable to growth in urban areas. It will exceed 100 when there has been an *absolute* decline in rural populations.

of the Metropolitan Area over the same period (Roberts, 1968: 279). In fact, in the light of diminished opportunities for external migration, Roberts regards the growth of non-primary economic activity in the small towns, with its concomitant urbanization, as the only chance to save declining per capita incomes in both the cities and the rural areas. It is certainly true for Jamaica that the small towns increased their share of the urban populations from 27.5 per cent to 36.7 per cent between 1960 and 1970, but there is little sign, apart from the tourist industry, of any major growth in employment potential.

In Trinidad and Tobago a similar pattern is revealed. Between 1946 and 1960 there is evidence of two strong movements; urbanization as the major part of inward movement consists of people from rural areas, and suburbanization as the city centre loses population to the wards of Diego Martin, St Ann's and Tacarigua. Thus during this period Port of Spain gained 10,400 people, 55 per cent of whom came from rural origins. But the loss was greater at 35,600 and nearly four fifths of these were relocated in suburban areas. Joy Simpson summarizes this process when she writes: 'between 1946 and 1960, a great exodus began. There was a dramatic movement from both rural and urban areas to urban and suburban areas; a movement so large as to overshadow all other aspects of the re-distribution of population within the territory' (Simpson, 1973: 13). Later survey data suggest the same process continuing. Thus during 1966–71, all of the gain of population in Port of Spain itself came from rural origins (largely Tobago) while 81 per cent of the loss (which greatly exceeded the gain) went to the suburban area of St George, which actually received 68 per cent of all migrant gains (Trinidad and Tobago, 1974b: Table 5).

The experience of other large Caribbean cities is very similar. San Juan, for example, reveals almost identical processes. The population of this city, with its companion town of Rio Piedras, comprised only 4 per cent of the total population in 1960 (Caplow, et al., 1964). By 1970 the Metropolitan Area had grown to over 30 per cent of the population of 2.7m. In the previous decade overall growth was 15.4 per cent; rural population falling by 13.3 per cent and urban population rising by 51.6 per cent. However, within the Metropolitan Area, suburbanization was the dominant move; the city centre rising by 19.5 per cent while the urban fringe exploded by 213 per cent in one decade (Puerto Rico, 1970). This latter process has also been characteristic of Western cities although in this case the suburban move is usually motivated by the promise of substantial rises in income. San Juan has undergone the same process but a much higher proportion of the movers remain poor by any standards, although marginally less so than on their arrival from the rural periphery. Thus Safa documents the migrants moving into the shantytown of 'Los

Peloteros': 'There is a constant flow of people into the shantytown from the rural area, and from the shantytown to other urban neighbourhood's (Safa, 1974: 13). In this case the whole settlement was razed and the people moved to an *urbanización*, thus contributing to suburban growth. The original settlement and the subsequent move have obvious relevance for understanding the social structure of this and other Caribbean societies, and it is to this question we now turn, having first concluded this chapter with a brief comment on the peculiar city formations that have emerged as a result of the dominant economic and trading ties with external markets.

The primate Caribbean city

The incorporation of Caribbean economies into those of metropolitan societies produced the inevitable consequence that one city tended to emerge as dominant. This is hardly unique but the need to establish administrative and commercial services near the main focal point for the shipment of raw materials and commodities produced a degree of concentration which is striking and important. It has also meant that not only do Caribbean societies have to face massive urbanization without the growth of wealth that ennobled the process in the West, but also that they are forced to tackle the problems of really large cities with, paradoxically, limited human resources. Table 4.10 summarizes the position with respect to six capital cities that together comprise the greater part of Caribbean urban population. The extent of first city dominance is so great, and the history of external migration so pronounced, that for many Caribbean societies the second city is actually located in the metropolis. Thus there are more Cubans in Miami than in Santiago de Cuba, more Haitians in New York than in Cap-Haïtien and more Jamaicans in London than in Montego Bay (Segal, 1975: 23). The 'two city index' is simply formed by dividing the population of the second city into the first and this indicates by what factor the latter was dominant in 1970. Other largest cities in the underdeveloped world rarely reveal such preeminence: in Ghana the index is 1.96, in Nigeria 1.05, in Brazil 1.16, in India 1.44 although in smaller countries, whether industrialized or not, it tends to be slightly higher. Even within the Caribbean, however, a simple correlation does not exist with size since Trinidad has one of the highest rates, but a relatively small population. The table also shows the degree to which the primate city dominates the urban population and in three societies it is moving close to containing a third of total population. In the tiny Leeward and Windward Islands the same situation obtains with the main urban centres containing 31.5 per cent of total population in 1970, which is a substantial rise over a decade earlier.

TABLE 4.10 *Measures of first city primacy for selected Caribbean countries 1970*

Country (population) (1)	First city (2)	Second city (3)	Urban total* (4)	Two city index (2:3)	First city as per cent Urban (2:4)%	First city as per cent total (2:1)%	Urban as per cent total (4:1)%
Dominican Republic 4,006,405	Santo Domingo 673,470	Santiago de los Caballeros 155,000	1,297,905	4.34	51.9	16.8	32.4
Guyana 699,848	Georgetown 167,078	Linden 29,000	233,078	5.76	71.7	23.9	33.3
Haiti 4,856,000	Port au Prince 506,525	Cap-Haïtien 54,691	879,708	9.26	57.6	10.4	18.1
Jamaica 1,797,401	Kingston metropolitan area 506,200	Montego Bay 42,800	652,300	11.83	77.6	28.2	36.3
Puerto Rico 2,712,033	San Juan 820,442	Ponce 128,233	1,291,889	6.40	63.5	30.2	47.6
Trinidad and Tobago 931,071	Port of Spain (Greater) 347,372	San Fernando 36,879	417,334	9.42	83.2	37.3	44.8

Sources: Dominican Republic – *Simposia Sobre el uso de los datos de Poblacion del Censo de 1970* (Santo Domingo, Oficiana Nacional de Estadistica, 1972): 132.

Guyana – *Guyana Handbook, 1976* (Georgetown, Guyana Manufacturers' Association, 1976): 15.

Haiti – *Resultats Preliminaires du Recensement General* (Port au Prince, Institut Haïtien de Statistique, 1973): 33.

Jamaica – *Population Census, 1970 – Preliminary Report* (Kingston, Division of Censuses and Surveys 1972).

Puerto Rico – *Census of Population, 1970 General Population Characteristics* (Washington, Bureau of the Census, 1971): Table 14.

Trinidad and Tobago – *Population Census, 1970 Bulletin No. 1A* (Port of Spain, Trinidad Central Statistical Office, 1974): Table 1.

* 'Urban' is defined as places with populations over 10,000 except for Trinidad and Tobago where it is defined as Port of Spain, San

5 Social structure and social organization

The preceding chapters have sought to identify some of the main reasons for Caribbean urban growth. But this process is also one with profound consequences for social organization itself. In this and subsequent chapters we look at the nature of Caribbean social structure and assess the directions of change, suggesting that the inequalities arising from the colonial past and the continuing ties of dependence, which underlie the patterns of urban transformation, have also to be seen as affecting social organization. Urbanization itself is both a symptom and a cause; it is a human reaction to relative deprivation and a creator of new environments which themselves redound upon family patterns, voluntary associations, ethnic relations and social stratification. All these changes set the parameters of political choice.

We start by examining social structure at the primary and secondary levels, focussing attention on family and kinship in the first part of this chapter but concluding with some observations on voluntary associations such as churches, trade unions, friendly societies and other forms of secondary grouping.

Caribbean family and kinship

Studies of Caribbean family forms and household groupings are numerous and varied.[1] They tend to concentrate on black families, and certain cultural similarities within the family and kinship patterns of black Americans have given rise to the phrase the 'Afro-American family' (see Marks, 1976). Moreover, research interest in the Afro-American family has been concentrated almost exclusively on 'lower class' forms, by which is normally meant the mass of rural or urban, working or non-working, people whose situation is typified by relative poverty and low status. The essential characteristics of the Afro-American family, as identified by this tradition of inquiry and which would distinguish it from other family forms in the Western World, could be summarized as:

(i) A variety of union types, embracing co-residence without registered marriage, and sexual union without co-residence.

(ii) A developmental sequence moving from sexual union without co-residence to one or other form of cohabitation, often with different partners.

79

The inevitable consequences of this arrangement are that a minority of births are 'legitimate', in the sense of being formally registered to a married couple at the time of birth, and many homes do not contain the father of the children resident within that household.

While a great effort by social anthropologists has been expended on the explication of these patterns of union and household composition, it is probably fair comment to note that recent contributions have either stressed the degree to which similarities exist with cultural patterns else-where, but which may not be achieved because of economic marginality or social disorganization (see Blake, 1961; Wilson, 1974; Rodman, 1971; R. T. Smith, 1956), or that the evidence suggests cultures fractured into distinct sections, usually coextensive with racial or class divisions (M. G. Smith, 1962; M. G. Smith, 1966).

Both of the approaches appear to be defective. The argument that there is no one typical pattern of Caribbean kinship is belied by the common features identified in almost all the research so far completed. On the other hand, the view that there is one system, not really any different from Western patterns, is equally untenable. We will examine some of the general features from characteristic locations and then suggest possible determining influences.

The general pattern

It is as well to record that an overview of the general features of marriage and kinship in black Caribbean family life is not a guide to the form they may take in any one territory. There is considerable variability, although not enough to render nugatory the attempt to paint an overall view. In one way or another nearly all studies point to different types of union. Aside from legal marriage there are 'common-law' unions defined by co-residence without marriage and 'visiting' unions defined by the presence of sexual relationship without cohabitation. The data presented in Table 5–1 show that in Jamaica the modal type of union changes with age. So called 'visiting' unions characterize the age groups up to 24, while thereafter co-residential unions predominate, so that for the last years of child bearing more than half the female population in unions of any type is married. It is this which gives rise to a 'developmental cycle' where early unions in lower class communities are marked by the 'visiting' pattern which is superseded by either 'common law' unions or legal marriage, although not necessarily with the same partner. However, work by George Roberts has shown that despite the increasing proportion of legally married couples with age, the cycle rarely embraces all three stages. Thus in a comparative study of Jamaica and Trinidad (excluding East Indians), he showed that the modal number of different types of

TABLE 5.1   *Distribution of women in unions in Jamaica by type of union and age group 1970*

Type of union	Age group					
	15–19	20–4	25–9	30–4	35–9	40–4
Married	1·3	11·5	26·1	39·4	47·5	51·2
Common law	10·3	28·8	36·4	32·0	27·3	21·2
Visiting	86·8	54·8	30·2	19·7	14·9	13·3
No longer living with partner	1·6	5·0	7·4	8·8	10·3	14·3
Total	100·0	100·0	100·0	100·0	100·0	100·0

Source: Commonwealth Caribbean, 1970.

unions is two and not three (Roberts and Sinclair, 1977). In fact, only 14 per cent of women in Trinidad and 10 per cent in Jamaica actually move into a third union type. Mating tables show a remarkable degree of similarity between the two countries in terms of age of entry into different unions. Thus the visiting relationship is entered into around twenty, and is followed by either common law relationships at twenty-six or marriage at twenty-eight.[2] There is a slight tendency for non-Indian women in Trinidad to prefer marriage to other forms of relationship at younger ages but overall the pattern is remarkably similar for two societies with pronounced historical differences. Cohort analysis shows that whereas in Trinidad 9.55 years are contributed by women passing through the average thirty-one years of child bearing in marriage, in Jamaica the figure is slightly less at 8.78 years (Roberts and Sinclair, 1977).

The problem of explanation

It is easy to understand the interest that Caribbean kinship and mating patterns have prompted. In societies with obvious European and African connections it is fascinating to trace or identify elements of cultural survival. Some of those who have done so have suggested a segmented cultural order which parallels the racial components of the population, while others have stressed the influence of the dominant European form. Both views are illuminating but both fail to account for the evidence that many studies (even those in one or other tradition) have adduced. It appears to be the case that there is a West Indian family form, also found in other parts of the Caribbean, that owes much to cultural survival *and* the colonial past, but which cannot simply be accounted for in terms of either.

One line of reasoning that at least identifies the relevant variables in the indigenous societies themselves is that characteristic patterns of mating and marriage must be seen within a socio-economic context. That is, the 'visiting' and 'common law' relationships are more common with low or uncertain economic returns. For example, Schlesinger (1968) writes: 'Where labour is casual and wages uncertain, it is very difficult for men to carry a sustained economic responsibility, and one tends to find a prevalence of short term common-law unions coupled with the development of either a female headed type of household or severe familial disorganization' (Schlesinger, 1968: 146). In Edith Clarke's work too, considerable emphasis is laid on the land tenure system and the disrupting effects of poverty in 'Sugartown', one of three locations for her Jamaican study (Clarke, 1966). Similarly, Hyman Rodman writes that the 'man's role as a worker–earner lies at the center of an explanation of lower class family relationships in Trinidad' (Rodman, 1971: 177), while Sidney Greenfield predicts for Barbados that 'a possible future rise in the standard of living ... would bring with it an increase in the percentage of stable nuclear families based on marriage' (Greenfield, 1966: 173).

It is almost certainly the case that the class correlation for types of unions throughout the French, Dutch and English speaking Caribbean possesses causative elements. These are not simply dependent upon the *ability* of wealthier men to offer marriage earlier but also derive from a greater concern for 'respect' which may be taken to refer to rules of conduct deriving from European middle class norms. It is equally clear that in some important respects such standards are not strictly adhered to, at least by men, whatever level of society one examines. It is this which gives rise to the label 'Victorian' for West Indian mating patterns, when by this is meant marked sex role differentiation and the acceptance of extra-familial unions for men. Whether aptly described as 'Victorian' or not this provides us with a crucial element of explanation. West Indian societies are indeed marked by extreme forms of sexual inequality and it is this which goes a long way towards providing a complete understanding of marriage and kinship.

This inequality is found in the sex role differentiation which may itself be the initial reason why a man may establish a cohabiting union. He does so in order to have someone who, aside from sexual services, may provide domestic facilities which hitherto have been provided by his mother, grandmother or other female relative. At all levels of society it is unlikely that this will greatly inhibit extra-marital relations. Commonly, the man will spend a great deal of time away from home and will often retain a high level of physical and social segregation within the home. Entertainment and friendship patterns for both sexes will also be highly segregated, although this feature declines in middle class relationships.

As Freilich and Coser point out, the 'sex-fame game', as they call the pattern of extra residential mating, has inbuilt conflicts (Freilich and Coser, 1972). Men receive prestige from other men in a local community by being successful in their affairs. They may increase the possibility of this occurring by being particularly adept at verbal wooing even though this may involve blatant dishonesty. The conflict is engendered because the interests of the women, over and above a sexual partner, are for security, stability and, if illicit relationships are involved, secrecy. Men, on the other hand, seeking status enhancement, engage in more or less discreet broadcasting of their conquests and, moreover, their stories gain credence by resultant pregnancies. The inequalities of the system are obvious and pronounced; men often responding with violence to putative or actual infidelities on the part of their 'wives'.

It is this inequality which appears to be associated with many of the chief characteristics of Caribbean kinship. Although empirical data are needed to confirm this judgement, it appears likely that fears of infidelity or violence are among the main reasons why many women continue 'visiting' relationships after their initial sexual encounters. Once in a 'common law' union with children, whoever their father, it is in a woman's interest to legalize the relationship for the benefit of the children and herself should the marriage fail to last.

The same pattern of sexual separation and inequality also accounts to some degree for two other features that are commonly, though falsely, confused. So called 'matrifocality' is the natural result of a situation where men spend so much time and seek so much gratification beyond the home. The term refers to the evident fact that mature women, usually mothers, emerge as the central focus of domestic groupings. It is they who often hold families together, partly because this is culturally defined as their main function and partly because there is no one else to do it. This does not mean that West Indian societies are matriarchies; far from it, the dominance of men is seldom questioned and in some respects it is the peculiar exercise of this dominance that produces adaptive patterns of relationship that minimize the man's importance.

The second resultant feature is that of the female headed household which is usually formed by the retention of 'visiting' relationships or the permanent departure of the male head. As elsewhere, the greater longevity of women is also a contributing factor but it is not unusual to find in excess of one in three households with female heads.

The most likely line of explanation then is to emphasize the sexual as well as the economic inequalities of the mating system. In many ways these may themselves interact to compound the pattern. Thus women may remain 'single' in order to continue work, particularly in urban areas where domestic employment is possible. However, greater equality within relationships would lessen the necessity of giving up employment

since being 'single' has rather little to do with fertility.[3] Without wanting
to enter the perilous area of marital psychodynamics, it could well be the
case that so called 'matrifocality' once established could serve to increase
the likelihood of male 'friending' or extra residential mating. This is
because a man may become more threatened by the functionally necessary emergence of a central kin figure and possibly less convinced of his
own ability to contribute, especially if the woman or some of the children
are working and he is not (see Buschkens, 1974: 175–218).

The extensive web of kin groupings produced by serial mating and the
common practice of leaving children to be raised with grandmothers or
aunts produces a system where there is a relatively low correlation between kin groupings and households. This is important, especially among
poorer communities, because it provides a network of interlocking loy-
alties which, in the absence of state aid, can be used in times of excessive
financial difficulty. In fact, despite the obvious inequalities between the
sexes, it is quite false to label male behaviour as 'irresponsible'. We have
already shown that status rewards may accrue precisely from accepting
responsibility for extra-residential relationships and there is considerable
evidence to suggest that men usually make some provision for their
children wherever they are living (Stycos and Back, 1964: 330).

There are some anthropologists who argue that the household with the
male absent is actually a functional or adaptive response to externally
generated pressures. Thus Nancie Gonzalez (1970) suggests that what
she terms 'consanguineal kinship' acts as a safety net for a man unable to
support his family. He is able to turn to his mother or sisters, while wives
are able to look for other providers if one man fails. A tradition of
extreme sexual division and inequality, combined with oppressive conditions of wage labour or inadequate returns from peasant agriculture,
may be disrupting, destabilizing influences on relationships, but the consanguineal alternative does at least provide a more or less stable household unit for the raising of children.

It is hard to say, however, what influence this common mating pattern
has on the actual number of children born to any woman. On the one hand
the higher incidence of cosanguineal households has a negative effect on
overall fertility, because even with age controlled, so called 'visiting'
relationships reveal on average a lower child/mother ratio. However, it
could be argued that cosanguineal households must raise the probabilities
of serial mating, and in societies where male virility is perceived as
problematic until extant children furnish positive evidence, the pressure
on fertility trends would be upward. Moreover, it is not simply men who
stand to gain in terms of community status by procreation. Where familial
roles and childbearing are the only avenues to status enhancement,
women too will do little to avoid pregnancy – especially where a new

relationship is concerned. Audvil King graphically describes the common situation where poor women from the slums of Kingston, who by any estimate have 'nuff pickney', may produce more as a way of trying to retain a man. As he puts it: 'Questioned as to why they pursue the folly of child after child, with different men, none of whom remains, they many times give the reply, "Then me noh a'fe try, sah?"' (King et al., 1971: 29.) That is, they have to try and hold a man who will help share the domestic burdens of poverty, and the only way they can do it so is to have his children. The question arises whether this cruel dilemma is exacerbated or relieved by progressive urbanization.

The urban household

There is no very clear picture of the kind of changes wrought on the pattern of West Indian and Caribbean kinship or family systems by urbanization. It rather depends on the perspective one has on urbanization itself. If it is perceived as a 'modernizing' influence encapsulating the supposedly egalitarian ideologies of advanced industrialism, then it is natural to suppose that one effect will be a change in the relationships between the sexes. This appears to be Freilich and Coser's position when they argue: 'When the forces of industrialization or urbanization begin seriously to impinge on the system, the male–female relationship will emerge as one of the weakest links in the structure. Hence, as elsewhere, exploitive relationships will be resisted, and strains toward complete reciprocity will emerge in full force once traditional impediments to equalization have begun to crumble' (Freilich and Coser, 1972: 18). It follows too that if urbanization is accompanied by greater affluence then this ought to affect the so-called 'marginality' of men whose enhanced status and self respect should be reflected in more stable mating patterns. If we look at the more advanced and industrialized territories there is, indeed, support for this proposition. Curaçao, for example, is more urbanized and industrialized than any other Caribbean territory and A. F. Marks found that 'legal marriage and the nuclear family composition of the household group occupied an important place' (Marks, 1976: 313). Moreover, he summarizes the changes in the Afro-Curaçaoan family as follows:

'There has emerged a more explicitly egalitarian ideology, together with an emphasis on greater equality between the sexes, a drop in the average age at marriage, a sharp rise in the relative number of marriages, a substantive decrease in the number of illegitimate births, a change in the power structure of the household group and different ideas concerning child care and child rearing [Marks, 1976: 56].'

There seems every reason for supposing that this is a true reflection of the position in Curaçao and it is likely to be replicated elsewhere provided that urbanization is accompanied by greater wealth and enhanced opportunities for men and women. Unfortunately, in other parts of the Caribbean there is very little reason for supposing that this is the case.

The picture emerging from Colin Clarke's excellent study of Kingston, Jamaica, is one of rapid urbanization accompanied by widespread poverty. Around the commercial core lie the tenements and rent yards of East and West Kingston. The latter simply consist of leased yards in which the tenant builds a single storey shack out of whatever materials are available, usually wooden flotsam. One room tenements, however, have become more important in the recent past; the 1943 Census showed that 28.5 per cent of Kingston's population was in tenements compared to only 8.2 per cent in the country as a whole. By 1960 these proportions had risen to 52.2 per cent and 16.2 per cent respectively (Clarke, 1975: 143, 150), but there is little evidence that the living conditions of the greatly enlarged population had improved. Clarke notes that the 1960 Census revealed the full extent of the housing problem 'when it was estimated that 120,000 people, or one third of the city's inhabitants, were living in delapidated accommodation, the greater proportion being concentrated in West Kingston' (Clarke, 1975: 91). Moreover, it is precisely these areas of the city that receive the rural migrants, rather than the government financed housing schemes. Clarke found that the yards and tenements were characterized by high rates of residential mobility often reaching 40 per cent in any one year but, despite this mobility, rural migrants rarely escaped upward to middle income housing nor, indeed, slipped downward to the even more impoverished squatter camps such as Moonlight City or Boy's Town (Clarke, 1975: 100–2).

Similar patterns are evident elsewhere. Urban growth has exacerbated overcrowding and pressure on all services and facilities. Many of those in shantytown areas move in time to others, possibly improving their housing conditions slightly as they do so. Helen Safa notes a move in San Juan towards squatter settlements even when rents were low in public housing, largely because of the wish to become independent of public authorities (Safa, 1974: 14–19), but the truth of Clarke's observation remains: 'Urbanization without adequate industrialization has condemned much of the increase in urban dwellers to high density, sub-divided accommodation' (Clarke, 1974: 227).

Despite the proliferation of poor housing and overcrowded accommodation, it is by no means true to say that urban facilities are necessarily worse than those in rural parts. Indeed this may be a factor in migration since, however rudimentary and unequal urban housing may appear there may be the *promise* of better income and facilities. The evidence is that rural movers seldom share these better conditions but, as Table 5.2 shows, the urban areas have a higher proportion of households with the basic amenity of piped water. The Cuban example is of interest here since, although post revolutionary Cuba has been remarkably successful in preventing the ravages of uncontrolled urbanization, the housing problem has proved to be one of the most intractable. A recent report on health in Cuba noted that: 'More than 70 per cent of the population live in inadequate houses, dwellings that do not provide the sanitary environment indispensable for a healthy people' (Valdés, 1971: 321). However, the important point is that even though the Revolution has only managed to provide a tenth of the annual number of new houses that Castro himself maintains are needed, a new system of priorities has been established. In contrast to other parts of the Caribbean, where resources have progressively shifted to the urban commercial core producing rural impoverishment and the familiar kind of urban squalor, Cuba has placed rural housing at the head of the priority list, followed by projects to rebuild urban slums and tenements. Urban–rural differentials continue to exist, of course, in both housing provision and health care, but the gap is being narrowed, and with it another motive for migration.

TABLE 5.2 *Percentage of household units with internal piped water in selected Caribbean countries (1972)*

	Urban	Rural	Both
Barbados	49.0	33.0	40.0
Cuba	58.1	6.6	39.1
Haiti	5.5	0.1	0.5
Jamaica	40.2	6.4	21.6
Dominican Republic	18.1	0.7	2.1

Source: America en Cifras 1974 (Washington, IDB, 1975).

In fact the Cuban case is outstanding for it represents the only systematic attempt to understand and reverse the inevitable tendency for uncontrolled and unplanned development to concentrate human and physical resources at the hub of the economic wheel. It is not simply the dismantling of the plantation system nor in itself the adoption of a socialist path that has produced this change of direction, although the Urban Reform Law of 1960, on which much of the subsequent policy has been based, is premised upon the need to promote the interests of the nation through mobilizing the support and participation of the peasantry and rural workers.

Among the first actions taken by the revolutionary government were the Agrarian Reform Laws of 1959 and 1963. The first law radically altered the basis of rural land tenancy and created 100,000 peasant proprietors, while the second nationalized the remaining *latifundia* to bring 60 per cent of productive land under state control, mostly in large state farms. During the first phase of agrarian reform, a great deal of attention was given to coping with communications problems and providing rural nuclei in the form of tiny new towns, eighty-three of which were established for populations of 300–500 between 1959 and 1962 (Acosta and Hardoy, 1973).

Even with the re-emergence of a sugar monoculture after 1965, the Cubans did not ignore agricultural diversification and this was specifically planned to lower the burdens of an inefficient and underdeveloped transport system and to help prevent an increased dichotomy between the city and countryside. For example, the policy of 'provincial self-sufficiency' under the Urban Reform Law of 1960 was applied to Havana and a strip of potential suburban, undercultivated land around the city was given over to the production of food for urban needs (*Cordón Urbano de la Havana*). The land was not, however, to be developed by peasants but by mobilizing urban residents under state direction with the object of diminishing the barrier between city and country, raising the status of rural work and lowering the reliance of the city on 'imports' from other provinces or from abroad.

The statutes of the Cuban Urban Reform Law are mainly concerned with the supply of adequate housing. The 1953 Census had shown that 30 per cent of urban housing was either 'poor' (*mala*) or 'very poor' (*ruinosa*), while in rural areas the figure rose to over 75 per cent. In the cities these problems have not been solved, but land speculation has ended and attempts have been made to plan development with integrated services. As Acosta and Hardoy put it: 'Although production has not yet reached a level that would assure adequate housing for the natural annual growth rate of the population, new housing projects are being constructed in all the cities on the island, complementing industrial, educational, and health investments and regional and urban infrastructure programs' (1973: 69). However, despite all the attention that has been given to planned urban housing programmes, the central focus of the revolutionary government has remained resolutely rural. Castro himself has emphasized in speech after speech the importance of housing and services in the countryside in order to stimulate production and correct the inequalities and shift of resources to the city. In 1967 he affirmed 'we are sure that if we build housing in the countryside, if we create adequate housing conditions in the countryside, the traditional exodus of country people to the cities will cease' (Castro, 1968: 81–2).

On the whole the attempt at righting the balance appears to have been more successful than improving the housing conditions of the average Cuban.[4] The reason for this is largely the continued natural increase in population, unrelieved as earlier by extensive migration. At the time of the Revolution the annual growth rate of Greater Havana was 2.19 per cent, although the city centre was increasing its population at a much slower rate. By 1965/66 the growth rate had been cut to under one per cent and it is now claimed that 'there has been no appreciable increase in population since the end of 1965' (Acosta and Hardoy, 1973: 36). Although planned growth is expected through natural increase, the Regional Plan for Havana specifically asserts the necessity to stop excessive growth.

The controlled rate of increase in Havana, and the diversion of urban expansion to other cities, is evident from the fact that 49 per cent of urban growth in the intercensal period 1931–43 was accounted for by the growth of Havana, whereas in 1953–69 this figure had declined to 31 per cent, even though at 1.7m it still constituted more than one fifth of Cuba's total population (Acosta and Hardoy, 1973: 78). A major reversal of the primacy indices is also evident, as Table 5.3 shows:

TABLE 5.3 *Two city and four city primacy indices in Cuba 1919—69*

	1919	1931	1943	1953	1969
Four city index	2.98	3.05	3.71	3.46	2.61
Two city index	7.01	6.44	7.25	7.46	6.15

Source: Acosta and Hardoy, 1973: 79.

It would be astonishing indeed if the typical primate city pattern had been reversed so quickly, but there is evidence that centralized administration, cognizant of the economic and social relations that produce uncontrolled urban growth, can at least halt these tendencies, although, of course, this has only been attained at the expense of an unbridled market system in jobs, land and capital.

Trade unions

In common with many aspects of social structure, trade unions in the Caribbean context occupy a wide variety of roles and exert divergent pressures, over and above their everyday concerns for the economic and occupational well being of their members. Our concern is simply to record some widespread patterns, noting the degree to which union activity may unwittingly exacerbate the concentration of resources in cities and towns.

Insofar as trade unions represent associations of free labour, their Caribbean role could hardly predate the middle of the nineteenth century. In fact, some forms of labour grouping began to emerge towards the end of the century but never obtained great importance in the Anglophone Caribbean until the critical decade in the 1930s. That is not to say that organized opposition to oppressive conditions did not exist before this time; the difference is that slave rebellions, insurrection and *marronage*, although as characteristic a feature of Caribbean history as the repression they opposed, sought to overthrow the system. Trade unionism on the other hand was essentially collaborative and reformist and it is for this reason that pressures for social change result in the institutionalizing of unions through official regulation and control.

In the English speaking Caribbean the first registered unions occurred in what was then British Guiana. The British Guiana Labour Union was established in 1919 and registered in 1922 under an Ordinance that was modelled on British trade union regulations of 1906. Trinidad had seen attempts to organize labour as early as 1897 with the founding of a Workingman's Association by Alfred Richards, while in Jamaica a series of relatively short lived unions had started after 1895 and disappeared by 1920. In the Spanish speaking Caribbean the starting points for organization were not dissimilar; Spanish oriented anarchists had formed a number of labour movements in Cuba from the 1880s while legal recognition for emergent unions was obtained in Puerto Rico in 1902.

Throughout the Caribbean the decade of the 1930s represents a turning point; strikes and disturbances broke out from one end of the region to the other. Reactions ranged from attempts at banning unions in Cuba (during Batista's first period of power) to trying to ensure in Trinidad that the new sophistication in labour organization took a form that was acceptable to continued Crown Colony rule and did not embrace 'agitators' like Uriah Butler. Evidence laid before the Commission of Inquiry under Lord Moyne, sent out from Britain to investigate the labour disturbances in the British West Indies, revealed a disturbing situation. In rural areas in particular wages had hardly risen, even in money terms, since the middle of the previous century. In Trinidad and British Guiana, where ordinances had governed the conditions of indentured Indian labour brought on to the estates up until 1917, there was virtually no improvement. Underemployment meant that a field labourer would be lucky to work 180–200 days a year or earn more than £20.00–£25.00 per annum, and conditions elsewhere in the British Caribbean were even worse. Discussing the plight of rural workers, the Moyne Commissioners wrote: 'When rates of earnings are inadequate, employment is seasonal and generally scarce and public assistance is thus limited, there can be little wonder that the standard of life of many of the working people throughout the West Indies is deplorably low' (West India Royal Commission, 1945: 196). They went on to point out that, although employers were organized, employees were not, and that as a result earnings were determined solely by the managers and owners of plantations.

The solution to the problem advocated by the Moyne Commission is instructive and important. It was not, of course, to alter the pattern of ownership, loosen the ties of dependence or increase the revenue gained from the sale of sugar to the 'mother country'. Rather, it was to organize labour under 'responsible' leadership, that is leadership that would not challenge these arrangements but would seek amelioration of conditions by following an evolutionary path on British lines.

The problem is that trade unions, like political parties, have tended to follow precedents and policies that are fundamentally derived from Western experience. That is they have been largely urban based and industrially oriented, serving the function of freeing labour from the traditional ties of the craft guilds and loosening attachments to a rural way of life. As such they have been crucially important in capitalist societies in aiding the industrialization process. The accent on wages and conditions of employment at a national level has aided labour mobility, increased productivity and promoted mechanization, and a manufacturing system based on advanced technology. But what effect has the same policy had on dependent societies which lack the industrialization that has ultimately made trade unions successful?

In the first place, it is vital to realize how readily trade unions have adopted foreign, developed society precedents. In his exhaustive study of foreign influences in the Caribbean, Jeffrey Harrod points out that: 'Because of a degree of autonomy from governments, their origins as imports, and their nominal, if not substantive, imitation of their industrial country counterparts, trade unions in less developed countries have been readily open to foreign involvement' (Harrod, 1972). Of course, this does not mean that these influences are all representative of Western liberal democracies. Indeed the Caribbean area has been a major site for the vying attentions of the pro-Western International Confederation of Free Trade Unions and the more leftward World Federation of Trade Unions, after the split between these international bodies in 1949. In recent years the former body has supported a regional affiliate in the form of the Caribbean Congress of Labour, while the latter now lacks a regional body, but could formerly rely on the Caribbean Labour Congress. However, whatever the line-up in terms of such groupings, the point is clear: trade unions have been remarkably pervious to international influence both in terms of their aims and their structure. For example, in 1939, the Trinidad Labour Party, which in spite of its name was more of a trade union than a party, declared in evidence to the Moyne Commissioners that it wanted to see a prosperous self governing dominion in the West Indies 'devoted to the service of the British Crown and working in accordance with British Traditions, British methods and educating itself on British lines'. Similarly, in the case of Puerto Rico the recent past has seen labour organizations that reflect the US style of operation. Indeed, the island's labour groups have been dominated by the enormous US unions like the Teamsters and as a result unions lack professional staff, training organizations and eschew all matters of social and economic reform (Lewis, 1963: 140)

It is only partly true that the obvious lack of effective union organization in rural areas is the product of seasonal employment, a dispersed membership and high levels of underemployment. Clearly this has not helped, but the more important reason is that the unions are essentially urban in focus. The structure of dependent economies has aided this tendency so that union successes have been greatest in precisely those areas where labour conditions were, in any event, least bad. In particular successes have occurred in capital intensive sectors of the economies, that is those where labour costs are a relatively small proportion of total costs. For example, there is a wide disparity between incomes in the Trinidad oil industry and the traditional sugar based plantation sector. The 1970 Census revealed that male full time employees might expect to earn an average of TT$117.50 (US$58.75) per month in sugar planting or TT$83.50 (US$41.75) per month in the rest of agricultural employment. Male workers in the oil industry, on the other hand, could expect to receive a gross income of TT$433.50 (US$216.75) per month or 3.7 times that of the sugar worker (Trinidad and Tobago, 1974c: 4–5). In 1975 a well organized and largely successful attempt was made to bring the Oil Workers Trade Union and the representative unions of the sugar industry (sugar workers: All Trinidad Sugar Estates and Factory Workers Trade Union; cane farmers: Island Wide Cane Farmers Trade Union) together to campaign, inter alia, for higher wages. This conflict, which was significant in popularizing the new official opposition – the United Labour Front, was directly political in tone. It represented powerful unions, co-operating across a historically significant racial divide, for political and economic goals. What is interesting however, is that the obvious prosperity of the oil industry allowed the oil workers to make an initial demand for a 147 per cent wage rise on already high rates of pay, while sugar workers had to be content with a doubling of their far lower gross incomes.

Thus imbalances within the economy mean that labour becomes divided, and unions, even while attempting a self-conscious drive for unity, find it difficult not to exacerbate those divisions. This has two consequences. In the first place it divides urban labour from the pool of unemployed as those working in capital intensive industries, whether manufacturing, mining or services, benefit greatly from union organization. Relatively low rates of direct taxation in the typical colonial economy make wage increases worth fighting for and increased urban wages stimulate the demand for the goods and services upon which urban prosperity is based. The mass of urban unemployed on the other hand, can only watch and wonder at this process. Carl Stone writes: 'in the Jamaican case it can be argued that the two main unions represent the more privileged sectors of the labour force and to this extent they have become partially specialized interest groups that do not provide a positive and general point of reference for the non-unionized sector of the mass public' (Stone, 1973: 87). Later in the same study he argues that trade unionism has 'dichotomized and severed the working class from the lumpenproletariat' (Stone, 1973: 146).

For similar reasons, unions have tended to divide the rural from the urban workers. As Frantz Fanon pointed out with characteristic force, union leaders who learnt their skills in the 'mother country', and were permitted to exercise them so long as they emulated Western precedent, do not know how to organize a peasantry. What is more they are not particularly interested, except in order to placate rural populations who might otherwise rise against them. The town is the battle ground for union activity and it is a battle between the propertied middle classes and the newly emergent labour aristocracy. The rural poor represent a threat to both but, more important for our purposes, the existence of both provides an undeniable magnet for urban living. This fact, and its concomitant that the resultant migration may only trade one kind of marginality for another, has political consequences that will be considered in a separate chapter.

Religious organizations

Of all forms of secondary association in the Caribbean, religious institutions are numerically the most important.[5] Church attendance seldom falls below seventy per cent of the population and religious ritual and belief provide some of the strongest strands of community organization at both national and local levels. But beliefs differ widely, and although the Caribbean has been an area responsive to missionary activity, variations in colonial experience have produced a complicated pattern, which intrasocietal stratification serves to compound. For our purposes, there are three questions of interest: Given the widespread influence of Christianity, has this been a force for change or stability? Do the fundamentalist elements of Christianity and the syncretic cults of folk religion play any part in the balance between town and city? And finally, in what way do religious beliefs themselves arise in response to poor urban and rural conditions? These are only some of many relevant questions and each will only be answered with some tentative observations.

It is hardly surprising to find that Roman Catholicism dominates the religious observance in islands subject to Spanish or French colonialism, or that Protestantism predominates in most former British or Dutch colonies. In fact the picture is slightly more complex, although the colonial influence is still of major significance. For example, 36 per cent of the population of Trinidad and Tobago declare themselves to be Roman Catholic, an influence largely due to colonial rule by Spain prior to the Napoleonic Wars, and the settlements of French speaking Creoles from Martinique and Guadeloupe. Similarly St Lucia and Dominica have extraordinary histories of colonial conquest in which French control has occurred on numerous occasions. In each case the proportion of Catholics exceeds ninety per cent. Barbados on the other hand contains a clear majority (53 per cent) who claim adherence to the Anglican denomination.

Unlike the Spanish and French speaking Caribbean which appear in census returns as remarkably homogeneous in their commitment to Catholicism, societies like Surinam, Guyana and Trinidad betray complex religious patterns because of their peculiar poly-ethnic structures. Moreover the areal distribution patterns of ethnic groups within these societies produce a pronounced difference between the city and the rest of the society. Table 5.4 shows the overall picture for Trinidad and Surinam using recent data. Thus in both societies Protestants and Catholics are overrepresented in the primate city area and this is especially true in Surinam. On the other hand the East Indians (or Hindustanis as they are collectively referred to in Surinam) are more likely to be found outside the main urban area, and this is particularly pronounced in the Trinidad case.[6]

Of course tables such as this often hide as much as they reveal. 'Protestant' for example covers a multitude of different denominations which are themselves adhered to by different social classes. In Trinidad two thirds of Protestants are Anglicans and they are widely distributed across the social scale. The largest remaining group are Presbyterians (17 per cent of Protestants) and they are interesting for a special reason. Trinidad during the nineteenth century was a focal point for missionary activity by Canadian Presbyterians. Their attentions were concentrated in rural areas, amongst the East Indian estate labourers and cane farmers. In fact in no part of the Caribbean were they particularly successful in separating Indians from the beliefs and traditions of the sub-continent and the

TABLE 5.4 *Percentage distribution of population by religion and residence in Trinidad (1970) and Surinam (1964)*

Religion	Trinidad		Surinam	
	Port of Spain	Remainder of country	Paramaribo	Remainder of country
Roman Catholic	55	35	33	16
Protestant	36	25	34	16
Hindu	2	28	15	33
Muslim	2	7	12	24
Other (including not stated or unknown)	5	5	6	11
Total	100	100	100	100
(N)	(62,680)	(829,637)	(110,093)	(214,118)

Sources: Surinam Census, 1964; Trinidad Census, 1970 (Bulletin No. 5) 1975.

success that was achieved is largely due to the educational and occupational advantages which often come with conversion. There is no doubt that the nominal adoption of Presbyterian belief opened up hitherto closed opportunities for advancement, and the results of that process are still discernible today. East Indians who are Presbyterians are more likely to be in urban white collar employment than their traditionalist cousins. In fact 36 per cent of Indians living in urban areas in Trinidad were described by the 1960 census as 'Christian' compared to 16 per cent in the country districts. Most of these were Presbyterians although converts to Roman Catholicism are also well represented, but are not so obvious amongst the more socially mobile (Harewood, 1975: 111). In Surinam, the 'Protestant' category is equally diverse, the vast majority being Moravians, nearly all of whom are drawn from the Creole lower class. The social significance of the Lutheran and Reformed Dutch Churches far outweighs their numerical strength (7 and 17 per cent of Protestants respectively) for supporters of these religions are drawn almost exclusively from middle class circles.

The element of class is central to understanding the response of poor people in the Caribbean to Christianity. In a colonial context the orthodox denominations served as buttresses to the imperial presence. They were, and in many places still are, intimately bound up with the stratification system, acting as brokers for the colonizer. Despite the obvious appeal that religiosity possesses for people pursuing hard, simple lives, particularly for those separated from the springs of their culture by the savage experience of a slave past, religious observance for most Caribbean people possesses an element, more or less powerful, of rejection of colonial orthodoxy.

This rejection may be seen in a number of forms, and in either a negative or positive sense. That is either through specific rejections of orthodox Christianity itself or through the substitution of alternative avenues of worship. It is not coincidence for example, that the Roman Catholic Cathedral in Port of Spain was occupied during the disturbances in that island in February 1970, or indeed that disputes between that Church and the current Prime Minister were amongst the most acerbic during the period prior to his first victory at the polls in 1956. Nationalist sentiments too lay behind François Duvalier's continual attempts (largely successful) to reduce the power of the Catholic Church in Haiti. The Church had aligned itself with the Mulatto élite and was inevitably identified with the French language and culture. At the other end of the social scale, and with data from tiny communities, it is relevant that both Horowitz in Martinique and Safa in Puerto Rico found relatively low levels of support for Catholicism despite almost total adherence in principle to this establishment belief (Horowitz, 1967: 81–82). In Safa's sample of shanty town dwellers in San Juan, half the men and a third of the women claimed that they never attended Church which, in Caribbean terms, represents a powerful rejection of official religions (Safa, 1974: 70–1).

The alternatives take three general forms which can be discussed in relation to the questions posed earlier. The first of these is hardly a very radical rejection of orthodox Christianity yet it is of great importance. Just as the establishment bias in the orientation of the Church of England permitted the advance of nonconformist proselytizing, so too the colonial identity of both leading Christian denominations gave a readily grasped opportunity to nonconformist sects in the Caribbean. The Baptists in Jamaica are an outstanding case, being founded by the Black American preacher George Lisle in 1783, and now claiming more adherents than the Anglican Church. Methodism and Seventh Day Adventism have also flourished in working class communities in rural and in urban areas and have come, with other nonconformist beliefs, to represent the 'respectable' end of working class religious observance. Of perhaps even greater interest has been the success of pentecostalism in a wide variety of forms. The 1970 Census indicates that in Jamaica 29 per cent of the population claimed adherence to either the Church of God or other pentecostalist faiths. These fundamentalist beliefs are divided into a multitude of sects with little in common except the probability of frenzied observance involving possession by the Holy Spirit, speaking in tongues and the achievement of trance-like ecstasy. They often entail attempts to heal the sick, baptism by total immersion and public confessions of sinful conduct.

The element of orthodox rejection in these religious practices lies in the warmth, camaraderie and intensity that they invoke. And yet it is not a form of rejection that has any wider political or social significance. The emphasis is placed on ritualized observance and if anything serves to canalize frustration and despair into the cul de sac of guilt and individual failure. It is striking that pentecostalism, widely construed, is one of the strongest zones of continued missionary activity – largely from Canada or North America. The message presented and driven home on these occasions emphasizes passivity and fatalism, even in the face of considerable poverty. There is little research evidence on which to draw but Helen Safa probably comes near to the truth when, in commenting on the growth of pentecostalist sects, she says: 'The very poor ... tend to drift into the other-worldly orientation of the Pentecostal churches, which offer the poor a momentary escape from reality rather than an improvement in their present condition' (Safa, 1974: 73). Whereas nonconformism has an ideology tending to promote material acquisition and individualized advancement, pentecostalism represents an avenue of mental, but not social or economic, escape. There is some research evidence to suggest that it is particularly likely to occur in times of disruption and change. La Ruffa, for example, presents data from Puerto Rico that specifically links the growth of pentecostalism with urbanization and high levels of external migration (La Ruffa, 1969).

The second line of religious rejection of colonial orthodoxy is much more characteristic of rural communities who have fewer contacts with the unsettling experience of urban migration. It is characterized by a retreat into real or imagined threads of the African past. In fact, of course, the dividing line between the popular Christian sects of the first group and those under present discussion is not that neat or clear. For example, Jamaica experienced a 'great revival' in 1860 and 1861 during which so called Native Baptists and others espoused a form of belief which incorporated many African elements. It did so, however, mainly to gain credence, for it was violently opposed to obeah or any other African sorcerous practice. 'Revivalism', as all Jamaican ecstatic religion became to be called, was thus an amalgam of Christianity and elements of African religious practice, but at all times the latter was a vehicle for the former. Even the most famous revivalist preacher during the 1880s, Alexander Bedward (famous for his espousal of black nationalism) was more committed to popular Christianity than the resurrection of African religions.

Moving further along the spectrum of retreatism towards the African past, the Pocomania cult in Jamaica certainly incorporates many more elements of obeah and far fewer aspects of Christian fundamentalism, although it still involves readings from the scriptures. It seems likely that these forms of escape and release arise in particular at times of ferment, depression and despair. They have no direct political function but share with more well known pentecostalist sects the quality of individual release from oppressive conditions. The particularly frenzied rites and the sounds made by devotees have suggested to some strong elements of Africanisms, but this is uncertain. The argument has more validity in the Jamaican Convince Cult which is found in the eastern parishes of St Thomas and Portland and is thought to be particularly strong amongst the Maroons or descendants of escaped slaves settled in inaccessible parts of the Jamaican hills.[7] The Bongo Men, as adherents to Convince are called, reject the notion of Christian salvation, preferring instead to propitiate the spirits or ghosts of former believers. These possess devotees in order to have access to worldly pleasures, and in return offer their corporeal partners opportunities to practice obeah or magic. Although most actual ceremonies will start with hymns and prayers, subsequent dancing, spirit possessions and animal sacrifices indicate West African antecedents (Hogg, 1960). The point is not simply that cults such as Convince represent survivals of African culture, but that they imply rejection of Western influence in a rural, isolated setting. As Donald Hogg stresses, devotees 'could show their resentment of European authorities and of their restrictions by rejecting Christian deities and defying Christian moral rules' (Hogg, 1960: 21).

The same rejection, made possible by rural isolation, is implicit in other Caribbean cults, some of which have gained considerable notoriety. These include Kumana in Jamaica, Voodoo in Haiti, Shango in Trinidad, Santéria in Cuba and Kelé in St Lucia. It is not that these cults only practice in rural areas but tradition and folklore are fundamental to their survival. Each involves spirits, possession and elements of sorcery combined with some Christian symbolism. For example, in Trinidad Shango (Shango, Chango or Xango is the Yoruba God of Thunder), has spirits with alternate African and Christian names (Simpson, 1970: 17–20). All these cults have many functions for devotees and undoubtedly serve as a way of making some sense out of a frustrating, alienating existence. They often provide low cost healing services and the *Hounfor* of Voodoo or the *Palais* of Shango may also serve as a focal point for community involvement. At times of strain and tension they may prosper and they can, of course, have wider political significance as in the tacit support given by *houngans* and *mambas* (or Voodoo priests and priestesses) for François Duvalier in the Haitian elections of 1957. Nearly all studies of these cults suggest that they will decline as societies become more urbanized and as the spread of Western culture proceeds through education and the mass media. What is perhaps also true is that frustrations and resentment, communicated by literacy and exacerbated by comparison, tend to transform the mystical into the militant. The Jamaican cult of Rastafari, the subject of our last brief comment, has grown and not declined in the recent past. And it has grown in precisely those areas of Kingston that have suffered the worst consequences of uncontrolled urbanization and peripheral poverty.

The Rastafari sect has been called the 'cult of outcasts' and a 'millennial' cult (Simpson, 1970). It started in 1930 among the poverty stricken unemployed of West Kingston and there its centre has remained, not in the tenements and yards peopled by the rural migrants, but in the even poorer slums of the squatter camps. It is possible to trace its origins to Pocomania and it has certainly borrowed the theme of an eventual African return from the black nationalist leader, and symbol of racial pride, Marcus Garvey. The cult took Rastafari (the emperor Haile Selassie of Ethiopia) as the living God and is committed to the belief that the black man is the exiled descendant of the ancient Israelites, destined to invert white oppression and reclaim ascendance and leadership (Barrett, 1968).[8]

The economic circumstances in which many of the Rastafarians live, their appearance (the 'locks' or long hair in particular), the use of ganja (marijuana) and elements of the ideology which express revolutionary intent have served to alarm the Jamaican middle class and to excite the attention of radical leaders. And there is indeed a rebellious element in Rastafarianism, an unwillingness to accept the racial and economic implications of a capitalist society wedded to a consumer led emulation of Western materialism. In fact the cult itself, although divided into a number of factions, is far too gentle and concerned with brotherhood and the compatibility of man with nature ever to be the central focus of, say, urban terrorism, but its significance lies in the vision of a better, more egalitarian future in which the majority of Jamaicans can feel themselves involved. It is for this reason that the present Prime Minister in his successful election campaigns of 1972 and 1976 carried with him 'Joshua's Rod' (a walking stick given him by Haile Selassie) as a symbol of his sympathy with the 'Rastas' and thus with the black radicalism in politics which they themselves had come to represent (see Kuper, 1976: 105–6).

Rastafarianism is a product of enforced marginality on the rim of a major Caribbean city. It seems unlikely, given the continuation of forces that have created marginality, that it will decline in importance. But that is not to say whether it will have a direct and immediate political significance as a movement (aside from its symbolic relevance). That is a complex matter on which expert opinion is divided. It may be, as George Simpson wrote in 1955, that 'doctrines which stress the complete hopelessness of the Jamaican situation and which advocate an early return to Africa may serve to discourage any effort to modify present conditions' (Simpson, 1955: 148). On the other hand, if Fanon is right that it is with the people of the shanty towns that 'the rebellion will find its urban spearhead' then, in the Jamaican case at least, they may well march under the banner of the Lion of Judah (Fanon, 1967: 103; cf. Llewellyn Watson, 1973; Nettleford, 1970: 41–111).

Trade and religious organizations do not by any means exhaust all examples of voluntary associations. Others range from friendly societies, which are widespread, to other forms of mutual benefit association such as the Trinidadian *susu* (a clear cultural retention of the Yoriba *esusu*) where members benefit in turn from the collective payments of all participants. At the middle class level urban based associations abound in the recreational and professional spheres and few identifiable ethnic groups are without an organization specifically formed to promote ethnic identity and act as a pressure group when collective interests are threatened. However, unlike West Africa, there is little evidence to suggest that these associations have a direct or immediate relevance for socializing the rural migrant into the ways of the city. The cultural and physical differences are seldom that great, although this is not to gainsay the importance of these associations as major secondary groupings in urban areas which may serve to *attract* the potential migrant. In particular, musical and artistic associations are widespread and actively supported. In some cases these groupings serve as the hub of a community for an age group, as in many of Trinidad's justly famous steelbands, in others they serve as vehicles for artistic expression at a national level, which is true of Jamaica's internationally recognized dance company. The revived concern for expressions of racial and national identity has universally spurred on such efforts in these fields and in others. The outstanding Cuban success at the 1976 Olympic Games in Montreal, for example, has been a spur to even greater involvement by young people in local clubs. In Jamaica and Trinidad too, outstanding athletic performances have renewed pressure on available training facilities. Unlike the case of Cuba, however, where the government has deliberately promoted sporting activities in the provinces, the Trinidadian or Jamaican aspirant is forced towards the main centres of population in order to have an adequate opportunity for training and coaching.

6 Race, class and education

The inequalities of Caribbean societies did not emerge over centuries; they did not become gradually embodied in an evolving culture, sanctified by tradition and supported by the nuances of privilege, as we find in many other societies. Rather, they were an integral, savage part of the controlled explosion that obliterated indigenous peoples and founded the plantations. Naked, unmasked force is everywhere used to defend wealth and privilege when no other alternative is available, but it is not a comfortable or indeed very stable form of domination. The powerful normally seek to stabilize their position by persuading those whom they control that the extant divisions in society are equitable, inevitable or necessary for collective survival. Failing complete success in this endeavour (although it rarely *fails* completely), the powerful will resort to force, but not without inventing justifications for their actions. In the absence of ready made legitimacy, and denied access to slowly evolved justifications of class mythology, the dominant groups of the Caribbean turned to the obvious, compelling divide of race or ethnicity. Distinctiveness of origin and peculiarity of custom was both a means of persuasion and a justification for force. Racial mythology, founded upon the proclamation that blackness was inferior to whiteness, served the same purpose. It could be used to try and convince blacks of their inferiority and if this was not completely successful (which it never was) then it could rationalize the use of force.

Despite the immense variability in Caribbean societies in terms of their racial and ethnic composition, and the diverse form that inter-relations have taken, race is historically the most obvious feature of their structure. After all, what is slavery in the New World except a rigid system of black degradation and white exploitation? To both white and black the blindingly obvious divide is that of race. But to think in these terms is a mistake; the plantations existed before slavery and they continued after its decline. Race may well be a mirror of social structure but it is also its mask. To see any Caribbean society as nothing more than an ethnic mosaic or a racial collage is to confuse the shadow with the substance. But extreme caution is also necessary, for cultures never stand still and what may be a shadow today can be a substance tomorrow. Black power and *négritude* may owe their origins to social and economic inequalities buttressed by racial mythologies, but that does not mean they can never act as

102

independent influences on, say, elections or political disputes. It is precisely for this reason that Caribbean social research is a graveyard of fallen sociologies (cf. Cross, 1977).

This chapter will be concerned to sketch a few of the essential features of Caribbean social stratification. To this end, Max Weber's analytical division between class, status and political party will be employed. At each stage, we can examine the relevance of racial and ethnic divisions and point to the consequences of these many structured inequalities for understanding the emergent and varied properties of contemporary urbanization. One particular feature, educational provision, will be given separate attention. But first a look at some of the varied population compositions within the region.

Patterns of racial and ethnic composition

It comes of something of a surprise to realize that there are about as many people in the Caribbean who would describe themselves as 'white' to a census enumerator as there are those who would identify themselves as 'black', if the latter is taken to mean of African descent. There are approximately 10,000,000 of each, comprising together slightly less than four fifths of the total. The remainder are mostly 'mixed', being descendants of white/black unions, many of which originated with white planters and their black slave mistresses. After that, the picture is more exotic and less clear, ranging from the Asiatic or so-called 'East' Indians of Guyana, Trinidad and Surinam to the remnants of aboriginal Indians in Belize, Guyana and Surinam, by way of Portugese, Chinese and Syrians who are scattered widely and thinly throughout the region.

Table 6.1 gives the overall picture for the main countries of the Caribbean and is divided into figures that are recent and more likely to be accurate and those that are older and contain a higher element of estimation. We can look briefly at how each society came to comprise its present ethnic groupings.

When Jamaica was taken by the British from the Spanish in 1655, the previous reliance upon white European indentured labour was in decline and by the turn of the century, as large scale plantation cultivation grew, so did the reliance on imported West African slaves. Eric Williams reports that in 1703 Jamaica had 3,500 whites and 45,000 slaves and although seventy-three years later in 1778 the whites had grown to 18,420, the slave population had risen almost as fast to 205,261 (Williams, 1970: 104). At that time approximately 18,000 slaves were being added annually as the sugar colony reached the zenith of its sugar fortunes. Overall 610,000 slaves were sent to Jamaica from 1700–86 (Williams, 1970: 145). Increasingly, however, other categories were

TABLE 6.1   *Percentage distribution of population by ethnic group*

Country	Ethnic group						
(a)	African	Mixed	White	Chinese	East Indian	Other	Total
Jamaica (1970)	91	6	0.5	0.5	2	0	100
Barbados (1970)	91	4	4	0	0.5	0.5	100
Belize (1970)	31	33	4	0	2	30	100
Trinidad and Tobago (1970)	43	14	1	1	40	1	100
Guyana (1970)	31	10	0.5	0.5	52	6	100
Surinam (1971)	(31)*		0	0	37	32	100
(b)							
Cuba	13	14	73	0	0	0	100
Dominican Republic	12	60	28	0	0	0	100
Haiti	90	7	3	0	0	0	100
Puerto Rico	(20)†		80	0	0	0	100

Sources: (a) Commonwealth Caribbean, 1970; Dew, 1976
(b) Rodriguez, 1965: Table 3 (1958 Estimates)

* Defined as 'Creoles'.
† Defined as *'no blancos'*
n.b. Percentages have been rounded so that zero does not necessarily indicate total absence

added to these two major groups and fell between them in the rigid caste-like system of inequality, sanctioned by law and justified by racial mythology. These were the manumitted slaves and free blacks, often imported from elsewhere in the Caribbean, and the 'free people of colour', largely the result of miscegenation between white master and black slave. Although 'free' the coloureds were denied equality with whites in every sphere. Inheritance rules limited the amount they could obtain on their father's death, legal constraints limited their occupational choices and educational opportunities and an Act in 1733 'provided that no one who was not three degrees removed in lineal descent from a Negro ancestor should be allowed to vote' (Williams, 1970: 188). By 1787, there were 4,093 free people of colour in Jamaica and they became in time a genuine middle class gradually winning privileges until they obtained formal parity with whites in 1830, four years before emancipation.

The ethnic structure of Barbados corresponds even more closely to an archetypal society of slave origins since, if anything, the whites preserved greater social and physical distance than in Jamaica. From the settlement of the colony in 1627 the population of Barbados expanded rapidly but the island changed character from being predominantly white in the 1650s to being mainly black a hundred years later. This was both a relative and absolute white decline; indeed there were three times as many whites in Barbados in 1624 as there are today. In the eighteenth century the population rose only very slowly which was primarily due to slave deaths. Lowenthal reports that although 150,000 African slaves were imported from 1712 until 1782, the total population itself only rose from 42,000 to 70,000 (Lowenthal, 1957: 452). Greater prosperity in the following century and fewer deaths among the black population led to considerable increases up to 1900 when the population exceeded 200,000 and the island became one of the most crowded places on earth. The 'mixed' population was given as 17 per cent in 1946, 6 per cent in 1960 and 4 per cent in 1970 which may be in part a reflection of declining levels of miscegenation, but it is also the result of differential fertility and changed self perceptions by the coloured group, who may now be more likely to describe themselves as black. Although it was written twenty years ago, before independence, Lowenthal's comment is not invalid today: 'Barbados is generally considered the most rigid of the British West Indies with respect to colour distinctions, and although there is no legal discrimination, social barriers are strong and enduring. While the whites no longer monopolise the chief administrative posts in the government, they own almost all the estates and control the major business concerns' (Lowenthal, 1957: 468).

It should not be thought, however, that all Barbadian whites were, or are, rich. The same reason that prevented Barbados experiencing the shortage of labour after emancipation that led to other West Indian societies adding yet more migrant groups to their numbers, a total absence of further land for settlement, also prevented planters offering former white servants land as an inducement to stay after their contracts expired. The result was that many returned to Britain or looked elsewhere, but some remained and provided Barbados with its small population of poor whites or 'Redlegs', mostly concentrated in the northern part of the island.

Although a slave owning colony in its time, Belize has always been somewhat outside the mainstream of West Indian societies, partly because of its mainland location but, more important, because it never developed sugar plantations or any other field crop for export. It had a slave based monoculture by 1800, however, but this was founded on the export of logwood and mahogany. The simplified distribution of population in Table 6.1 hides some unique elements in Belize's history. The 'mixed' category, for example, includes some who are Spanish speaking *Mestizos*, descendants of Mayan Indians from the Yucatan and Spanish settlers. The 'other' category is even more diverse, including 22,000 or 18.7 per cent of the total population who are Amerindians, mostly of the Kekchi and Mayan groups. The remainder are nearly all Black Caribs whose story is extraordinary – even by Caribbean standards. Originally runaway slaves from Barbados, they settled in the hills of St Vincent where they fraternized, and periodically fought, the indigenous 'Yellow' or 'Red' Caribs who they gradually supplanted after the latter's decimation by English attack. The second Carib War of 1795, which the Black Caribs fought with the English to try and retain their land, resulted in defeat and the deportation of nearly 5,000 survivors to the Bay Island of Roatán off the coast of Honduras. From there they migrated to the mainland where, preserved by relatively high rates of endogomy, they still retain a separate language and distinctive folk traditions (Lowenthal, 1972: 179–181; cf. Wilson, 1974).

Unlike many other West Indian islands, the Spanish colony of Trinidad could hardly have been called thriving by the close of the eighteenth century. In 1777 there were only 1,400 inhabitants, other than a handful of indigenous Indians, of whom three hundred were European, and the balance slaves or freed blacks and coloureds. Following an attempt by the Spanish in 1783 to stimulate colonization, white French speaking Creoles arrived, fleeing from the radical changes induced in Martinique and Guadeloupe by the French Revolution. By 1811, fourteen years after being ceded to the English, 8 per cent of the population was white (but of English, Spanish and Dutch descent), 21 per cent free men of colour and free blacks, and the balance slaves in a total population of 32,000 (Wood, 1968: 32).

The most significant event in forming the ethnic composition of Trinidad occurred after emancipation. Unlike Barbados, there was an ample supply of land in Trinidad for the relatively small population, and the immediate reaction of the ex-slaves was to seek an independent existence, particularly in the expanding cocoa industry that exceeded sugar in importance until the turn of the nineteenth century. The shortage of labour resultant from this exodus prompted what Hugh Tinker has called the 'new system of slavery' which brought 144,000 Indians through the port of Calcutta to serve an indentured term of five years on the sugar estates of Trinidad in the period up to the abolition of this trade in 1917. Some two and a half thousand Chinese, a thousand Portugese speaking white residents of Madeira and an equivalent number of 'Syrians' also crossed the middle passage during this period to add to what on any reasoning must be described as a poly-ethnic community.

The Guyanese situation is not dissimilar. Formerly three Dutch slave colonies cultivating sugar on an empoldered ribbon of coast divided by two giant rivers, British Guiana emerged as a united colony after centuries of political vicissitude in 1831. The population in 1834 numbered 92,824, the greater proportion being slaves. Wages on the sugar plantations in the years immediately after emancipation were relatively high in order to dissuade labourers from setting up on their own. This had the opposite effect, for by the mid 1840s freed blacks were using their savings collectively to purchase estates such as Bel Air in Berbice and Buxton and Friendship on East Coast Demerara. These and other concentrations later became the basis for Guyana's black villages, but they created an enormous labour problem for the planters who responded by devising a scheme for mass immigration which introduced 239,000 Indians, 32,000 Portugese from Madeira, 14,000 Africans and 13,000 Chinese into the colony in the years through to 1917.

The Portugese and Chinese rapidly moved off the plantations into trading and the expanding service sector in Georgetown, and many of the Africans became displaced from their peasant holdings by poor returns, ill health and the relentless competition of the Indians. By 1921 the majority of Africans had moved to Georgetown, New Amsterdam or to the Upper Demerara River where the new bauxite mine was rapidly expanding. By that year nearly 80 per cent of the agricultural labourers were East Indian, creating a racial division of labour which still characterizes the society.

Surinam was expanded as a plantation society based on African slavery in the century after the Dutch acquisition in 1667. Political and economic upheavals in the last quarter of the eighteenth century lessened the prosperity of the colony which was deprived of further slave supplies by the historical accident of being in a period of British reoccupation at the time of abolition (1804–16). Surinam had always had a history of losing slaves through desertion, and their descendants (the Bush Creoles), who have always formed a distinctive ethnic component, now constitute 10 per cent of the population. Following the abolition of slavery itself in 1863 and further massive, though legitimate, migration from the estates, Surinam experienced the familiar pattern of chronic labour shortage. After experimenting with small-scale immigration from the Azores, Madeira, the Canary and Cape Verde Islands and Hong Kong, the Dutch Government settled on two main sources – 35,000 East Indians (Hindustanis) from the British connection through Calcutta and 33,000 Javanese from the Netherlands East Indies. The Indonesians are now 15 per cent of the population and together with the Hindustanis they dominate the rural areas of Surinam, excelling in the rice industry and forming the backbone of the small-scale agriculture which now accounts for more than 90 per cent of agrarian output. Some measure of the extraordinary complexity this heritage creates may be gauged by the realization that although Dutch is the official language, the lingua franca is usually Sranan (or Creole English), while the Hindustanis still speak Hindi, the Indonesians, Javanese, the Chinese, Hakka and the Bush Creoles and residual Amerindians their own separate languages. It is hardly any wonder that such cultural distinctiveness and occupational specialization creates enduring political difficulties.

The major reason why the Spanish colonies have never acquired such large proportions of blacks as the French or British possessions was that they never had so long a history of slavery nor in most cases were they ever as dependent on sugar plantations. In 1768 the Cuban population of 204,155 was 54 per cent white and tobacco planters were frequently supplementing their labour force by white or mestizo recruits from Spain or the Yucatan. From 1790 until the abolition of slavery in Cuba in 1865, as the country developed sugar plantations, more than half a million slaves were imported, nearly a third of them arriving after emancipation in the British West Indies (Thomas, 1971: 1532–3). With the assimilation or annihilation of the indigenous Indians, Cuba's population, in Caribbean ethnic terms at least, became relatively simple, although there are frequently wild variations in the proportions who are ascribed to the three main categories. Table 6.1 represents the last official estimate, but unofficial figures have put the Afro-Cuban proportions at nearly half and the whites at only 30 per cent (M. G. Smith, 1974: 277).

Eric Williams records that the Spanish part of Hispaniola, which was later to declare itself independent of Spain as the Dominican Republic in 1821 (and again in 1844 after twenty-three years of annexation by Haiti), had only 12 per cent as slaves out of its total population of 125,000 at the end of the eighteenth century (Williams, 1970: 110). Nearly two hundred years later, despite the most complex vicissitudes of political and economic fortunes, the proportion of Africans remains approximately the same. Definitional problems are again legion but there seems little doubt that while the vast majority of the black population is at the lower end of the socioeconomic spectrum, so too are large numbers of the *mestizo* group. For this reason the phrase 'coloured middle class', so commonly used in Jamaica, is far less apposite.

The considerable variation in ethnic composition between Hispanic and non-Hispanic societies in the Caribbean is well illustrated by Haiti which as the French colony of Saint-Domingue from 1697 was a classic black slave colony. In 1779, eighty-two years after the Spanish capitulation, the population was nearly 90 per cent black through slave importation. Although high rates of mortality caused by sickness and ill-treatment cut the net addition considerably, Saint-Domingue was the major destination for slave ships from the African coast during the eighteenth century. At the time of the French Revolution, which was to have such a profound effect upon the colony's political history, Saint-Domingue had a white élite of planters, senior officials and lesser functionaries comprising 7 per cent of the population while the Mulatto group, whose temporary and opportunistic alliance with the slave rebellion was soon to create the first black republic in 1804, numbered 28,000 or 5 per cent. Once again today's ethnic structure is hardly very different (Williams, 1970: 246).

Puerto Rican migration history is parallel in many ways to Spain's other leading Caribbean colony, Cuba. Although coffee rather than tobacco was the leading crop before sugar cultivation, the pattern of small-scale farming was similar and without the plantation there was no need for the slave. The census of 1827 recorded that whites were just half the population and that only 10 per cent were black slaves. Thereafter continued miscegenation between mestizos and whites blurred the distinction with the effect that census reports have progressively reported an increasing proportion of whites, despite the importation of black slaves up until 1865. The four fifths of the population who are now recorded as 'white' derive as much from changed self perceptions as they do from a genuinely altered racial composition (Hoetink 1867: 185).

In this brief review it will be noted that in most cases the ethnic composition of the major Caribbean societies was firmly established a century ago. Although groups have differed in terms of their rate of natural increase and their propensity to return to their land of origin or re-emigrate elsewhere, there is a surprising consistency in the retention of previous patterns. This is also true for settlement in terms of urban or rural location. The Javanese of Surinam and the East Indians of Trinidad and Guyana were the last sizeable groups to settle, and they are still largely confined to the rural areas. For example, only 16 per cent of Indonesians lived in Paramaribo at the time of the 1964 census in Surinam, compared with 23 per cent of the Hindustanis. The Bush Creoles, however, retaining the aptness of their title, are 98 per cent outside the capital city. The general pattern for other Commonwealth Caribbean countries may be seen in Table 6.2 which effectively demonstrates the spatial divisions of racial location. Comparisons are only valid within a country, however, since the definitions of 'urban' differ, but it is possible to see the degree to which Africans in Jamaica and Indians in Trinidad and Guyana are mainly located on the rural periphery.[1] This is important because the city is the nexus of the dependent economy, the nodal point without whose control no group can expect to be influential in altering the nature of economic or political processes. Of course, Table 6.2 does not show the relative power of each group, which is partly a function of numbers but also of political and economic position. The same data may be redistributed as shown in Table 6.3 to give the ethnic distribution in urban areas and in the rest of the country.

It is readily apparent that Trinidad and Guyana possess a pronounced division of ethnic location which is particularly obvious in the latter case. For example, the ratio of Africans to Indians in rural areas of Trinidad is 1:1.5, whereas the comparable figure for Guyana is 1:3, indicating that not only are a very high percentage of Guyanese Indians in rural areas but that they are three times as numerous as the second largest group.

TABLE 6.2   *Proportion of main ethnic groups in urban locations for Commonwealth Caribbean 1970 (per cent)*

	African	Mixed	White	Chinese	East Indian	All
Jamaica	27	43	62	70	25	29
Trinidad	54	65	74	74	27	45
Guyana	52	52	76	76	13	30
Barbados	55	78	72	100	97	56

Source: Commonwealth Caribbean, 1970.
'Urban' definitions:
   Jamaica – Kingston and St Andrew
   Trinidad – Port of Spain, St George, San Fernando and Arima
   Guyana – Georgetown, Suburbs of Georgetown, New Amsterdam and Upper Demerara River
   Barbados – St Michael and Christ Church

In societies such as these the relevance of ethnic group distribution can only be understood in the whole context of group inequality. The urban/ rural distinction is one, but by no means the only facet to that inequality. We need to consider occupational and economic distinctions, differentials of prestige entitlement and access to educational opportunity.

The structure of social inequality

The dependent societies of the New World are fundamentally class societies but nowhere do they conform to the capitalist pattern of the West. Even today the majority of the labour force survives directly off the land so that any investigation of classes has to start with this fact. And that in turn must mean starting with the plantations. Before examining in some detail the nature of the various classes involved in the development of the plantations it is important to note a transformation in this productive unit from what we would call a 'pre-capitalist' to a capitalist form.

In the early years of their existence plantations were typified by

TABLE 6.3 *Percentage distribution of urban and rural populations by ethnic group in main Commonwealth Caribbean countries 1970*

	Jamaica		Trinidad		Guyana		Barbados	
	Urban	Rural	Urban	Rural	Urban	Rural	Urban	Rural
African	86	93	51	36	54	21	88	95
Mixed	9	5	20	9	18	7	5	2
White	1	0	2	1	1	0	5	3
Chinese	2	0	1	0	1	0	0	0
East Indian	2	2	24	54	23	64	1	0
Other	0	0	1	0	3	7	1	0
Total	100	100	100	100	100	100	100	100
	(516,865)	(1,280,536)	(423,280)	(507,791)	(210,767)	(489,077)	(132,754)	(102,473)

Source: Commonwealth Caribbean, 1970.
Urban definitions: Same as table 6.2

a simple division between master and slave, a paternalist, caste-like relationship, changing little, where production surpluses were directly repatriated to an absentee owner residing in London or Paris. A small European class dominated the mass of Africans and sought to run the colony in their own interests. The metropolitan government on the other hand was relatively uninterested in problems of administration and content to allow the colony to go its own way unhindered. In the latter half of the eighteenth century the picture changes as the wealth of the colonies came to be realized, a wealth which was both an aid to and a result of the burgeoning prosperity of the newly emergent European industrial societies. The planters as a class began to give way to the corporation as new foreign capital amalgamated plantations, rationalized production and strived for efficiency and low cost. Part of this incorporation of the plantations into the capitalist economies of Europe and North America entailed the removal of support for such pre-capitalist restrictions on labour mobility and manpower flexibility as slavery, which gave way to a new system of wage labour (cf. Williams, 1964a).

In the earlier period there was no need for the development of towns or cities since the nexus of economic activity was the plantation. A port grew up, of course, to ship and service the export trade on which the colony depended, but urbanization was minimal due to the lack of an alternative source of employment and the impossibility for most of breaking the chains of slavery. With the emergence of the corporate plantation, however, the whole structure was altered and, in addition to new foreign intervention in the rural regions of our ideal type sugar based colony, there were two urban influences. First the emergent interest in empire, consequent upon the obvious wealth of the West Indian colonies and, later, the scramble for the lands from where the slaves had been abducted, demanded a greater say by the metropolitan power in the affairs of each colony. In the British West Indies this was the time for development of the Crown Colony form of administration. Second, the new interest in these 'underdeveloped estates' prompted the export of surplus capital from the industrial society to develop the manufacturing, service and commercial sectors of the colonies. Both these forces acted as a spur to growth in the main urban area, usually based on the old port of the pre-capitalist colony. In the previous period the labour problem was solved by migration, either forced or semi-forced (as in the indenture system), but now these opportunities gradually declined and the only possibility was to aim for efficiency through utilizing less labour while at the same time attempting to ensure that labour costs were kept as low as possible. One way of achieving the latter was to aim for a proportion of the labour force always unemployed or underemployed so that competition for work kept wages low. This was relatively easy to achieve in rural areas, because of the seasonal nature of the crop, but it was also helped by high rates of natural population growth.

The investment of capital in urban areas (often capital raised by or in association with the corporate plantations and originally representing horizontal or vertical integration) created a proletariat or body of wage labourers who in time became wealthier than their rural cousins. This disjunction created or sustained a migrant flow to the city where pressure on jobs served to limit wages and free more surplus for repatriation or possibly more urban investment.

This simplified scenario could hardly be presented as an accurate description of every Caribbean economy but the broad framework of this dynamic process is a fair summary of dominant trends in the history of the plantations. There is a real sense in which the end of slavery was the end of a pre-capitalist plantation structure and with it the end of a relatively simple class system, certainly based on needs emanating from a commercial capitalism in Britain and Europe, but fundamentally pre-capitalist in social form. It is only from this time that the primate city emerges as the centre of the colony and although linked in important ways with the rural periphery each develops a more complex class structure.

Naturally, the first instinct of manumitted slaves, before or after emancipation, was to leave the plantation or, failing that, to seek to lessen their total dependence. The only alternative in the years before urban development started was to lease, buy or occupy land for peasant cultivation. This was much easier in some Caribbean territories than in others. In Jamaica, for example, the small trickle of ex-slaves into their own holdings became a flood after 1838 although very many failed to break completely with the plantations. The fear of labour shortage was the prime reason why plantations extended the system of *métayage* used for slaves to feed themselves, and permitted the cultivation of small plots of estate land in return for wage labour at croptime. Of course, over time some small-holders became genuine farmers, often emulating the plantations in cultivating cash crops (as with the sugar farmers of Trinidad) or developing new cash crops for export (e.g. the banana industry in Jamaica or the rice farmers of Guyana). Rarely, however, did such groups free themselves from the influence of the corporate plantation, either because they had to rely on the processing and transport systems of the estates or because their seed, supplies and equipment came through companies or stores owned by the diversified plantation.

Although the corporate plantations share with their pre-capitalist forms a clear separation of employers from labour, backed up by racial mythology, they came to depend more and more upon impersonal regulation and control. As Sidney Mintz writes: 'Control over the labour force, like control over other factors of production, is impersonal, standardized and essentially commercial. Such control is backed by the existence of a state political system which is stable and monopolizes force within the society' (Mintz, 1959: 46).

It is tenable to regard the Caribbean peasantries as a form of resistance to the domination of the plantations. However it is also true that not all societies proceeded in the same way. For example, as the peasantry mushroomed in Jamaica, it was declining in Cuba and Puerto Rico as the newly founded slave based sugar industry grew to its pre-eminent position in the latter half of the nineteenth century. Rural classes often appear in a symbiotic relationship, trading labour for land, but in fact the relationship is heavy with contradiction. Peasants rely on land, capital and access to markets. Plantations own the finest land, forcing independent peasants on to the rural periphery. They are rich in capital and have a well oiled marketing mechanism. Mintz again has an apposite word when he writes: 'Typically, the history of Caribbean peasantries is full of false starts, regressions, and struggles for power between plantation and peasant adaptions' (Mintz, 1974: 133). He is also perceptive in noting that the contradictions between the demand for a large quiescent labour force and the allocation of land for food cultivation necessary before and after slavery to ensure its supply, was one way in which the system weakened itself by lessening the dependence of labour on the plantations (Mintz, 1974: 211–12). One might add that the internal marketing system which developed to distribute the food surplus thus generated also had the effect of bringing rural women into contact with the emerging city. Even today the majority of rural migrants to the city are women.

In the city the development of an urban proletariat proceeded apace once capital investment from indigenous and foreign sources had begun to flow into the primate city. A typical urban class system emerged, although with one or two special features. For example, although a genuine bourgeoisie or productive class did exist in the typical Caribbean colony, it was a relatively small part of the new middle class. This was because much of the capital originated in the metropolitan society and was controlled from there. This meant that a large proportion of the middle class was really comprised of functionaries, either in administration or in management. The 'coloured middle class' of Jamaica is a good example: a group who owed their position to foreign capital and who because of this were more of a consumption than productive class. The upper class might contain local and foreign whites, some of whom were also landed but, at least in the twentieth century, it is not they who constitute the dynamic element in the class system. In fact, one feature of the typical neo-colonial society is that it lacks that dynamism. A typical bourgeoisie is, in one sense, a revolutionary class creating the productive capacity and wealth for change: Caribbean societies have often lacked that group and instead revealed a middle class who, despite being the most privileged in terms of access to educational opportunity, are rightly, if somewhat harshly, said to be characterized by: 'Their own struggle for posts and pay, their ceaseless promising of new jobs, their sole idea of national development as one where everybody can aim at getting something more, the gross and vulgar materialism, the absence of any idea of elementary originality of thought' (James, 1973: 84).

A genuine bourgeoisie in a capitalist, industrialized society would scarcely waste the human labour power constituted by the urban unemployed. Rather the productive capacity would be utilized as cheap labour, as indeed has been the case in Puerto Rico where foreign capital has been allowed the greatest penetration. That is not to say that urban unemployment does not exist on that island but simply that manufacturing would be expected to grow apace despite, rather than because of, the local middle class.

In terms of the structure of Caribbean classes, we can draw a distinction between the rural and urban system, although both have come to be dominated by the multinational corporation. This can be represented in the following diagram. It is quite mistaken to imagine that these two systems are any more than analytically separate; they interpenetrate in important ways. Thus with the advent of corporate plantations, the old conflict between the planters and urban classes gives way to co-operation as both depend upon the same capital sources. Similarly the urban proletariat is constantly replenished from the displaced peasantry and estate labourers are forced towards the city by lack of land and rural opportunity.

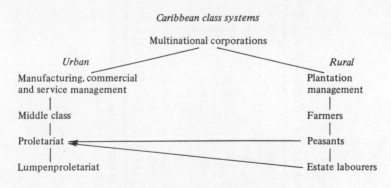

Caribbean class systems

Caribbean class systems

Of course there are many exceptions to this pattern. In Martinique, for example, and to a lesser extent in Barbados, the old landed planter class

TABLE 6.4 *Percentage distribution of wage earners in urban Jamaica by sex and race 1960**

Income	African		Mixed		White		Other		Total	
	M	F	M	F	M	F	M	F	M	F
(J£)										
0–99	28	60	16	32	2	4	17	33	25	52
100–199	31	23	20	20	3	5	18	18	27	22
200–499	33	14	37	31	11	35	34	29	33	18
500–999	6	3	17	16	19	47	20	19	10	8
1,000 +	2	0	10	1	65	9	11	1	5	0
	100	100	100	100	100	100	100	100	100	100
Number	(52,761)	(41,400)	(11,470)	(10,484)	(1,598)	(817)	(5,151)	(3,717)	(70,980)	(56,418)

Source: Adapted from Clarke, 1975: table 32.
* 'Not stated' have been excluded.

have rebuffed corporate control and have retained an extraordinary dominance (Kovats-Beaudoux, 1973). The Béké of Martinique are a historical anachronism who by dint of racial solidarity and staunch endogamy still control the land and have a more significant role than Metropolitan Frenchmen in the affairs of the island.[2] At the other extreme the diagram takes no account of the Cuban case where all large plantations are now publicly owned co-operatives, nor of the more recent attempts by other countries to control the multinationals through nationalization (e.g. Guyana) or by majority participation (e.g. Jamaica and Trinidad and Tobago).

The particular form that Caribbean classes take is a direct result of ties of economic dependence and the legal and political systems and traditions which these have created. It is invariably the case that racial categories are reflected in the composition of urban and rural classes, although often their structure is further complicated by divisions between Creole and foreign elements. However, all the evidence suggests the persistence of a strong positive correlation between wealth or income and white or coloured phenotype. This can be demonstrated without too much difficulty, although recent censuses and surveys have tended to eschew racial categorization and income data can only be accepted with the usual caution. Table 6.4 provides a distribution of income by the main racial groups in urban Jamaica (Kingston and St Andrew). It shows very clearly indeed that the majority of black urban wage earning men (it excludes the unemployed) earnt less than J£4.00 (US$9.60) a week in 1960, whereas nearly two thirds of white men earnt more than five times as much. The 'mixed' group, who are mostly 'coloured' or white/black mixtures, fell in between, as does the very similar 'other' category which is mostly comprised of East Indians, Syrians and Chinese.

One obvious feature of social structure which explains why these gross inequalities exist is, of course, that the occupational distribution of the races is entirely different. For example, 61 per cent of the European or white men in urban Jamaica were classified as in 'professional or supervisory' employment in 1960 compared with only 5 per cent of the Africans. That may explain a large part of the income differential, although it only begs the deeper question for the existence of such an unbalanced occupational structure. It is a problem for a simple class analysis of Caribbean societies, at least based on the normal indices of socio-economic status, that occupational groupings do not explain *all* the income differential. For example, 1960 data from Trinidad suggest a more complex pattern. Jack Harewood (1971) reports that median monthly incomes for male employees by race in 1960 were as follows:

	TT$
African	104.03
East Indian	76.98
White	500.00
Mixed	112.85
Other	132.77

However, controlling for occupational categories still gave a range of medium income for 'professional and technical' employees from TT$162.15 for Indians and TT$175.36 for Africans to TT$972.17 for whites, which is as extreme within this top occupational category as it is overall. The reason is probably a combination of three factors: first that the 'professional and technical' employee category is itself heterogeneous in terms of skill and educational level; second, that the 'white' group contains a substantial proportion of foreigners representing multinational companies and paid at international salary levels and, finally, that 'race' is still employed as a relevant ascriptive criterion in occupational placement and salary assessment. A study of the 'business élite' in Trinidad found that nearly four out of five could be described as of white or 'light' complexion and that although social mobility of members of darker races did occur into the business élite, racial discrimination and family contacts assured that they had to achieve a higher level of educational and occupational performance (Camejo, 1971).

The development of capitalist class relations in dependent economies alters the caste-like proscriptions of the early colonial period, but nowhere does it destroy them. This is partly the effect of 'cultural lag', the retention of social categories used to bolster and justify a grossly inegalitarian system in the first moments of its existence. More important, it signifies the presence of a pattern of deference which in one form or another can be found in all societies whether they be capitalist or not. What sets the colonial connection in the Caribbean apart is that this pattern of deference is firmly based on 'race' and the degree of approximation to white ethnicity. It is a system which has endured and justified discriminatory action from Carriacou to Cuba and which has had the unanticipated consequence of encouraging urban residence and deepening the mythology that places a rural way of life at the lowest point on a hierarchy of personal aspiration.

Max Weber's original designation of status groups (*ständé*), as communities ranked in terms of a positive or negative estimation of social honour or prestige as revealed by preferences of association and differential life styles, is an appropriate analytical category for understanding Caribbean social stratification in two ways. It permits an assessment of the degree to which historically important criteria for group membership, such as race, continue to influence the distribution of material and non-material resources and it also illuminates the manner in which primordial cultural traits may be retained or regenerated under appropriate conditions.

Research material on the first question is extensive, largely because many sociological and anthropological investigators have tended to assume that the frequent and pervasive references to race and colour in Caribbean literature, and in the patterning of personal relations, is evidence that here lies the true core of Caribbean societies. David Lowenthal, for example, in one of the most detailed, thorough and well researched investigations into West Indian societies, takes the persistence of the 'white bias', or positive evaluation of European culture and Caucasian phenotype, as the single most important feature of their structure (Lowenthal, 1972). The difference between Lowenthal's approach and that advanced here may be seen from the following summary of one main argument he employs. Commenting on the retention of racial categories, he says: 'If colour no longer determines class boundaries, it increasingly symbolizes the differences that lie beyond them. Precisely because status and rewards are in flux, racial inequalities are no longer accepted as inevitable concomitants of a hierarchical system but are construed as deliberate, malign, and hence corrigible' (Lowenthal, 1972: 299). However, colour never did *determine* class boundaries but once reflected them, and to a considerable extent still does. Although status may be in flux in some areas because political power has become redistributed through adult suffrage, rewards on the whole have not reflected this change, and it is for this reason that racial inequalities are viewed as unacceptable, becoming a major topic for political debate.

Another, more complex and sophisticated variant of the same theme is contained in most theories of 'social and cultural pluralism', a theoretical approach to Caribbean societies claiming descent from J. S. Furnivall's thesis on colonialism in Southeast Asia (see Cross, 1971). It is premised on the belief that the original cultures of the constituent groups in slave society have persisted, albeit modified, so that today sectionalized cultures frozen in their original rank order of prestige typify many Caribbean societies, particularly the British, French and Dutch West Indies (M. G. Smith, 1965; 1974). While this approach aptly describes an important historical fact, that whites have traditionally dominated blacks in Caribbean cultures, it fails to generate any understanding of the dynamics in this process and does not permit an adequate appraisal of the degree to which the external ties of dependence or the internal relations between social classes sustain and modify racial ascription (see Stone, 1973).

A more fruitful line of reasoning, equally committed to the determining force of cultural distinctiveness, is that of H. Hoetink (1967). Hoetink's approach to the sources of deference and racial contact in Caribbean cultures is to emphasize the fundamental difference between the more open and mobile race system of the Spanish speaking Caribbean and the harsher 'Northern European variant', as he describes the form in the British, French and Dutch West Indies. Many have commented on an apparent difference of race relations between the two and the usual approach is to suggest that cultural factors, such as the egalitarian implications of Catholicism or the early accommodation to Moorish influence, provide the answers to this comparative puzzle. Although it is perfectly tenable to suppose that the strident individualism of radical Protestantism lent itself well to myths of black inferiority, and it has certainly been the case that North America and Northern Europe have revealed deep and enduring strains of racism, it is dangerous to place too much store by this theory for it tends to suggest little or no racial elements in the hierarchy of deference in the Hispanic Caribbean and Latin America.

It is not appropriate to trace the lacunae of this debate, which have generated a massive literature on differing interpretations of New World slavery, but it is pertinent to note that recent writing on the Hispanic Caribbean does not support the thesis that racial evaluations are irrelevant for status placement.[3] Gordon Lewis, for example, who has effectively argued that Puerto Rico is a class stratified dependent society, is unequivocal in the judgement that 'To be black in Puerto Rico ... is to suffer the stigmata of a negative image' (Lewis, 1974b: 143). An even more powerful example is provided by post revolutionary Cuba where the combination of an open Hispanic heritage, coupled with burgeoning socialism and rejection of North American racism, might be expected to provide ample evidence that racial categorization is irrelevant. David Booth's fine essay on this topic testifies to the 'war against racism' in Castro's Cuba but avers that 'while the revolution has a number of solid achievements to its credit, there are wide areas where its effects remain uncertain, and yet others where only modest successes have been scored up to now' (Booth, 1976: 169).

There remains therefore, a racial element in deference within the Caribbean: to be black is still to be placed lower in a hierarchy of prestige than any other group. The force of these evaluations varies from society to society and is dependent upon ecological and demographic factors, moral and religious sentiments, the complex interplay of historical events and, perhaps more important than anything else, the degree to which racial ascription has correlated with access to economic and political power. But criteria of deference must be understood to have an important independent effect, albeit constrained by other factors. Certainly if to be black carries a greater probability of being poor and powerless then, in materialist cultures at least, it must come to represent negative evaluation. Children imbibe that judgement by the time they can see themselves in a context wider than their own families or peers. Just as class mythology may lower horizons and constrain ambition, so too with race. The historical fallacy of racial inferiority becomes the certainty of a fulfilled prophecy as young people locate themselves in what appears to be a natural order. Ideology may serve dominant interests, but it does so in a dynamic way which is, of course, one reason why change occurs.

In terms of urbanization, patterns of racial deference take on a particular significance. The 'white bias' must become an urban bias if, as is the case, white life style is increasingly identified as 'urban'. The caste-like relationship of the traditional rural racial dichotomy, characteristic of the pre-corporate plantation, did not have this implication, but the more impersonal and bureaucratic development of the new plantation sector, together with the integration of the corporate plantation into shipping and services has altered this prior pattern. Industrialization, the growth of a service sector and the massive intrusion of Western advertising has also promoted the urban life style. Advertising and the media in particular can be seen to have a dramatic impact. In nearly all cases the products and messages, whether strictly commercial or contained in films or programmes, are imported from Europe or North America. They feature white actors and a consumption oriented life style which is profoundly urban in its implications. Except in Cuba, where specific attempts have been made to counteract this tendency, the message is stark and compelling: rural life is at best a monotonous struggle for survival with little chance of improvement while the city offers escape and the promise of sophistication. It is the chance to trade the marginality of the *jibaro* for the ease and opulence of the executive. The city is the shop window of a wanted world; the crowd gathers round it to see and be seen.

It is common for writers on the Caribbean to cite the experience of slavery as a major reason for the low prestige which attaches to agricultural labour. But this view is historically inaccurate and sociologically improbable. Emancipated slaves tried desperately to leave the plantations because their lives continued to be unfree. But they desired more than anything else to work on the land, their *own* land. Some succeeded but most did not, because the plantations owned the best arable land and *controlled* nearly all the rest. When commentators attribute urban migration to lack of interest in farming or agricultural employment they oversimplify the reality and conflate symptoms with causes. The reaction against the land is an attempt to reject the certainty of poverty. Despite governmental exhortation, people learn by observation and exemplar. The clarion call that issues by example from those Caribbean middle classes that are oriented to North American or European life styles contains the unambiguous message that all but the foolish should try to make it in the city. On the whole, the education that people receive encourages them in the wisdom of that belief.

Education

In all societies differential prestige attaches to occupational position. Slave societies of the Caribbean were no exception but it was not until the caste-like rigidity of the pre-capitalist plantations gave way to the more modern form that education became a relevant factor in occupational placement, and thus an avenue of social mobility. In this process the rise of the free coloureds during the nineteenth century is perhaps the most important watershed. The *gens de couleur* or the free people of colour were inevitably destined to occupy an intermediate position in slave society once racial mythology had come to buttress and explain its gross inequalities. But, as Raymond Smith comments, 'they also became the main bearers of the idea that they had the right of access to high status positions and to better life chances in relation to the market *in spite of colour*' (Smith, 1970: 61; emphasis in original). The changed occupational structure, consequent upon the rise of corporate plantations and the concomitant growth of their new handmaidens, the primate cities, enable that claim to be heard, because the free coloureds could offer the educational standards that European civilization decreed as appropriate for commercial, professional or mercantile roles.

The rise of education as an avenue of occupational mobility did not occur in isolation from other transformations. It marked the deepened incorporation of Caribbean societies into the web of European economic and political connections. The coloureds were the vehicle for this revolutionary process in many parts of the region. In Martinique, for example, which had long been the French model of plantation society after the liberation of Haiti, Michael Leiris writes: 'Creole whites have not for the most part been interested in furthering their studies beyond the minimum required for the management of their enterprises, and the Negroes have found themselves in practice deprived of all the avenues of culture, while for a number of *mulattoes* education appeared as a means by which they could rise socially' (Leiris, 1955: 152). Education thus came to betray two essential aspects in Caribbean life: it was perceived as a pathway to affluence and status by non-whites but it was, at the same time, an escape route that was only recognized as legitimate when it manifestly underpinned the European connection and buttressed the survival of colonial dependency.

This is clear on two levels. Secondary education for the coloured group, or later the children of the new black middle class, strictly emulated the putative standards of Europe in content and form. Primary education on the other hand served a different purpose, albeit equally ideological; it replaced the immediate and external control of the overseer's whip with the self-discipline of religious and moral conviction. Universal literacy also had the inestimable advantage of both enabling political control to become centralized, as rules could now be read, and permitting business to grow, as the populace could practise their newly won abilities on advertisements and other trade announcements.

This directs our attention to the two main levels of Caribbean educational systems when assessing their impact on urbanization – the form that secondary education takes prepares a majority of children with privileged backgrounds for élite status while the primary level functions to inculcate values conducive to a materialist culture based on European and, increasingly, North American industrial needs. The minority from each group who have not simply emulated the attainment level of their parents provide the vibrant element to a system of status placement without which the myth of 'open' opportunity would be untenable. Moreover, that degree of rigidity would prevent adaptation to changing technology and produce an obvious disjunction in local and metropolitan interests.

At the primary school level, the Caribbean school system is now all but universal. As early as 1901, barely a generation after the abolition of slavery, Cuba had a compulsory primary school system and 'upper level' primary schools (termed 'post-primary' elsewhere in the Caribbean) were added under Machado. Prior to the Revolution, however, the spread of primary schooling had stagnated and Samuel Bowles records that by 1958–59 the proportion of the age group attending school had fallen to under one half (Bowles, 1976). This was about the proportion actually *attending* primary schools in the Anglophone Caribbean at the time of the Moyne Commission in 1938 (although 77 per cent of the age group were enrolled).

These figures manifest the opposition that universal education, of even the most rudimentary kind, had received. What there was, was largely the result of denominational interest, which was itself at least partly motivated by a desire to further missionary ambitions. As late as 1926, Eric Williams records a Creole planter's view on education for agricultural labourers as: 'Give them some education in the way of reading and writing but no more. Even then I would say educate only the bright ones; not the whole mass. If you do educate the whole mass of the agricultural population, you will be deliberately ruining the country' (quoted by Williams, 1964b: 213). However, despite such opposition the denominational view prevailed, even though, for the Anglophone Caribbean at least, many commissions of inquiry and inspectorate reports noted the poverty of provision, characterized in the years before independence by overcrowding, irrelevant curricula and untrained teachers (Cross, 1973a: 55–6).

From the very earliest days of public provision following emancipation, there had been frequent comments from varied sources bemoaning the apparent irrelevance of much that was taught in primary schools for the practical needs of the colonies. Shirley Gordon's compilation of material on the development of education in the West Indies includes the following protest from a Barbadian agricultural paper of 1892:

'The sons and daughters of the labouring classes have become impregnated with the idea that the education which is imparted to them makes them better than their fathers; and they have begun to look with disdain upon mere manual labour. Field labour, in particular, they regard as an abomination. Rather than work in the fields they prefer to gravitate to town and recruit the army of loafers to be seen about Bridgetown [Gordon, 1963: 135].'

Typically, as the colonial planter quoted by Eric Williams knew, there was no chance of an independent rural existence. The individual's future was wage labour in oppressive conditions on a plantation, and nobody acting rationally would pursue any education which did not apparently promote escape from this fate. As a result the 'best' schools produced the lowest proportion of agriculturalists. Even in 1938, the Moyne Commissioners had noted the contradiction between economic need and educational provision when they wrote: 'If education is to fit the West Indian to make the most of the opportunities afforded by his own country, those opportunities in their turn must be sufficient to attract those who have a good education' (West India Royal Commission, 1945: 108). Again in a forceful denunciation of previous educational practice, Eric Williams wrote in 1946 about his vision as one where:

'The children learn to read, but they learn to read about their own lives. They learn to write, but they learn to write about the farm, their crops and their livestock. They learn arithmetic, though arithmetic is no longer the multiplication table, but the amount of vegetables which should be raised to supply a given number of people and the measurement of a plot for the garden [Williams, 1951: 46].'

For most parts of the region, these aspirations have yet to be attained; a fact which merely testifies to the longevity of the colonial tradition. It is perhaps only in Cuba that a determined effort has been made to reorientate the content of primary education so as to instil the importance of the land and the pride that should be associated with its cultivation. As elsewhere, education has tended to be less the initiator of change and more the consequence of history.

The demands for adult literacy have however ensured that primary education is now all but universal, as Table 6.5 demonstrates. Only in

Haiti is there evidence of a serious lack of primary level education; the 84 per cent coverage in Guyana being largely occasioned by the presence of remote Amerindian peoples. The gross enrolment ratios have the limitation of not showing precise coverage because of the common practice whereby children stay on beyond the official learning age in 'post-primary' streams. At the secondary level and beyond, the picture is very different and there is less consistency. Jamaica, for example, had only 8.6 per cent of the 15–19 year old age group in secondary schools in 1971 although the aim is for a third by 1990. Although many states have pressed ahead with schooling beyond the primary level (variously termed 'post-primary', 'junior secondary' etc), all have retained a selective element at the higher secondary level. An important segment of this provision has been in schools that have been primarily concerned to provide education for an élite group, who would otherwise be forced to go abroad. On the whole they have served to provide an avenue for the sons and daughters of the local middle class to enter business or the liberal professions. The content of the education in these schools has been even more closely imitative of the perceived metropolitan norm than at the primary level. In the Anglophone West Indies, the zenith of educational achievement has been an outstanding performance in foreign examinations sat locally, followed by the award of a public scholarship to read for history, law or medicine at an ancient British University. Even though a local University has existed since 1948, with agricultural and engineering faculties in Trinidad, this institution itself is redolent of British precedent (Cross, 1973a: 68–9).

The implications of these patterns of educational provision for tilting the balance in favour of an urban life style are immensely important. Fluency in Western culture and the intrusion of Western perceptions of occupational prestige are bound to concentrate effort on educational achievement. But facilities for this achievement are more easily accessible to middle class urban dwellers than any others. In Trinidad, for example, survey data show that in 1967, the children of parents in professional or managerial employment were at least three times as likely to be attending selective secondary schools as their representation in the population would suggest (Cross and Schwartzbaum, 1969: 196–9). Moreover, children living in rural areas were only just over half as likely to be attending the more prestigious public funded secondary schools as they would if provision and performance were equally distributed. More recent data underline the point. Using the definitions of 'rural' and 'urban' previously employed, the 1970 Population Census for the Commonwealth Caribbean reveals that at age fourteen, 63 per cent of children living in urban areas of Trinidad attended secondary schools, compared with only 40 per cent in rural areas. Unfortunately the census does not control for parental

TABLE 6.5 *Enrolment ratios* and primary school pupil teacher ratios in selected Caribbean countries 1973*

Country	Enrolment ratios			Pupil teacher ratios
	Primary	Secondary	Higher	
Barbados	100	–	(6.75)	–
Cuba	100	26	(7.58)	25
Dominican Republic	(105)	–	(9.08)	55
Guadeloupe	(129)	(68)	–	29
Haiti (1971)	(50)	–	–	45
Jamaica	(132)	(28)	(6.68)	40
Puerto Rico (1972)	(149)	(39)	(30.14)	22
Trinidad and Tobago (1971)	91	35	(2.28)	33
Guyana	84	48	(3.44)	32

Source: *Unesco Yearbook,* 1975 (tables 3.2; 4.2).
* Enrolment ratios express the proportion of the relevant age group actually enrolled in the schools. The gross ratio (given in parentheses) may exceed 100 because the schools commonly contain children outside the official age ranges. Where possible net enrolment ratios are given, which compare the number of pupils within the actual age range with the group's representation in the total population.

occupation so there is no way of knowing whether this is an effect independent of residence.

The anti-rural bias of education is further demonstrated by Table 6.6 which shows the proportion of tertiary or higher education students studying agriculture or graduating from agricultural courses. Two features stand out: although 44 per cent of the Jamaican work force still earn their living from the land (1970) only 2.3 per cent of higher education students on that island are studying agriculture, most at the Jamaica School of Agriculture. On the other hand, whereas in pre-revolutionary Cuba 4.7 per cent were studying agriculture (1958/59), by 1968/69 it had risen to 6.2 per cent and had reached 11.7 per cent by 1973. Indeed the Cuban achievements are notable in other respects. The whole burden of the new educational policy is to deliberately counter the effect of Western education in alienating the people from the land. Both in terms of providing mass education in relevant skills, and channelling the talents of the educational élite towards developing agrarian technology, the Cuban approach is outstanding. Landmarks in this policy include the closure of the schools in 1961 in order to send teachers and senior pupils into the countryside to combat illiteracy (it has been claimed that illiteracy fell from 24 per cent to 4 per cent in a single year) and the *escuela al campo* policy which brought the secondary schools to the people rather than the other way round (Bowles, 1976: 77–8; cf. Gillette, 1972).

It may take such deliberate action to rectify the unintended consequences of educational development elsewhere, for there is little doubt that at the present time education at all levels serves to motivate migration, although evidence from Puerto Rico suggests that this is only a rational consideration, as far as income is concerned, at the higher educational levels (Carnoy, 1970). Martin Carnoy's careful study starts from the fact that the rural:urban income ratio has widened in Puerto Rico (as elsewhere) from 1:1.81 in 1950 to 1:2.24 in 1968 (Carnoy, 1970: 336). His data indicate that only about a fifth of the income differential between urban and rural locations is attributable to socio-economic factors, much of the balance being a reflection of qualitative differentials in educational provision. However, these differences in turn explain a relatively small proportion of the variance at low education levels, but progressively more through the higher grades of primary and junior secondary schools. Thus, improving the quality of primary schooling in rural areas is not likely to improve income by a great amount, which throws some doubt upon the capacity for education itself to be highly influential in slowing down rates of urbanization. But this only adds more weight to the argument that education is a blunt instrument for fashioning a new society and is no substitute for more direct action.

TABLE 6.6　*Proportion of students studying or graduating in agriculture 1973 (per cent)*

	Studying	Graduating
	(% of all higher education students)	(% of all higher education students graduating)
Cuba	11.7	14.7
Dominican Republic	2.0	4.3
Haiti (1967)	4.3	
Jamaica	2.3	3.3
Puerto Rico (1972)	–	0.6
Trinidad and Tobago (1971)	8.7	15.8
Guyana	4.8	5.6

Source: *Unesco Yearbook*, 1975 (tables 5.2; 5.3).

Indeed it could be argued that the proportion of public expenditure which is directed at improving educational provision is often higher than a country can realistically afford. In Barbados more than a fifth of public expenditure is allocated to education (21.2 per cent in 1973) while figures for other Caribbean countries are slightly less but comparable.[4] Moreover, as the West Indian economist Arthur Lewis has pointed out, high costs for teachers, buildings and equipment usually mean that poor countries receive less than developed countries for the same proportion of public expenditure (Lewis, 1961: 16). It is for these reasons that some have advocated 'deschooling' or the progressive shift of educational resources from formal schooling into various techniques of job related, adult education. Again Cuba seems to have dallied with this idea, but Castro's statements on the subject are unclear. On the one hand he has stressed the urgency of adopting radical new means of educational communication, such as educational television, and the need for 'uninterrupted, practically lifelong study' while, on the other, he declares: 'It is the intention of the Revolutionary Government to establish obligatory education through the pre-university level' (Castro, 1968: 261; 300).

It is precisely this latter view which has prompted the originator of the 'deschooling' thesis, Ivan Illich, to observe: 'As long as communist Cuba continues to promise obligatory high school completion by the end of this decade, it is, in this regard, institutionally no more promising than fascist Brazil, which has made a similar promise' (Illich, 1973: 153). When compared with the rest of the Caribbean, that appears to be an overly harsh judgement. It is true that advances in Cuban education, when assessed on a world scale, do not appear to have incorporated a new educational philosophy, but in the context of the Caribbean the changes are genuinely revolutionary. To call adapting an educational system to national needs 'revolutionary' is more an indication of the dead weight of the Caribbean's colonial past than it is to uncritically accept the Cuban alternative. It is certainly a moot point whether Cuba has escaped the progressive emphasis on certification, or what Ronald Dore (1976) has called the 'Diploma Disease', as the index of educational excellence.

For the rest of the Caribbean, the pursuit of educational advance has proceeded largely uncritically, and has consumed very significant proportions of national income (often in excess of 5 per cent). A judgement on whether it has significantly contributed to economic growth or development has yet to be made. The proposition advanced here, however, is that by legitimating a hierarchy of occupational prestige derived from the colonial connection, and by concentrating on subjects and skills adapted to foreign interests, it has cemented the urban areas more firmly into ties of economic dependence. And with that it has played its part in the shift of resources to the entrepôt city.

7 Politics and policies

It is a truism to observe that policies and approaches to urbanization, in any of their many dimensions, will depend upon whether they are conceived as a problem requiring official response and, if so, upon how they are defined and understood. This chapter will conclude with some consideration of the four main strands of understanding that may be discerned, although it will be stressed that specific governments may demonstrate two or more. Moreover, variations in the magnitude of urbanization, together with circumstances that make it more or less visible, ensure that wide divergences occur in the clarity of official perceptions, regardless of the vantage point that is preferred.

It is also clear that the selection of a perspective on urban issues is not a random process. Rather, it is intimately connected with the development strategy that is adopted, and this itself is constrained by the structure of political institutions and traditions bequeathed by a society's history. Politicians do, of course, help to make history, but within a framework that is not of their choosing. We start therefore with an overview of Caribbean political systems and then consider the directions in which politicians have sought to steer them. The thesis is that the strategies of development that men and history have conspired to produce, intimately affect the manner in which many economic and social problems are understood. The 'problem' of urbanization is then taken as an example of this process.

Political systems

Earlier, the tentative proposition was advanced that, despite immense and puzzling variability, it was possible to speak of a peculiar Caribbean identity on the level of political economy. Equally clearly, however, this consistency is absent when we seek to classify on the basis of political systems. Indeed, even the guidelines suggested here are oversimple, for barely two political structures appear similar. However, an important dimension of variation for economically dependent societies is their degree of *political* dependence, and on that basis the Caribbean may be divided into three. There are, first, sovereign states without formal, institutional or constitutional dependence on any other; there are those in a variety of semi-independent political statuses that have been categorized as in a state of 'federal dependence' (to suggest that their putative autonomy is more apparent than real), and, finally, there are those that still exhibit the same structure as in the past and these have been labelled 'colonial dependent' states.

Haiti, the second republic in the New World and an independent country for more than 170 years, is obviously in the first category, together with the eastern part of Hispaniola which formally became independent forty years later as the Dominican Republic. Cuba followed with political independence in May 1902 – a period that was preceded by hitherto unequalled US investment and, somewhat ironically, followed by massive immigration from the former motherland, Spain. Sixty years elapsed before the next addition to this category with the political independence of the four main Commonwealth Caribbean countries following the collapse of the short lived West Indies Federation that had struggled into being after a generation or more of political debate in 1958. Alexander Bustamante's victory over the Jamaican People's National Party, led by Norman Manley, at a referendum on the federation and at a subsequent general election in April 1962 permitted independence in August of that year. This was the same year that Trinidad and Tobago became independent under the People's National Movement of Dr Eric Williams, as those islands declined to accept the mantle of federal leadership, while another four years was to pass until first Guyana (formerly British Guiana) and then Barbados joined their ranks. Recent minor additions include the Bahamas (1973), Grenada (1974), Surinam (1975) and, most recent of all, Dominica in November 1978.

The most important member of the second category, those societies in a state of federal dependence with a metropolitan power, is Puerto Rico. It is fair comment to observe that the question of political status has been one of the most enduring concerns in recent Puerto Rican politics. Indeed, since the establishment of the formal relationship with the United States (*Estado Libre Asociado*) in 1952 one of the main divisions separating political parties has been whether to consolidate this so called 'Commonwealth' relationship into full statehood, with all the repercussions for federal taxation and loss of national identity that this would imply, to maintain the existing relationship and concentrate attention on pressing problems of economic development, or to negotiate full independence as a sovereign state. The most recent election in November 1976 removed the Popular Democratic Party, which is identified with the maintenance of the present relationship and replaced it by the pro-statehood New Progressive Party, but it is unlikely that any change of status will occur in the foreseeable future.

The six islands of the Netherlands Antilles (Aruba, Bonaire, Curaçao,

Sint Eustatius Saba and Sint Maarten) also occupy a semi-independent status, being technically in an equal partnership with the Kingdom of the Netherlands. The original Charter of 1954, which included what is now the Republic of Surinam, made provision for reciprocal co-operation and assistance with common regulations governing nationality and liability to conscription. There are two levels of government in the Netherland Antilles; the Central Government, consisting of a Crown-appointed Governor, a twenty-two seat legislative chamber (*Staten*) and a Council of Ministers, and four island governments, one each for Aruba, Bonaire and Curaçao and one for the three Dutch Windward Islands situated 500 miles to the north. The similarity between this system and the previous colonial administration, together with the massive degree of economic dependency upon the Netherlands, makes it clear that this is far from being a partnership of equals.

The policy of the French government towards Martinique, Guadeloupe and French Guiana is in some respects similar. Each is a *département* of the French state returning a Member to the National Assembly in Paris. Although citizens of Martinique and Guadeloupe had been technically French since 1848, the Law of Assimilation of 1946 clarified and codified the position, and lessened the power of local political institutions. Although the system was modified in 1960, mainly by making the prefect of each *département* more responsive to local demands, the French Caribbean islands remain politically dependent upon France. As in Puerto Rico, elections in the past twenty years have suggested that public opinion supports the continuation of this dependence, largely because it entails generous welfare services and unrestricted emigration possibilities to the metropolitan country.

The last group of territories are all dependent upon the UK in a form of relationship which can only be described as 'colonial'. They include the 'Associated States' of the Leeward and Windward islands, Belize, the Turks and Caicos Islands, the British Virgin Islands and the Cayman Islands. Apart from Belize, they are small in both land area and population. The Associated States were brought into being after the collapse of the West Indian federation and their constitutions prescribe full internal self-government. They originally consisted of St Kitts/Nevis/Anguilla, Antigua, Dominica, St Lucia, St Vincent and Grenada. However, Anguilla's attempted secession from the three-island federation dominated by St Kitts led to British occupation in 1969 and the granting of individual Associated Statehood in 1976. Grenada became independent in 1974, a development which the original constitutional arrangements permits with two thirds majority support in the local legislature. In the case of Belize, independence will occur when settlement of the long standing border feud with Guatemala is reached. At the moment, however, the palpable threat of annexation, and the British military forces assigned to prevent it, ensure the continued colonial status for this under-populated, multi-racial society in Central America.

For the Associated States the position with regard to eventual political independence is unclear. On the one hand, the British government, although concerned about internal stability and freedom from other external influences, would be happy to accede to independence requests – as the Grenada and Dominican cases made abundantly clear. However, traditions of dependence, coupled with a real lack of human and physical resources, have created widespread perceptions of non-viability from local politicians and electorates alike. In 1976, for example, Antigua, which looked like following Grenada to political independence, re-elected Vere Bird to power, which will probably ensure the continuation of the *status quo*. On the whole the Leeward and Windward islands have tended to place their confidence in regional integration through CARICOM rather than strive for complete separation, although these strategies are by no means exclusive. They may become so, however, if CARICOM ever achieves its intended goal of political rather than economic union, but strains within the Market, occasioned by the widening gap between the growth rates of the larger member territories as opposed to the smaller, make this itself an improbable event.

Despite their tiny size, the Associated States are not free from the same forces that produce rural decline and urban growth. For example, in St Lucia the main urban centre (Castries) contained 11.4 per cent of the population in 1921 and 40.5 per cent in 1970. Again in St Vincent, Kingstown contained 8.6 per cent of the population in 1921 and 20.7 per cent fifty years later. Only in tiny Montserrat, which has always felt it necessary to cling rather more closely to the metropolitan coat tails, had the urban proportion of the total population declined, and that is the result of massive out-migration.

Ideologies and strategies

Caribbean states demonstrate numerous positions on the orthodox continuum between right and left. Nearly all have experienced a version of agrarian capitalism, implicit in the rise of the corporate plantation, and have urban regions strongly influenced by the peculiar economic and social relationships that this entails. However, whereas some, like Puerto Rico in particular but also increasingly Haiti, have welcomed foreign capital and pursued what has been termed 'industrialization by invitation', others have rejected the involvement of multinational corporations and adopted a policy of public ownership of the means of production. It is indeed worth noting that the Caribbean contains two fine examples of alternative strategies. Puerto Rico, on the one hand, has been prepared to accept the role of an economic satellite in return for investment, direct access to the North American market and easy immigration controls. Cuba, however, represents the complete antithesis to this approach; ties of dependence may exist with the Soviet Union but these exclude foreign ownership of resources and only entail loans, technical assistance and trade agreements.

However, such a simple division by no means exhausts the political ideologies of the Caribbean and thus falls short of indicating the overall development strategies, which themselves include attempts to counteract the undesirable facets of uncontrolled urban migration. Another crosscutting distinction relates to the form of nationalism that is adopted, or perhaps more accurately the stage of development of nationalist ideas that has been attained. The present writer has argued elsewhere that in the Anglophone Caribbean, nationalism or insular identity had first to overcome the racial divide implicit in the colonial connections and subsequently attempt to counter the alienating influence of metropolitan values (Cross, 1973b). This tended to take the form of asserting political independence prior to developing strategies for economic self determination. Indeed the latter have been approached very gingerly, and one reason why this is so is that these societies have traditionally lacked a sense of their own identity.

As Sidney Mintz has effectively argued, one of the major divides between the Hispanic Caribbean and elsewhere in the region is that during the seventeenth and eighteenth centuries Spanish attention had shifted largely to the mainland of South America (Mintz, 1974). Left much more to their own devices, Spanish colonizers set about the task of creating new societies without the continual surveillance and dominating influence of the metropolis. As Mintz writes:

'it seems probable that the planters of the Hispanic colonies were outstanding to the degree to which they developed insular – that is, creole, as opposed to metropolitan or Spanish – identities. They also seem to have been the colonies in which genetic intermixture proceeded most rapidly, and in which the rise of intermediate groups of freemen was rapid and more or less continuous [Mintz, 1974: 310–11].'

Moreover, the late growth of the plantations, and thus the early establishment of peasant sectors, lessened the impact of the metropolitan power in the rural areas (Mintz, 1974: 314).

In the English, French and Dutch Caribbean, on the other hand, the greater domination and influence of the metropolis stimulated rather than healed the racial divide. The all pervading influence of the plantation system constrained rather than encouraged an independent peasantry and the lack of local decision making activated a demand for progress on political rather than economic grounds. The recent history of the non-Hispanic Caribbean is studded with examples of political leaders and writers who have been primarily concerned with problems of local identity. That is, attempting to challenge the continued hegemony of colonial values and metropolitan standards. A generation ago, these critiques tended to be couched in terms which revealed assumptions of the very kind they apparently sought to overcome. Such was the case with Aimé Césaire's apotheosis of blackness in the early statements on *negritude*, or with C. L. R. James' attacks upon continued colonial rule. The ambivalence is demonstrated by the Martiniquan writer's unwitting acceptance of a fundamentally right-wing idealism in which to cast the thesis, while for the Trinidadian Marxist it is possible to demand revolution, while at the same time writing panegyrics on the game of cricket!

More recently the situation has changed. The West Indian described by Frantz Fanon may have been Europeanized but his future lies not in idealizing his 'blackness' but in transforming the economic base of his society. The Francophone and the Anglophone West Indies, for example, have experienced a wave of radicalism in the past five years, starting with the uprising in Trinidad in February 1970. There are very few islands which do not now possess groups who normally seek a clearer commitment to an indigenous identity coupled with the adoption of economic policies whose prime intention is the creation of a greater degree of economic independence. The existence of such groups, drawing their support mainly from the urban dispossessed and often led by university educated intellectuals, is evidence however of the original thesis – that the non-Hispanic Caribbean in particular has suffered greatly from the colonial dilemma of a deracinated people socialized into a culture that denies them autonomy and a legitimate creole identity.

This may seem to carry us far from the problem of urbanization, but this is not so. These cross cutting dimensions may be used to suggest a highly schematic framework for appraising current strategies of development. We are then in a position to examine the significance of these policies for emerging problems of uncontrolled urban growth. The figure below tentatively suggests a Caribbean society for each quadrant. While such a scheme represents a gross oversimplification of history, it does suggest a series of assumptions and constraints that have influenced current policies. We need to examine each example in a little more detail, together with two others whose recent changes of direction or equivocation deny the possibility of ready categorization. The following section considers in brief overview some salient dimensions of development strategies in Puerto Rico, Haiti, Trinidad, Jamaica, Guyana and Cuba, who together contain 75 per cent of Caribbean people.

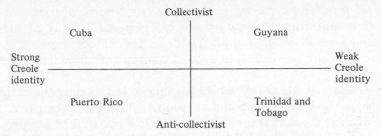

Puerto Rico

In 1940, the Puerto Rican economy was still dependent for employment, income and exports on the traditional industries of sugar and tobacco cultivation. The only other industry of any importance was needlework, which engaged more than 60 per cent of employees in manufacturing. In that year more than 80 per cent of export revenue was earned from these three industries. The period after the Second World War was one of astonishing transformation. Guided by the dynamic Economic Development Administration (usually termed FOMENTO), Puerto Rico launched an aggressive policy of national transformation aimed at turning the Caribbean island into a modern industrial economy. 'Operation Bootstrap' had managed by 1973 to boost per capita income in Puerto Rico at current prices to US $2,180 from only US $343 in 1950. In the latter year, manufacturing had contributed only 14.5 per cent to net national income, and much of that was processing associated with sugar or tobacco, while by 1964 it had risen to 23.2 per cent and is now beyond that figure (González, 1971: 93). Moreover, the dependence on agriculturally based manufacturing has changed so that more than three quarters of exports (nearly all of which are destined for the mainland US) are now composed of products from the new textile, clothing and light manufacturing industries. Fomento's contribution over this period has been equally spectacular. In 1950 only 0.5 per cent of national income came from sources supported by this newly formed agency, while in 1972, 18 per cent was directly attributable to its activites (Díaz, 1973: 7).

Supporters of this policy, which has dominated Puerto Rican development strategy for almost a generation and which is intimately associated with the name of the island's most famous governor, Luis Muñoz Marín, frequently point to the contrast between the poverty and ignorance of the past and the sophistication and comparative affluence of the present. Moreover, they may refer to research data (e.g. Andic, 1964) that suggest that structural changes consequent upon economic development, such as growing skill levels in the working population and an enhanced share of national income derived from wages and salaries, have begun to narrow the extreme inequalities of personal income. Massive federal transfer payments, ready access to North American capital markets, unrestricted migration and the personal security of welfare payments are also adduced as arguments for the continuation of the Commonwealth connection or even its transmogrification into full state federation.

Detractors of the policy, which has indeed led to an economy more permeated by mainland demands than most colonies at the height of their dependence, argue that the economic miracle has worked wonders for United States investors at the cost of Puerto Rican independence. They point to the continued high unemployment rates which, despite massive outmigration of Puerto Ricans to New York and elsewhere, have remained as high as before (12.9 per cent in 1950; 12.3 per cent in 1970). Moreover, the dominance of North American capital, seduced from the mainland by tax exemption regulations and cheaper labour, is said to buttress rather than counteract the poverty and dependence of the Puerto Rican economy. As Gordon Lewis (1963) reminds us, the island has a per capita income little more than half the poorest state in the union.

It is hard to deny that when a society develops a form of association whose *raison d'être* is the submissive acceptance of a subordinate role, it will be unlikely, within the confines of mutual agreement, to close the gap between itself and the dominant power. The logic of the arrangement is that, at best, prosperity will be contagious, but the implication of satellite status is also that economic crises at the core will be felt with greater severity at the periphery. This, indeed, has been the case with the recent recession of the US economy and it is noteworthy that these problems proved severe enough to provoke investigation into a new development strategy for Puerto Rico. A Committee presided over by Dr James Tobin of Yale University recommended a policy of savage austerity, largely, it seems, in order to ensure that Puerto Rico can still offer lower costs and easier profits than domestic investment. As they admit 'Puerto Rico cannot pursue an independent monetary policy' and on that account the gubernatorial Committee advocated a deflationary policy based on public expenditure cuts, wage restraint (including the suspension of mainland regulations on the minimum wage levels) and tax increases (*Caribbean Monthly Bulletin*, November–December 1975).

It may seem strange to characterize the Puerto Rican case as strong on Creole identity when the island seems ready to acquiesce to such subservience. However, consciousness of a unique identity is not the same as the radical assertion of independence. There is quite clearly little demand for the latter (the 'independence' vote scarcely tops five per cent and reached 4.5 per cent in November 1976) but the strength of a unified identity, albeit passively projected, is evident elsewhere. Political ideology cross-cuts racial and socio-economic divisions, and the commitment to a *Puertorriqueñan* culture and national language is a powerful unifying force, even though few are apparently clear as to the identifying features of the former. However, for all that, the impression is clear that Puerto Ricans have *chosen* to remain in their present relationship with the US and that despite the unmistakable presence of mainland materialism they *could* choose otherwise. The fractured identities of many other Caribbean societies frequently suggest that elements within them have taken over much more than the way of life of their ascendant affines.

Haiti

The Haitian case is harder to categorize, largely because in the period before the death of François Duvalier in 1971 it was not easy to discern a coherent development strategy of any kind. Since the succession to the ethnologist's hard won title of 'président à vie' by his young son Jean Claude, there is some evidence that greater acceptance of US capital investment is being encouraged.

While in this century Haiti has been subjected to almost continual foreign interference, for the period before occupation by the United States in 1915 Haiti was left relatively free to make its own way (although there was British and US involvement in the revolt of 1865, a periodic German naval presence and continued economic pressure from France and the United States). Sidney Mintz suggests that 'Haiti was probably less affected by external developments than any other country in the Hemisphere' (Mintz, 1974: 270). Throughout that period the issue of economic dependence was widely debated amongst members of the tiny élite, and many advocated changes in the laws designed to prevent foreigners owning land (Nicholls, 1974). In one form or another these regulations had been in force since the Republican Constitution of 1806 and, although by the end of the century foreign influence was mounting, the sustained opposition to colonial penetration is one reason why the large plantations were never resurrected.[1] This in turn limited the growth of capitalism, separated the urban and rural areas almost completely and produced the lowest shift of resources to the primate city in the whole of Latin America. Even now only 18 per cent of the population is urban and the comparative lack of development in Haiti has meant that the economic and political system has not produced the contradictions and conflicts that would lead to radical change. Indeed it is striking how excluded the peasantry in Haiti, who are almost four fifths of the population, have been from national decision making. The sordid and often violent transfers of power in the recent past are the outcome of battles between contending urban groups, often representing the perceived interests of those descended from the *Affranchis* (free coloureds) on the one hand, and the emergent black middle class on the other. The fact that debates take place in French, a language that the vast majority of the population do not speak, adds further poignancy to the Haitian malaise, which is more profound and important than the repressive activities of individual presidents or the infamous exertions of the *Tonton Macoute*.

Despite the sophistication of debates on economic nationalism which, as David Nicholls (1974) demonstrates, had little to learn from modern contributions, the absence of a clear alternative development plan and the urgent demand from US strategists that European roles be minimized in the Caribbean to enhance North American interests, soon resulted in major capital investment. The new constitution of 1918 was written to suit US interests and from that time on increasing areas of land and manufacturing concerns were owned by North American capital.

Feelings of national identity, like other manifestations of ethnicity, are seldom stimulated in periods of comparative isolation. The American occupation of Haiti thus gave rise to a reactive nationalism that produced the *noiriste* groups, such as the *griots* (of which François Duvalier was a founder member) and the reopening of bitter hostilities between the Mulatto and black élites. Indeed the characteristic feature of Duvalierism (or 'papadocracy'!) is not ideological but pragmatic. The 'success' of Duvalier *père*, (and incidentally the reason that he died in his bed) was in destroying the power of the Church and the Army, and nullifying the influence of the intelligentsia (see Nicholls, 1971; 1970). The strengthening of US interests in the past few years is equally a strategy of survival; a desperate attempt to overcome destabilizing pressures of poverty and squalor. But, unlike Puerto Rico, it does not represent a popular decision. The Haitian people are as muted on this as they have always been on matters of significance.

However, a new period of foreign investment has begun, and Haiti now has tax concessions to add to the attractions of a ready supply of cheap labour. In fact, as membership of mainland trade unions pushes up wages and labour costs in Puerto Rico, so called 'screwdriver' industries (final assembly of light manufactures) tend to move elsewhere, and Haiti may well become a favoured location. Already between 1967 and 1971, export of small manufactures rose from 9 per cent of total exports to 30 per cent (Nicholls, 1974: 32).

Trinidad and Tobago

It is no surprise to discover the Prime Minister of Trinidad and Tobago declaring in 1968, seven years after political independence, that the 'future way forward for the peoples of the Caribbean must be one which would impel them to start making their own history, to be the subjects rather than the objects of history, to stop being the playthings of other people' (Williams, 1970: 504). While it would be false to suggest that the lack of a strong cultural identity was unique to the Commonwealth Caribbean, it is an element of dependence more profound and compelling here than elsewhere. The peculiar demand of British colonialism for psychological as well as economic and political subjection was perhaps necessary to stimulate the arrogance on which the innovation of modern imperialism depended. Its consequence was an imitative system of such power that many subjected to it, even now, do not perceive the lie on which it is based. For these reasons, it is possible to characterize most parts of the Commonwealth Caribbean as having a weak Creole identity, although this is not to say that their development strategies in the recent past have always coincided.

Since the beginning of decolonization after the Second World War, Trinidad has tended towards an 'open economy' solution to development. In 1951 a third of direct investment came from foreign sources, largely the UK or the US, while international public borrowing raised this figure to 45 per cent (Carrington, 1971a: 137–8). In 1950, the island passed an Aid to Pioneer Industries Ordinance, based on the advocacy of the distinguished West Indian economist Sir Arthur Lewis, and the policy of encouraging foreign capital in manufacturing investment became consolidated in the period after 1956, when the People's National Movement under the present Prime Minister, Eric Williams, achieved the first of its five consecutive election victories. The Trinidad experience parallels that in Puerto Rico with rapid economic growth running hand in hand with high and sustained levels of unemployment. Capital intensive rather than labour intensive investment assured that in 1967 it would have required more than three times the five year development budget to provide jobs in pioneer manufacturing industries for the unemployed (Carrington, 1971b: 145). As others have found, this development strategy not only increases dependent ties with wealthier associates, it also demands massive infrastructure investment at a time when the expectations of high wages, profits and consumption levels reduce the tax base. It leads, therefore, to continual crises of public expenditure.

Trinidad has been helped in finding a way out of this dilemma by two events: the first was a political crisis that forced an urgent reappraisal of policy on a wide range of fronts and, the second was the oil crisis of 1974 that had overnight repercussions on the economy of this small island, and promoted successful drives for the exploration of off-shore sites. Even before the events of 1970, when the combined energies of radical dissidents, the urban unemployed and factions of the army, the sugar workers and the oilworkers brought the PNM nearer to collapse than any election has done before or since, Eric Williams had declared that

Trinidad's path was a third way between the laissez-faire submission of Puerto Rico and the collectivism of Cuba. The strategy was said to involve 'continued reliance on outside investment and trade with the outside world; but it also involves steady and increasing assumption of control over the commanding heights of the economy by the Government and nationals, a determined attempt to promote racial harmony and social equality, and the conscious development of a national and cultural identity' (Williams, 1970: 512). Undoubtedly the crisis of February 1970, which produced a prolonged state of emergency, draconian public order acts and a reorganized police force, did more than stimulate repression. Public investment has been pursued on a competitive basis in some areas, such as banking, while elsewhere a majority holding has been taken in companies with a monopoly or semi-monopoly position. The government now controls the major sugar and oil companies, and has a large stake in the mass media and in shipping, transport and telecommunications. The political adroitness that enabled these measures to have been painlessly achieved, coupled with hopelessly divided opposition forces and an economy booming in the wake of the oil crisis, seem to be the major reasons why the present government survived the various crises of the past few years to obtain twenty-four seats in the thirty-six seat legislature at the 1976 elections. Although turn out was low (55 per cent), the election marks the return of a viable opposition force in the Indian led, but socialist inspired, United Labour Front. The most probable scenario over the next few years is that Trinidad will retain a relatively open economy, collaborating with international capital – particularly in the field of oil exploration and extraction – but will seek to consolidate the major public stake in the economy.

Jamaica

The Jamaican case is in many respects similar to that of Trinidad. Although, unlike the latter, Jamaica has yet to promote local identity by declaring itself a republic, the policy of the People's National Party under the leadership of its founder's son, Michael Manley, has been more concerned with equality and the redistribution of wealth.

Post-war Jamaica pursued an open, pro-US capital policy through the late 1960s. The massive growth of the bauxite industry and tourism, together with derived demand for new construction, boosted the Jamaican economy at an unprecedented 7.2 per cent per annum from 1950–65. Again, however, the expansion did not produce a lessening unemployment problem, nor did it make any headway towards solving Jamaica's chronic inequalities of income. Moreover, as elsewhere, the constraints demanded by an aggressive, externally generated industrialization programme, such as low taxation and easy opportunities for the repatriation of profits, were felt by many to more than offset the advantages of new industries.

Prior to his overwhelming re-election victory in 1976, Michael Manley committed his government to a path of democratic socialism involving public ownership of utilities, worker participation in industry and a welcome to foreign capital 'provided the investment is consistent with national purposes'. However, buffeted by worsening terms of trade, population growth and the effects of the US recession, Jamaica has moved further than most West Indian governments in controlling the activities of foreign companies and nationals operating inside the country. For example, a policy of national control has been pursued in the all-important bauxite industry. The policy requires the reversion of lands owned by the bauxite firms to the Crown, a government majority stake in each mining company, an option to participate in processing, and an enhanced levy on ore or alumina exported. In October 1976, the Jamaican Government and the Aluminum Company of America signed the first agreement based on these principles which involved the return of 7,000 acres of land and the establishment of JAMALCO – a joint company mining bauxite and processing alumina at the giant Halse Hall plant in Clarendon. The new rates of production levy are expected to produce J$175m in 1977.

The control of the sugar companies is not as advanced, largely because the returns are likely to be so much smaller. However, Jamaica is unusual in providing a really concerted attack on the land problem. Although few inroads have yet been made on the rural dominance of the banana and sugar plantations, considerable amounts of land have been reallocated under Project Land Lease. Forty-five thousand acres of land previously held by bauxite or sugar companies have been taken over and allocated to 20,000 farmers grouped together as rural co-operatives on a scheme whose original genesis lay with a report prepared by Thomas Balogh for the Prime Minister's father, Norman Manley (Balogh, 1966: 293–318).

Of all the countries in the Anglophone Caribbean, Jamaica has displayed the most constructive attitude towards the Cubans. On his return from a visit in 1975, Michael Manley declared 'No people in the world have such a feeling of happiness and contentment. We found a unity of spirit unequalled anywhere among the Cuban people who work hard because they believe in what they are doing' (*Caribbean Monthly Bulletin*, July 1975). The Prime Minister's visit is to be returned by Fidel Castro and economic, trade and technical agreements have been reached which include the gifts from Cuba of a 'new style' boarding school at Twickenham Park, Spanish Town for 500 boarders.

Guyana

The 'Co-operative Republic' of Guyana, under the government of the People's National Congress led by Forbes Burnham, has sought to model itself on the Tanzanian precedent. The theory is to promote a policy of co-operative socialism under the slogan of working to make 'the little man a real man'. Since the founding of the republic in February 1970, four years after independence from Britain and a little over five years after the PNC, led by Burnham, had assumed power, a number of co-operative projects have been initiated and concerted attempts have been made to mobilize the Guyanese people for national development. An example of the latter is the National Self Help Road Project which aims to drive a new highway from the coastal regions through the mineral rich jungle and savannah of the interior to connect with roads in Northern Brazil. One hundred and twenty miles of this road, from Mahdia to Annai, are meant to be built by volunteer labour from Georgetown and the coastal belt.

However, while the rhetoric on development strategy has emphasized the 'small man', the reality has been rather different. Over the past twelve years Guyana has undergone a metamorphosis from a Crown colony with internal government, where most of the major companies were foreign owned, to a society where nearly all the important parts of the economy are state owned. In 1964, 18 per cent of national investment was on behalf of state concerns; in 1976 it was 87.8 per cent. In 1971 the Demerara Bauxite Company was nationalized to become Guyana Bauxite (GUYBAU), followed in 1972 by the founding of Guyana Timbers, in 1975 by the nationalizing of Jessels Securities (Sugar) and Reynolds Bauxite (to become BERMINE or Berbice Mining). The last bastion of private enterprise, the Bookers empire, which ran most of the sugar industry, was nationalized in May 1976 along with Berger paints and other concerns. Moreover, the state now runs two daily and three Sunday newspapers and a radio station and has recently passed legislation enabling it to ban the importation of publications critical of government policies. The Prime Minister, Forbes Burnham, also announced in December 1976 that: 'We are now in discussion with Cable and Wireless, so that the State, the representative of the people, will totally own and control our telecommunications in and out of Guyana.' State control and the repression of critical comment is well illustrated in the case of a radical newspaper called *Dayclean*, issued by the Working People's Alliance, which has been continually harried and opposed. An investigation initiated in 1974 by the Caribbean Publishing and Broadcasting Association came to the conclusion that the government owned media were subject to covert and overt control and that those elements that were not directly owned were also effectively limited in the criticism they could voice.

The Guyanese development strategy has been to found a state capitalist system where the state effectively controls all aspects of the economy and limits and restricts dissent and opposition. This is particularly evident from the policy employed over nationalization. Rather than found independent units with direct freedom of manoeuvre, all 23 public corporations are organized under Guyana State Corporation (GUYSTAC), worth over £100m, the president of which is the Prime Minister. The government recently announced the formation of a 'People's Militia', ostensibly to aid the security forces in resisting border incursions from Venezuela, but many are convinced that it will be a PNC dominated force designed to ensure conformity with government policy.

The concern expressed about developments in Guyana arises not from the attempts at redirecting public policy towards socialist goals but from the particularly bureaucratic and centralized form that this has taken. These moves have a peculiar poignancy in the Guyanese case because of the recent experience of ethnic conflict that the country has had to endure. The facts are that the present government derives its support from the minority African population. It came to power in 1964 as a result of a changed electoral system initiated by the British government, in collaboration with the United States, and designed to keep the Indian Marxist leader Cheddi Jagan from assuming power (see Henfrey, 1972). Jagan is the leader of the People's Progressive Party which had used its Indian majority support to win all previous elections under adult suffrage. In 1960 the Indians were 47.8 per cent of the population; by 1970 they had grown to 51.8 per cent. Africans meanwhile had declined from 32.8 per cent to 31.2 per cent over the period and it is widely accepted that the elections of 1968 and 1973 were rigged so as to enlarge the government vote. Certainly at the last election in 1973 the PNC secured thirty-seven seats in the fifty-three member legislature with a supported strength of 243,803 votes to the PPP's 92,734. Many commentators find these figures hard to accept and stories of rigging are widespread.

The pro-Soviet style of state ownership and control has brought the present government much nearer to the position adopted for many years by the PPP, or at least by its leaders. The result is that opposition and criticism is now largely extra-parliamentary and easily repressed or controlled.

Cuba

The Cuban model of development is also strongly influenced by the Soviet example although it differs in many important respects. The population is not divided as in Guyana, the system is less centralized and apparently far more responsive to local needs and aspirations. Indeed in the recent past an elaborate system of delegated administration has been introduced (*Organos del Poder Popular*). Members of a *circunscripción* (the smallest political division in Cuba) nominate candidates for the neighbourhood assembly (*Asambleas de Vecinos*). In October 1976, these then chose 10,725 delegates to a Municipal Assembly (*Asambleas Municipales*), there having to be more than two delegates and as many as eight from the 2,837 *circunscripcións* in Cuba. The Municipal Assemblies in turn send delegates to one of fourteen Provincial Assemblies (*Asambleas Provinciales*) which then supply the members of the National Assembly (*Asamblea Nacional*). At each level an executive committee is formed, the members of which are *ex officio* members of the next level, while the chairman and vice-chairman are paid, full-time incumbents. Eventually this system will ensure localized devolved administration and will feed back policy suggestions to the higher echelons of government. Aside from the state apparatus, this effectively means the Communist Party, whose main task is to ensure that the whole political process takes place within the context of a revolutionary frame of reference. The Party (membership 202,000) is an élite organization exercising a powerful influence on the country. Membership is only open to those revealing a profound commitment to revolutionary praxis and receiving a high degree of popular support, which is itself normally gauged by nomination from a union or a Committee for the Defence of the Revolution (a neighbourhood body designed to bolster morale and promote revolutionary zeal as well as undertake community services).

Cuba's policy on economic development does not appear to be unduly influenced by the USSR, although it is only with the Eastern European block that she runs a trade deficit.

Cuba is also supported by massive Soviet aid but there is little to suggest a blind emulation of Soviet development.[2] While economic growth is important, the Cubans are much more enthusiastic about health care and educational advance than they are about simply raising per capita income or developing a consumption led economy.[3] This idealism is, of course, one reason why Cuba shines so brightly as a beacon on the international horizon and why proponents of a similar philosophy tend to downplay the significance of Soviet aid.

The original Cuban plan for massive industrialization had been rethought by 1964/65 as problems of raw material supply and potential markets become clear. About that time a decision was taken to renew sugar development and strive for a harvest of ten million tons. This has never been attained although the harvest has exceeded a record 8,000,000 tons. A severe drought in Eastern Cuba has cut back sugar production recently and the latest estimate for 1976–77 is about 6,000,000 tons. Sugar cane still counts for approximately three quarters of Cuba's exports and about half the annual crop is sold under bilateral agreements with Eastern European countries. It is hoped gradually to mechanize sugar production and utilize the relocated labour force in an expanded industrial sector.

The consolidation of the Revolution will require continued economic growth and, like all primary producers, Cuba is very dependent on commodity prices. For example, high world prices for sugar in 1973 enabled her to obtain a positive trade balance for the first time since 1960. Since that time prices have fallen and the country has entered another age of austerity. Changes have occurred in the wage system which for the first time provides economic incentives to increase productivity and lower absenteeism. Overtime payments are now paid, for example, as well as bonuses for exceeding agreed productivity targets. The latter provide one per cent increase in wages for each percentage point in excess of a target – but also reduce wages by the same amount for an equivalent shortfall. The system of public commendation still survives and workers may be designated 'Advanced Workers' or receive the Moncada Flag (*Bandera de Moncada*, named after the barracks in Santiago where Castro made an unsuccessful attack in 1953). Additional community and revolutionary activity may also be rewarded with the title of National Hero of Labour (*Héroe Nacional de Trabajo*) which entitles the recipient to priority in buying scarce consumer goods and an enhanced pension.

There is little evidence to suggest that food and clothing rationing which started in 1962, will end in the foreseeable future. Indeed, the current economic difficulties have resulted in exhortations by the government for Cubans to consume less than their allowance. As in all systems of rationing a black market exists but it is also possible to buy some rationed goods at much higher prices on the free market.[4] Rum, the drink of the Caribbean, is not available on ration and on the free market costs 22 pesos (US$29.00) a bottle.

There is every sign that the Cuban development path will lie in the direction already well charted and surveyed. Successes have been genuinely impressive and few commentators doubt that if a Western style election was held in Cuba it would lead to an overwhelming vote of confidence in Castro and the Party. Memories of Batista and the sordid side effects of the US presence, together with the astonishing progress in health, education, employment and rural development, ensure that there will be no immediate decline in revolutionary zeal. The greater confidence of the government itself is likely to enhance Cuba's influence on the international stage, as re-established contacts with the rest of the Caribbean and Castro's African adventures suggest. What is particularly persuasive about the Cuban solution in an area of fractured identities is that despite all the Soviet aid it remains distinctly Creole.

The urbanization issue

Although it is possible to debate the exact location of these six Caribbean countries on our simple classification, there is little doubt that some important differences exist, and it would be surprising indeed if these did not extend to the appreciation of urbanization and urban growth as problems requiring a policy response. Countries vary in the degree to which they recognize urbanization as a problem at all and also in how they understand it. Future policies may be dependent upon the particular appraisal that wins out over competing alternatives. Categorization of countries is not easy, although lines of continuity do exist between the development strategies previously discussed and the probable stance on urbanization.

Among countries with an unambiguous national identity, but committed to an anti-collectivist political stance, urbanization is quite likely to be recognized as a national issue requiring governmental response, but one which is a necessary concomitant of the modernization process. Puerto Rico provides an outstanding example of this position. There is no doubt that the problem is perceived, but there is little attempt to control or limit the process, for to do so would effect the ready supply of cheap labour for the new factories or industries clustered around the urban core. Thus the solution is usually reported as one of planning, on the assumption that what is unfortunate about urbanization is not the process itself but the strain on existing resources that it produces if badly managed. For more than twenty years the Puerto Rican government has contained an active planning department whose main line of approach has been to guide the rural migrants into the new *urbanizaciones* that now crowd around the periphery of San Juan and other cities. The Puerto Rican Urban Renewal and Housing Corporation is responsible for a number of housing programmes and Helen Safa estimates that at least 78,000 people had benefited by 1965. She points out that where public housing has replaced shanty town living, it has led to greater dependence by the poor on the state, lowered mobility and an increased probability of matrifocal families (Safa, 1974: 86).

In these circumstances the planners may abound but they are constrained by the demands of business and foreign investors who fear the decline of cheap labour supplies or an unemployment rate low enough to permit opposition to poor wages. Gordon Lewis concluded that the planner, although ubiquitous, was 'denied any real power to address himself to what, in the sprawling growth of greater San Juan, is the massive driving power of the profit motive as it stimulates the building contractor, the real estate speculator, the finance company' (Lewis, 1963: 203).

The Haitian response is difficult to assess for although some attempts have been made at urban planning, the penurious state of the Haitian economy and the great divide between Port au Prince and the mass of the rural population prevent anything resembling co-ordinated development from occurring (CHISS, 1971). As Haiti is drawn more closely into the orbit of the US economy once again, we can expect to see increased urban migration and, if economic expansion permits, a more concerted attempt at planned urban growth through low cost housing schemes. In Trinidad, by contrast, the picture is clearer and different from the Puerto Rican experience. Although an urban planning system exists, the drift of the towns is not perceived as a necessary concomitant of modernization. Rather, another definition of the problem holds greater sway. In this definition, which is common throughout the Commonwealth Caribbean, urbanization is perceived as being the result of a colonial education system that emphasizes skills and talents relevant for urban living to the detriment of agriculture or rural crafts. Thus the solution is thought to lie with schooling and job training which, by combating this emphasis and promoting the virtues of rural living, will counteract the draw of the city and dull the pain associated with the past experience of slavery or indentureship. Thus, where the problem is recognized at all, it will not be in terms of the constraints upon employment in rural areas, or limits to the amount of land (although Trinidad has certainly tried to settle a considerable number of farmers on Crown lands) but rather in terms of the attitudes that rural folk have to the land. This is, perhaps, one of the most pervasive myths of the Anglophone Caribbean but is belied by the evidence from the rice farmers of Guyana, the cane farmers of Trinidad, or even the Jamaican peasantry.

In the past Jamaica adhered very closely to this perspective, tending not to identify urbanization as a problem at all, but where doing so adopting an individualized explanation. Thus Colin Clarke remarked recently: 'In Jamaica there is no conception that the urban hierarchy might be treated as a system, and used as a tool for correcting some of the more obvious disparities between Kingston and the rest of the island' (Clarke, 1974: 230). However, recent moves by the Jamaican Government have brought a reappraisal of the issue and it is possible now to identify a third perspective on urbanization. This is to conceive of the problem as essentially an imbalance of resources between the rural and urban locations. It follows from this standpoint that policies should be devised which channel resources to rural locations. This change of heart is evident in Project Land Lease, which aims to overhaul the rural sector and lessen the extraordinary strains imposed on the Jamaican peasantry by the retention of corporate plantations. Land is leased to farmers' co-operatives on very favourable terms. Also in 1972 the Jamaican government instigated operation GROW (Growing and Reaping our Wealth) and later phases of Land Lease are designed to ensure that new small farms yield a minimum of J \$2,00 per annum.

There is little evidence of any appreciation of urbanization in the Guyanese case, although the government now has all the necessary power to redirect resources into the rural areas.[5] It remains a moot point, however, whether it will choose to do so for fear of alienating the main body of its support – the urban located Africans. There is some indication that encouragement is being given for the highly successful rice industry but, as earlier discussion indicated, the returns from this activity are hardly conducive to a renaissance of rural fortunes.

It is to Cuba that we have to look for the most sophisticated understanding of the urbanization issue. Of course, long before the revolution Cuba had the highest proportion in towns. At the turn of the last century just under half of the population could have been described as 'urban'. This was because Cuba had the most advanced capitalist system; a fact which Marxist theory would suggest was directly responsible for the Revolution itself. Be that as it may, the post revolutionary Cuban government has been more aware than any other (with the possible exception of the People's Republic of China) that the only way to control the progressive shift of resources to the urban centre is to combine all three strands of understanding in a policy which has as its prime purpose the resurrection of rural employment to a position of prime national importance. Thus the Cuban government is committed to the planned growth of the rural economy, to a concerted education programme designed to enhance the dignity and status of praedial work and to specific measures intended to redress the imbalance between Havana, Santiago, Camagüey, Santa Clara, Guantánamo, Cienfuegos, Manzanillo, Holguín, Matanzas and the rest of the country. Rather than accept a situation where peasants migrate to the city, the Cubans have sought to lessen the motive for moving by stimulating rural employment and bringing the benefits of the city to the country. This has meant the founding of literally hundreds of small towns so that each of the 53 districts into which the country is divided has an urban centre (Acosta and Hardoy, 1973). The latest phase of this development involves more than a hundred towns consisting of two and three storey apartments, whereas the earlier developments made greater use of multi-storey blocks. It is notable that this aspect of Cuban policy has been emulated elsewhere and 'intermediate growth centres' have now become an important part of the solutions to urbanization propounded by United Nations agencies.

8 Conclusion

In the preceding chapters, urbanization as a social process has been set within the context of broader social changes and social problems. It needs to be reiterated that many aspects of the process are both inevitable and desirable. We can scarcely imagine progress in administration, achievement in the arts or developments in health care or scientific knowledge outside the city. And yet for dependent societies, whose very future must rely on creative solutions to problems long since controlled or ameliorated in the industrialized West, the dangers are great. A blind acceptance of urban growth as a natural concomitant of development appears likely to strengthen, not weaken, the ties of dependence. What has recently been termed 'urban bias' in the allocation of resources has also been called 'a main cause of the persistence of poverty' (Lipton, 1977: 71). The reasons are clear: if resources progressively shift from the land to the city they are not doing so to fuel a new wave of industrial revolutions. It is too late for that. They are concentrating in the hands of a minority who may then consume and behave as the wealthy in rich countries are perceived to do. Others may gather to observe, though seldom to participate. They may in time protest at their exclusion. If so, attempts may be made to improve housing or replan communities on the urban periphery – that is, more resources may be expended on the city. Meanwhile the only long-term hope for growth and equality, the land, is starved of human and material capital.

The recent Cuban experience suggests that this abject scenario is not inevitable, although even here the concerted attempt at counter-urbanization is dependent less on a propitious economic order and more on the exercise of an inordinately active and determined political motivation. For most other Caribbean economies the future is less clear. Rural economies barely appear to be holding their own; indeed there are strong reasons why out-migration from the countryside should rise as mechanization and a scarcity of fertile land in viable units increases under-employment and lowers net returns. Although notable advances have been made – such as Jamaica's Land Lease project – the colonial system of plantation ownership is still largely intact in many parts of the region although, increasingly, governmental intervention is altering the historical pattern of foreign ownership.

The diversification of Caribbean economies from dependence upon their traditional monocultures has proceeded at a rapid rate in the larger territories. Most successful, in some senses, have been the extractive industries such as oil and bauxite. The success story which these operations represent must be qualified by two observations. First, so far as the former British West Indies is concerned, they were originally established in the earlier part of this century when the area was perceived as comprising 'undeveloped estates', to use Joseph Chamberlain's expressive phrase. Accordingly they have had to come to terms with mounting waves of economic nationalism challenging the colonial assumption that raw materials must be used to further metropolitan interests. Second, unquestioning adoption of Western extraction techniques, devised in societies where labour is costly and scarce, has resulted in a minimal absorption of surplus labour and the creation of a 'labour aristocracy' whose easy rise to relative affluence serves as a persuasive precedent for other workers and further justification for capital intensive investment. Similar problems are not unknown in the emergent manufacturing sector which has the additional threat of promoting massive internal migration. In Puerto Rico, in particular, which has consolidated its development strategy around low cost manufacturing, the pressure on urban housing has grown as a direct result of this policy.

Problems of urban growth stem less from the process itself and more from the gulf between promise and fulfilment. Nowhere is this clearer than in the counterpoint between income and employment. With the progressive transfer of resources to the urban areas, real income levels tend to rise relative to rural returns. However, employment prospects are often worse, perhaps not for the migrants themselves, who often reveal the energy and motivation of the ambitious, but certainly for the youthful lumpenproletariat whose increasing presence is a sign of incipient crisis. In some areas the urban pressure is relieved by recourse to the traditional solution of emigration, largely to the developed countries whose interests have been paramount in determining the shape and form of Caribbean economies. Plagued by recessions, unexpected additions to the labour force created by such social changes as the altered expectations governing the labour force participation of married women, and the political repercussions of racism, these countries have made external migration progressively harder. The exception to this is where political affiliation of the dependent economy prevents the total suspension of migrant flows, although even here there are signs that the open access period of the immediate post-War years will not recur.

The pressures on urban growth through migration are compounded by higher rates of natural increase in most rural parts of the area. In nearly every case, policies of promoting artificial population control have been adopted with some apparent success. Once again, however, the Cuban case is based upon alternative assumptions. The accent here is less on devising technical programmes for avoiding unwanted pregnancies and more on the ways in which heightened levels of economic and political involvement may increase the motivation to curtail family size and thus improve the ratio between needs and resources. It remains to be seen which strategy proves to be more successful although, somewhat ironically, the Cuban approach can claim the experience of the industrial world as an effective precedent.

Social scientists have puzzled for many years over the reasons for the peculiar form that Afro-Caribbean working class families commonly reveal. Fascinating but ultimately unpersuasive accounts have been given of cultural retentions that have survived the predations of slavery, while others have assumed that modernization and the cultural dimension of urbanization would gradually alter the traditional pattern as affluence and the spread of middle class norms of more or less stable monogamy overcame the disruptive effects of economic marginality and male irresponsibility. If urbanization was itself predicated upon greater equality in the distribution of resources then indeed the latter argument at least might hold sway, but there is little evidence of this occurrence. Rather, the retention of informal sexual unions appears to be an adaptive response by men to the norm of sexual prowess (possibly in the absence of alternative avenues of status enhancement) while for women it serves to sustain a measure of independence in a world of male domination. In contrast to the 'modernization' perspective, therefore, urbanization through migration – which has a greater significance for women – might be expected to support rather than undermine the common pattern of serial mating and an evolution of union types from 'visiting' to 'common law' or legal marriage for most individuals.

The Cuban example is again outstanding when it comes to examining housing policy. It is not that the revolution has been particularly successful in providing adequate housing but that the attempts at urban and rural reform have been specifically intended to challenge the assumption that life in an urban household is preferable to remaining in a village. The Chinese, as well as the Cubans, have discovered that this philosophy is more easily propounded than achieved, and it is unlikely that it will ever be totally fulfilled, but a combination of education, exhortation and regulation is more likely to have this effect than official disinterest.

Voluntary associations are widespread in the Caribbean and membership of most positively correlated with urban residence. Indeed some, such as trade unions, may be said to have had an urbanizing influence by tending to promote consumption led economies. They have been especially successful in capital intensive industries whose affluent workers serve as role models for potential migrants. Religious associations may also serve as vehicles for the penetration of foreign values and they would have tended to take on a different flavour in urban contexts. Rather than simply reflecting the legacy of the colonial connection, unestablished sects or cults have often arisen to project the frustrations of the urban dispossessed. The Jamaican Rastafarians are an intriguing but not isolated case in point. Other associations abound, particularly at the middle class level, and while they undoubtedly function to propagate urban values they do not serve as primary agencies of socialization into the city culture as they often do in countries where town and country may be divided by enormous distances and differences of language and ethnicity.

There is no evidence for the simple diffusionist thesis in Caribbean societies. This may be because it confuses cause with effect, but whether that is so or not, any cultural diffusion that has occurred originally by-passed the urban areas by appearing as a concomitant of plantation dependence. True as the cities have grown up to accommodate emerging needs for trade, transport and services they have propagated urban values. The irony is that rural folk, usually able to comprehend metropolitan languages and well versed in Western life styles have accepted such values not as innovations but as extensions of their own culture. The Scottish crofter or the Irish peasant has more roots to lose than the average West Indian whose loss predates either his urban or rural existence. Of course, urban migration involves a different life style but small city size, as well as cultural affinity, adds to the impression that the two areas are not worlds apart. Even in societies where major ethnic divides are overlaid on urban–rural separation there is no real sense in which the sophistication of the former may be contrasted with the traditionalism of the latter. While there is no gainsaying the difference between Creole and East Indian culture in Trinidad and Guyana, for example, what divides them is not Western sophistication. Creole life style may appear on the surface to be more 'Westernized' but this is largely confined to the sphere of religion and does not betray a critical divergence. The rural African or urban Indian are similarly different and both are likely to be enmeshed in family relationships that straddle the rural–urban divide.

This is not to say that the Caribbean is anything less than a racial mosaic, nor that the peculiar origins of these compositions have not affected the areal distribution of the constituent parts. Indeed some racial groups appear to be almost totally urban in residence, often when they have been more than usually successful in penetrating the new trading and service sectors. The precise experience of inter-racial relations is not the result of chance juxtaposition but it is intimately tied to the social and economic division of labour and allied rewards that have accrued from membership of high status racial groups. The 'white bias' of all Caribbean societies, even when having its greatest impact through 'coloured' or

Mulatto groups, has had a profoundly urbanizing effect. The easy intrusion of Western advertising and material ideals has itself been made possible by the hitherto unchallenged acceptance of European or North American cultural superiority, which in its turn has propagated aspirations that can only be comprehended, let alone fulfilled, in an urban milieu.

Education in both its formal and informal aspects has buttressed this system of values. The importation of films, the showing of American television programmes and the foreign ownership of newspapers have achieved an even greater impact than is common in underdeveloped societies because of high levels of literacy in major world languages and the lack of indigenous cultural traditions. There is evidence that this may now be changing but formal education is still supportive of previous patterns. Even where concerted attempts have been made to develop syllabuses and styles of teaching as adapted to their surroundings as they are to those from whence they originated, they still tend to derogate rural employment and non-urban life styles. Again the form and content of Cuban education is counterposed to most of the others. All workers must engage in some activity that may be expected to promote greater sensitivity to agricultural employment while education in agriculture itself has grown to occupy nearly three times the proportion of the higher education age group since the revolution.

The need to promote alternative values through formal education and the desire to encourage a more creative orientation to rural crafts is widespread throughout the Caribbean. This is often because of the perceived need to develop local food production rather than because of a wish to rethink the nature of the rural–urban connection. Indeed in a society like Trinidad and Tobago there is little evidence that the rapid urbanization (and suburbanization) of Port of Spain is perceived as a cause for concern. Even where similar developments have aroused official reaction, as in Puerto Rico, the premise is that no policy can be implemented which might lessen the supply of cheap labour to the factories in major conurbations. Jamaica, on the other hand, has gone further than simply regarding the progressive shift of resources to the city as a necessary concomitant of growth, and has begun to instigate policies designed to correct the palpable imbalances of resource distribution. Only in Cuba, however, is there evidence in official policy of anything that could be described as a 'theory' of urban growth or progressive urbanization. Here a systematic, centrally directed and coherent attempt has been made to reverse the normal flow of human and physical resources. Leaving aside the unquestioned relevance of political leadership, the Cubans have been aided in this task by a strong sense of local identity and a collectivist ideology that lends commitment and purpose to strategies that are often painful in impact and long term in intention. Moreover, it is possible that the real cultural differences between pre-revolutionary Havana and the rural areas spotlighted the negative implications of the former and the positive values of the latter. Elsewhere, the apparent lack of awareness of the dangers of unplanned urban growth may be in part attributable to the lack of a clear divide and with it the absence of cultural clashes and problems of acculturation.

It would be unduly glib and simplistic to suggest that other Caribbean countries may overcome the negative effects of urbanization and uncontrolled urban growth simply by emulating the Cuban approach. And yet greater understanding of the forces that created the primate city in its local, consumption led form is a necessary prerequisite for any coherent and integrated strategy. Many Caribbean people are struggling to achieve hitherto unknown levels of international autonomy for their countries. Internally too they have inherited a legacy of imbalances and inequalities that could progressively undermine these new and hard won freedoms.

Notes

Epigraph

The literal translation of this verse of a poem by Nicolás Guillén, the famous Cuban poet, lacks the power and beauty of the original. So too does the following interpretation although it may carry more meaning than the dead prose of a perfect translation (see Sardinha, 1976: 41):

> The man from the land
> is lost,
> dead before he is born.
> And the man from the city,
> oh Cuba, is hungry and poor
> on nothing but charity's hand,
> but he can don a sombrero
> and dance to a popular band

Chapter 1: Introduction

1 Eric Williams records that in 1862 in Cuba it was estimated that the sugar production from 490 acres and 74 free workers could only be matched by 635 acres and 142 slaves (Williams, 1970: 290).
2 In fact the slave trade was abandoned by Britain in 1807, by France in 1817, by Holland in 1818 and by Spain in 1820. The abolition of slavery itself occurred in 1833 in British Colonies, 1848 in French Colonies, 1863 in Dutch Colonies. In Puerto Rico it lasted until 1873 and in Cuba until 1880.

Chapter 2: Theories of urbanization and dependence

1 In fact Boeke is far from consistent in his application of the dualism thesis. At times he actually refers to the relationships of dependence that exist between urban and rural sectors.
2 The 'Frankian' model is itself hardly static. In addition to new works by the author himself, there have been a number of recent critiques and developments. See in particular the perceptive comments of David Booth and the essay by O'Brien, both in Oxaal, et al. (1975).

Chapter 3: The economic order

1 The Caribbean Common Market is the latest stage in regional economic integration. It emerged out of the Caribbean Free Trade Association (CARIFTA) which was an agreement initiated on 1 May 1968. Other Com-

monwealth Caribbean territories acceded to the original agreement and by May 1971 the members consisted of Barbados, Antigua, Guyana, Trinidad and Tobago, Jamaica, Montserrat, Dominica, Grenada, St Kitts–Nevis–Anguilla, St Lucia, St Vincent and Belize (British Honduras). In January of the previous year the Caribbean Development Bank was formally established to provide a central banking facility for CARIFTA. All except Antigua and Montserrat signed an agreement known as the 'Georgetown accord' in April 1973 to press ahead with economic integration. On 4 July 1973 the Caribbean Common Market (CARICOM) was formerly established by the Chaguaramus Treaty, signed by the four major Commonwealth Caribbean countries – Barbados, Trinidad and Tobago, Guyana and Jamaica. These four, sometimes known as the More Developed Countries (MDCs) were joined the following year by the eight Less Developed Countries (LDCs) (Antigua, Belize, Dominica, Grenada, Montserrat, St Kitts–Nevis–Anguilla, St Lucia and St Vincent). The Secretariat of CARICOM is located in Georgetown, Guyana and the Caribbean Development Bank (CDB) is sited in Bridgetown, Barbados.

2 The case of Booker McConnell Ltd is a fascinating instance of a multinational company founded on West Indian sugar estate interests. The parent company, whose Guyana holdings have now been nationalized, diversified its activities in a number of different directions. Its original operations in Guyana had been vertically integrated to include a sugar engineering firm (Demerara Foundry Co.), a bulk carrier cargo line shipping sugar to the UK (Booker Line), a ship services, stevedoring and wharfowning firm (Bookers Shipping), sugar storage facilities (Demerara Sugar Terminals) and insurance services (Guyana Insurance Agencies). Second, diversification had occurred into other Guyanese operations based either on agriculture, manufacturing or services. Firms included East Coast Estates and the Kabawar Cattle Ranch Company, specializing in dairy farming and cattle ranching, Guyana Industrial Holdings which operated sixteen shrimp trawlers out of Georgetown, Guyana Distilleries which processed rum, gin and other alcoholic beverages, Guyana Lithographic Company which provided printing and packaging services and Guyana Stockfeeds in which there was a minority stake. Other Guyanese interests were in Bookers Stores and the Carib Drug Company which specialized in retailing, agricultural equipment and the manufacturing and marketing of pharmaceuticals and toiletry products.

The third area of diversification was into other overseas markets. In 1975 capital employed in Guyana was £32,000,000 but other Caribbean holdings employed a further £6,000,000. These included the major department store in Trinidad and St Lucia and a wholesaling and agency services firm in Barbados as well as Estate Industries in Jamaica producing the liqueur Tia Maria. Other overseas diversification was into Kenya, Nigeria, Malawi and Zambia with mainly minority holdings in sugar estates, pharmaceuticals, retailing and agency services.

The fourth strategy entailed an extension of investment in the UK where 55 per cent of investment capital was employed in 1975. These operations include a wide range of investments involving food distribution (53 per cent of UK turnover in 1975) and engineering (21 per cent of UK turnover). A small but interesting part of turnover now comes from Artist's Services, one of the eight divisions of the parent company which controls thirteen subsidiaries specializing in copyrights and artist's services. These include the works of Ian Fleming,

Agatha Christie, Georgette Heyer and Denis Wheatley and the services of Harold Pinter, Vivien Merchant and Hayley Mills.

The apparently changing relationship between companies such as this and the nationalist governments of underdeveloped societies may be gauged by the announcement from the Guyanese government on 14 February 1976 that it intended taking over all Booker, McConnell interests in that country from 26 May 1976, the tenth anniversary of independence. The 1975 Annual Report of the Company records that the Guyana subsidiaries were valued at £32m in that year, of which £19m was covered by parent company equity. The settlement reached on 26 May provided approximately £10m with only £1.8m in cash (none of which will actually leave Guyana since it will be absorbed as liabilities to be met from subsidiaries). The balance is due as Guyana Government promissory notes payable in instalments over twenty years at an annual interest of 6 per cent.

3 The Gini coefficient measures the ratio of the measured distribution of incomes to a perfect distribution. It ranges from 0 to 1, the higher figure indicating perfect *inequality*. It should be noted that Ahiram's data have been criticized. See Cumper, 1974: 478.

4 Although other factors, such as the ethnic divide between Indians, who predominate in the country areas, and Africans may increase the difference, the point is that Trinidad is a society where all are subject to powerful urban influences of a materialist culture.

5 The sources for these figures are the *Trinidad and Tobago Census Bulletin No. 20, (1965); Trinidad and Tobago Continuous Sample Survey of Population No. 6* (IN 1–1), 1966; *Trinidad and Tobago Manpower Income Report,* Vol. 1 No. 2, 1973.

6 The data for this and the following paragraphs are taken from *Trinidad and Tobago Continuous Sample Survey of Population* Labour force Series Publications Nos. 9, 1967; 13, 1968; 15, 1970; 24, 1974; 25, 1974.

Chapter 4: Population structure and change

1 'Urban' is defined as the parishes of Kingston and St Andrew; 'Semi-Urban' as St Thomas, Portland, Clarendon and St Catherine, while 'Rural' comprises the remaining eight parishes.

2 It is quite striking that the unrestricted migration to France and the Netherlands has not produced an enormous exodus from the French and Dutch West Indies. Approximately 60 per cent of the movement from the French territories to the metropolitan country is supported by an official agency, known by its initials as BUMIDOM (*Bureau pour le Développement des Migrations Interessant les Départements d'Outre-Mer*) founded in 1963, but this organization has a controlling interest rather than a facilitating role.

Chapter 5: Social structure and social organization

1 For an excellent review see R. T. Smith, (1963). M. G. Smith also surveys the relevant literature although his review suffers from a rather biased assessment of views that differ from his own. The compilation of Mintz and Davenport (1961) contains some particularly valuable papers.

2 In fact for a small minority these ages may refer to a three point progression.

3 It should be noted that fertility *does* vary with the type of union, being lower in

common-law unions than in legal marriage, and lower still in visiting relationships. For example, Sinclair reports that the child:mother ratio in Jamaica
in 1970, for women who had reached the end of childbearing (45–54), was
5.475 for married women, 5.154 for those in common law unions and 3.442 for
women in visiting relationships. These ratios show a change of −5.7, +6.4 and
−17.4 per cent respectively in the intercensal decade (Sinclair, 1974b: 163).

4 It has been estimated that Cuba in the mid 1970s has an accumulated shortfall
of adequate houses of 1,200,000 units. To overcome this in thirty years and
allow for increased demand through population growth would require an
annual output of 119,000 units, whereas annual output in recent years has been
only about a quarter of this figure (Acosta and Hardoy, 1973: 51).

5 Although this generalization is far from universally true. For example, Marks
reports from Curaçao that membership of religious associations was very low
indeed in his sample and church attendance was strongly correlated with age
(see Marks, 1976: 210–11).

6 Caution must be exercised in interpreting these data which are necessarily
highly dependent on the definition employed for the primate city. Thus in Table
5.4 a narrow definition of Port of Spain has been employed (following the
Census). The religious distribution would look different if St George was
included in the primate city region because of concentrations of East Indians in
the wards of Tacarigua, Arima and St Ann's.

7 The word 'Maroon' is thought to derive from the Spanish *cimarrones* or 'wild
ones'.

8 See, for example, the statement by Samuel Elisha Brown in which he says: 'We
the Rastafarians who are the true prophets of this age, the reincarnated
Moseses, Joshuas, Isaiahs, Jeremiahs who are the battle axes and weapons of
war; we are those who are destined to free not only the scattered Ethiopians but
all people, animals, herbs and all life forms' (Brown, 1966: 3).

Chapter 6: Race, class and education

1 The handful of East Indians in Barbados are an exception, being largely located
in the wholesale and retail trades.

2 This is despite the fact that they are themselves divided in important and often
subtle ways into the *Grands Békés, Békés Moyens* and *Petits Békés*.

3 It is possible to isolate a large number of positions in this debate but they would
include the extreme idealist positions of Gilberto Freyre (1946), the more
subtle idealism of Frank Tannenbaum (1947) and Stanley Elkins (1959), the
rather simple materialism of Marvin Harris (1964) and the more sophisticated
and complex historical materialism of Eugene Genovese (1965; 1966).

4 For example, the Dominican Republic spends 13.9 per cent of public expenditure and comparative figures for Jamaica, Trinidad and Guyana are 17.2 per
cent, 12.2 per cent and 13.5 per cent respectively (*Unesco yearbook, 1975*:
Table 6.1).

Chapter 7: Politics and policies

1 However, even as early as 1803, Dessaline had made it clear that land ownership by whites would be restricted and this regulation was contained in the
Republican Constitution of 1806 (Nicholls, 1974; 45).

2 In 1972 Cuba renegotiated repayment agreements with the USSR postponing

repayments until 1986 and spreading loans over twenty-five years. The total debt may exceed US $5,000m.
3 The Cuban economic plan for 1976–80 allocates US $2024.5m to health and education. This provides for 400 additional semi-boarding schools and 1,000 secondary schools, 49 hospitals, 110 health centres and 51 old peoples homes.
4 For example, cigarettes on ration cost 20 centavos (US $0.27) for twenty but off ration they are 1.70 pesos (US $2.30). Petrol is rationed at 60 centavos (US $0.8) a gallon but costs 2 pesos (US $2.70) on the free market.
5 Although Prime Minister Burnham has proposed a new capital city for Guyana at the Mathews Ridge – Arakaka–Kaituma Complex in the North West District this has to do with the claim by Venezuela for that mineral rich area, and has nothing to do with the expansion of Georgetown.

References

Acosta, M. and Hardoy, J. E. 1973 *Urban Reform in Revolutionary Cuba.* Occasional Papers No.1 (New Haven, Yale University).

Adams, N. A. 1969 'Internal Migration in Jamaica: An Economic Analysis'. *Social and Economic Studies.* **18**: 137–51.

Ahiram, E. 1965 'Income Distribution in Jamaica and Trinidad–Tobago' in Andic, F. M., and Mathews, T. E. (eds.) *Caribbean in Transition* (Institute of Caribbean Studies; Rio Piedras): 1–11.

1966 'Distribution of Income in Trinidad and Tobago and Comparison with Distribution of Income in Jamaica'. *Social and Economic Studies.* **15**: 103–20.

Andic, F. 1964 *Distribution of Family Incomes in Puerto Rico* (Rio Piedras, University of Puerto Rico).

Balandier, G. 1970 *The Sociology of Black Africa* (London, Andre Deutsch).

Balogh, T. 1966 *The Economics of Poverty* (London, Weidenfeld and Nicholson).

Barbados 1973 *Development Plan, 1973–77* (Bridgeton, Government Printer).

Barrett, L. E. 1968 *Rastafarians: A Study in Messianic Cultism in Jamaica* (Rio Piedras, University of Puerto Rico).

Beckford, G. L. 1969 'The Economics of Agriculture Resource Use and Development in Plantation Economies' in Bernstein, H. (ed.) *Underdevelopment and Development* (Harmondsworth, Penguin, 1973): 115–51.

1972 *Persistent Poverty* (New York, OUP).

1975 'Caribbean Rural Economy' in Beckford, G. (ed.) *Caribbean Economy* (Mona, ISER): 77–91.

Best, L. 1968 'Outlines of a Model of Pure Plantation Economy'. *Social and Economic Studies* **17** (3).

Blake, J. 1961 *Family Structure in Jamaica* (New York, Free Press).

Blakemore, H. 1975 'Limitations of Dependency: An Historian's View and Case Study'. *Buletin de Estudios Latinamericanos y del Caribe.* **18**: 74–87.

Boeke, J. H. 1953 *Economics and Economic Policy of Dual Societies* (New York, Institute of Pacific Relations).

Boland, B. 1974 'Labour Force' in Roberts, G. (ed.) *Recent Population Movements in Jamaica.* (Jamaica, CICRED).

Booth, D. 1975 'Andre Gunder Frank: An Introduction and Appreciation' in Oxaal, I. et al (eds.) *Beyond the Sociology of Development* (London, Routledge and Kegan Paul): 50–85.

1976 'Cuba, Colour and the Revolution'. *Science and Society.* **40** (2): 129–72.

Bowles, S. 1976 'Cuban Education and the Revolutionary Ideology' in Figueroa, P. M. E. and Persaud, G. (eds.) *Sociology of Education: A Caribbean Reader.* (London; Oxford University Press): 67–89.

Braithwaite, L. 1953 'Social Stratification in Trinidad'. *Social and Economic Studies.* **2** (2–3): 5–175.

1968 'Social and Political Aspects of Rural Development in the West Indies'. *Social and Economic Studies.* **17** (3).

Brewster, H. 1973 'Economic Dependence: A Quantitative Interpretation'. *Social and Economic Studies.* **22** (1).

Brown, S. E. 1966 'Statement of a Ras Tafari Leader' (Rio Piedras, University of Puerto Rico).

Buschkens, W. F. L. 1974 *The Family System of the Paramaribo Creoles* ('S-Gravenhage, Martinus Nijhoff).

Byrne, J. 1972 *Levels of Fertility in the Commonwealth Caribbean* (Jamaica, ISER).

Camejo, A. 1971 'Racial Discrimination in Employment in the Private Sector in Trinidad and Tobago'. *Social and Economic Studies.* **20** (3): 294–381.

Caplow, T. et. al. 1964 *The Urban Ambience: A Study of San Juan, Puerto Rico* (Totowa, NJ, Bedminster Press).

Carnoy, M. 1970 'The Quality of Education, Examination Performance and Urban–Rural Income Differences in Puerto Rico'. *Comparative Education Review.* **14** (3): 335–49.

Carrington, E. 1971a 'The Post War Political Economy of Trinidad and Tobago', in Norman Girvan and Owen Jefferson (eds.) *Readings in the Political Economy of the Caribbean* (Jamaica: New World Group): 121–42.

   1971b 'Industrialization in Trinidad and Tobago since 1950', in Norman Girvan and Owen Jefferson (eds.) *Readings in the Political Economy of the Caribbean* (Jamaica, New World Group): 143–50.

Castro, F. 1968 *Major Speeches,* (London, Stage 1).

CHISS, 1971 *Le Processes à Urbanization à Port au Prince* (Port au Prince, Les Cahiers au Centre Haitien d'Investigation en Sciences Sociales).

Clarke, C. G. 1971 'Population Problems in the Caribbean'. *Revista Geographica.* **75**: 31–48.

   1974 'Urbanization in the Caribbean'. *Geography.* **59** (264): 223–32.

   1975 *Kingston, Jamaica: Urban Development and Social Change 1692–1962* (Berkeley, University of California Press).

Clarke, E. 1966 *My Mother who Fathered Me* (London, George Allen and Unwin).

Comitas, L. and Lowenthal, D. (eds.) 1973 *Work and Family Life: West Indian* 1973 *Slaves, Free Men, Citizens: West Indian Perspectives* (New York, Doubleday).

Commonwealth Caribbean 1970 *1970 Population Census of the Commonwealth Caribbean* (University of the West Indies, Census Research Programme).

Commonwealth Secretariat 1970 *Youth and Development in the Caribbean* (London, Commonwealth Secretariat).

Cross, M. 1971 'On Conflict, Race Relations and the Theory of the Plural Society'. *Race.* **12**: 477–94.

   1973a 'Education and Job Opportunities' in Moss, R. (ed.) *The Stability of the Caribbean* (London, Institute for the Study of Conflict): 51–76.

   1973b 'Black Nationalism and Anti-Colonialism' in Benewick, R. et al. (eds.) *Knowledge and belief in Politics: The Problem of Ideology* (London, Allen and Unwin): 299–319.

   1977 'Problems and Prospects for Caribbean Social Research'. *Boletín de Estudios Latinamericanos y del Caribe.* Número 22: 92–111.

Cross, M. and Schwartzbaum, A. 1969 'Social Mobility and Secondary School Selection in Trinidad and Tobago'. *Social and Economic Studies.* **18** (2): 189–207.

Cumper, G. E. 1974 'Dependence, Development and the Sociology of Economic Thought'. *Social and Economic Studies*. **23** (3): 465–82.

Curtin, P. D. (ed.) 1971 *Imperialism: Selected Documents* (London, Macmillan).

Davis, K. 1969 *World Urbanization, 1950–1970*. Vol. 1 – *Basic Data for Cities, Countries and Population*. Monograph No. 4 (Berkeley, University of California).

　1972 *World Urbanization, 1950–1970*. Vol. 2 – *Analysis of Trends, Relationships and Development*. Population Monograph No. 9 (Berkeley, University of California).

Dew, E. 1976 'Anti-consociationalism and Independence in Surinam'. *Boletín de Estudios Latinamericanos y del Caribe.***21**: 3–15.

Dewey, R. 1960 'The Rural–Urban Continuum: Real but Relatively Unimportant'. *American Journal of Sociology*. **66**: 60–6.

Díaz, S. N. 1973 'La Economia Puertorrequeña: La Operation Manos a La Obra y Sus Consecuencias'. *Caribbean Monthly Bulletin*. **7** (5): 6–11.

Dominican Republic 1970 *Republica Dominica en Cifros 1970* (Santo Domingo, Oficina Nacional De Estadistica).

Dore, R 1976 *The Diploma Disease: Education, Qualifications and Development* (London, George Allen and Unwin).

Durkheim, E. 1964 *The Divisions of Labour in Society* (New York, The Free Press).

Ebanks, G. E. 1968 'Differential internal Migration in Jamaica, 1943–1960'. *Social and Economic Studies*. **17** (2): 197–214.

　1975 'Barbados' and 'Jamaica' in A. Segal *Population Policies in the Caribbean* (Lexington, Mass., D. C. Heath): 25–72.

Elkins, S. 1959 *Slavery: A Problem in American Institutional and Intellectual Life* (Chicago, University of Chicago Press).

Eyre, L. A. 1972 *Geographical Aspects of Population Dynamics in Jamaica* (Boca Ratan, Florida Atlantic University Press).

Fanon, F. 1967 *The Wretched of the Earth* (London, Penguin).

Foner, N. 1973 *Status and Power in Rural Jamaica* (New York and London, Teachers College Press).

Francis, O. C. 1965 'Characteristics of Emigrants just Prior to Changes in British Commonwealth Immigration Policies' in Andic, F. M. and Mathews, T. G. *The Caribbean in Transition* (Rio Piedras, University of Puerto Rico): 91–121.

Frank, A. G. 1969 *Latin America: Underdevelopment or Revolution* (New York and London, Monthly Review).

Frazier, F. 1939 *The Negro Family in the United States* (Chicago, University of Chicago Press).

Freilich, M. and Coser, L. A. 1972 'Structured Inbalances of Gratification: The Case of the Caribbean Mating System'. *British Journal of Sociology* 23 (1) : 1–19

Freyre, G. 1946 *The Masters and the Slaves: A Study in the Development of Brazilian Civilization* (New York, Knopf).

Frucht, R. 1967 'A Caribbean Social Type: Neither "Peasant" Nor "Proletarian"'. *Social and Economic Studies*. **16** (3): 295–300.

Furnivall, J. S. 1948 *Colonial Policy and Practice* (London, Cambridge University Press).

Genovese, E. 1965 'Materialism and Idealism in the History of Negro Slavery in the Americas' in Foner, L. and Genovese, E. (eds.) *Slavery in the New World* (Englewood Cliffs, N. J. Prentice Hall): 238–55.

1966 *The Political Economy of Slavery* (London, MacGibbons and Kee).

Gillette, A. 1972 *Cuba's Educational Revolution.* Fabian Research Series 302 (London, Fabian Society).

Girvan, N. 1975 'Caribbean Mineral Economy' in Beckford, G. (ed.) *Caribbean Economy* (Mona, Jamaica, ISER): 92–129.

Girvan, N. and Jefferson, O. 1971 *Readings in the Political Economy of the Caribbean* (Kingston, New World).

González, A. 1971 'The Macroeconomies of Puerto Rican Development' in Mathews, T. E. and Andic, F. M. *Politics and Economics in the Caribbean* (Rio Piedras, Institute of Caribbean Studies): 89–102.

González, N. L. S. 1970 'Towards a Definition of Matrifocality', in Whitten, N. E. and Szwed, J. F. (eds.) *Afro-African Anthropology: Contemporary Perspectives* (New York; Free Press).

Gordon, S. C. 1963 *A Century of West Indian Education* (London, Longman).

Greenfield, S. 1966 *English Rustics in Black Skin: A Study of Modern Family Forms in Pre-Industrialized Society* (New Haven, College and University Publishers).

Guyana 1973 *Economic Survey of Guyana* (Georgetown, Ministry of Economic Development).

Hanley, E. 1975 'Rice, Politics and Development in Guyana' in Oxaal, I. et al. (eds.) *Beyond the Sociology of Development* (London, Routledge and Kegan Paul): 131–53.

1976 'All ah we is Hustlin', unpublished paper.

Harewood, J. 1971 'Racial Discrimination in Employment in Trinidad and Tobago'. *Social and Economic Studies.* **20** (3): 267–93.

1972 'Changes in the Demand for and the Supply of Labour in the Commonwealth Caribbean'. *Social and Economic Studies.* **21** (1): 44–59.

1975 *The Population of Trinidad and Tobago* (St Augustine, CICRED).

Harris, M. 1964 *Patterns of Race in the Americas* (New York, Walker and Co.).

Harrod, J. 1972 *Trade Union Foreign Policy: A Study of British and American Trade Union Activities in Jamaica* (New York, Anchor Books).

Henfrey, C. 1972 'Foreign Influence in Guyana: The Struggle for Independence' in de Kadt, E. (ed.) *Patterns of Foreign Influence in the Caribbean* (London, OUP): 49–81.

Hewitt, L. 1974 'Internal Migration and Urban Growth' in Roberts, G. W. (ed.) *Recent Population Movements in Jamaica* (Mona, CICRED): 24–55.

Hoetink, H. 1967 *Two Variants in Caribbean Race Relations* (London, OUP).

Hogg, D. 1960 *The Convince Cult in Jamaica.* Yale University Publications in Anthropology No. 58 (New Haven, Yale University).

Horowitz, M. M. 1967 *Morne Paysan: Peasant Village in Martinique* (New York: Holt, Rinehart and Winston).

Horvath, R. J. 1972 'A Definition of Colonialism'. *Current Anthropology.* **13** (1): 45–57.

Hoselitz, B. 1960 *Sociological Aspects of Economic Growth* (New York, The Free Press).

Illich, I. 1973 *Celebration of Awareness: A Case for Institutional Revolution* (London, Penguin).

James, C. L. R. 1973 'The Middle Classes' in Lowenthal, D. and Comitas, L.

(eds.) *Consequences of Class and Colour: West Indian Perspectives* (New York, Doubleday): 79–92.

Jones, W.O. 1968 'Plantations'. *International Encyclopaedia of the Social Sciences* (New York, Macmillan). **12**: 154.

Kahl, J. A. 1968 *The Measurement of Modernism: A Study of Values in Brazil and Mexico* (Austin and London, University of Texas Press).

King, A. et al. 1971 *One Love* (London, Bogle-L'Ouverture Publications).

Kovats–Beaudoux, E. 1973 'A Dominant Minority: The White Creoles of Martinique' in Comitas, L. and Lowenthal, D. (eds.) *Slaves, Free Men, Citizens* (New York, Doubleday): 241–75.

Kuper, A. 1976 *Changing Jamaica* (London, Routledge and Kegan Paul).

Landstreet, B. 1975 'Cuba' in Segal, A. *Population Policies in the Caribbean* (Lexington, Mass., D. C. Heath and Co.): 127–58.

La Ruffa, A. L. 1969 'Culture Change and Pentecostalism in Puerto Rico'. *Social and Economic Studies*. **18** (3): 273–81.

Leigh Fermor, P. 1950 *The Traveller's Tree: A Journey Through the Caribbean Islands* (London, John Murray).

Leiris, M. 1955 *Contacts de Civilisations en Martinique et Guadeloupe* (Paris, UNESCO/Gallimard).

Levitt, K. & Best, L. 1975 'Character of Caribbean Economy' in Beckford, E. (ed.) *Caribbean Economy* (Jamaica, Institute of Social and Economic Research): 34–60.

Levitt, K. & McIntyre, A. 1967 *Canada–West Indies Economic Relations* (Montreal, McGill University).

Lewis, G. K. 1963 *Puerto Rico: Freedom and Power in the Caribbean* (New York, Monthly Review).

1968 *The Growth of the Modern West Indies* (London, McGibbon and Kee).

1974a 'On the Dangers of Composing a West Indian Anthology'. *Caribbean Studies*. **14**(1).

1974b *Notes on the Puerto Rican Revolution* (New York and London, Monthly Review Press).

Lewis, W. A. 1961 'Education and Economic Development'. *Social and Economic Studies*. **10**(2).

Lipton, M. 1977 *Why Poor People Stay Poor: A Study of Urban Bias in World Development* (London, Temple Smith).

Little, K. 1965 *West African Urbanization: A Study of Voluntary Associations in Social Change* (Cambridge University Press).

Llewellyn Watson, G. 1973 'Social Structure and Social Movements: the Black Muslims in the USA and the Rastafarians in Jamaica'. *British Journal of Sociology*. **24**(2): 188–204.

Logan, R. W. 1968 *Haiti and the Dominican Republic* (London, OUP).

Lojkine, J. 1976 'Contributions to a Marxist Theory of Capitalist Urbanization' in Pickvance, C. G. (ed.) *Urban Sociology: Critical Essays* (London, Tavistock): 119–46.

Loomis, C. P. & McKinney, J. C. 1963 'Introduction' in Toennies, F. *Community and Society* (New York, Harper and Row).

Lowenthal, D. 1957 'The Population of Barbados'. *Social and Economic Studies*. **6**(4): 445–501.

1960 'The Range and Variation of Caribbean Societies' in Rubin, V. (ed.) *Social and Cultural Pluralism in the Caribbean, Annals*, **83** (art 5): 786–95.

1968 'Race and Colour in the West Indies' in Franklin, J. H. (ed.) *Color and Race* (Boston, Houghton Mifflin): 302–48.

1972 *West Indian Societies* (London, Oxford University Press for the Institute of Race Relations).

Lowenthal, D. & Comitas, L. 1973 *Consequences of Class and Colour: West Indian Perspectives* (New York, Doubleday).

1973 *The Aftermath of Sovereignty: West Indian Perspectives* (New York, Doubleday).

MacGaffey, W. & Barnett, C. R. 1965 *Twentieth-Century Cuba* (New York, Anchor Books).

McGee, T. G. 1971 *The Urbanisation Process in the Third World* (London, G. Bell and Sons).

McKinney, J. C. 1966 *Constructive Typology and Social Theory* (New York, Appleton-Century-Crofts).

McNulty, M. L. 1976 'West African Urbanization' in Berry, B. J. L. (ed.) *Urbanization and Counterurbanization* (California, Sage): 213–32.

Mandle, J. R. 1972 'The Plantation Economy: An Essay in Definition'. *Science and Society.* **36**: 49–62.

1973 *The Recent Decline in Fertility in Trinidad and Tobago* (Preliminary Paper No. 5: International Population and Urban Research, University of California).

Marino, A. 1970 'Family, Fertility and Sex Ratios in the British Caribbean'. *Population Studies.* **24**(2): 159–72.

Marks, A. F. 1976 *Male and Female and the Afro-Curaçaon Household* (The Hague, Martinus Nijhoff).

Marx, K. 1973 *Grundrisse: Foundations of the Critique of Political Economy* (London, Penguin).

Maunder, W. F. 1960 *Employment in an Underdeveloped Area: A Sample Survey of Kingston* (New Haven, Yale University Press).

Mintz, S. W. 1959 'The Plantation as a Socio-cultural Type' in Pan American Union, *Plantation Systems of the New World* (Washington, DC): 42–54.

1974 *Caribbean Transformations* (Chicago: Aldine).

Mintz, S. W. & Davenport, W. (eds.) 1961 *Caribbean Social Organisation, Social and Economic Studies* (special issue). **10**(4): 380–535.

Nettleford, R. 1970 *Mirror, Mirror: Identity, Race and Protest in Jamaica* (Jamaica, Collins and Sangster).

Nicholls, D. 1970 'Politics and Religion in Haiti'. *Canadian Journal of Political Science.* **3**(3): 400–14.

1971 'Embryo-Politics in Haiti'. *Government and Opposition.* **6**(1): 76–85.

1974 *Economic Dependence and Political Autonomy.* Occasional Paper Series No. 9 (Montreal, Centre for Developing Area Studies, McGill).

Nortman, D. 1975 *Population and Family Planning Programs: A Factbook.* Reports on Population/Family Planning No. 2.

Olivier, S. 1929 *White Capital and Coloured Labour* (London, Hogarth Press).

Ortiz Ména, A. 1976 'Address by the President of the Inter-American Development Bank at the Inaugural Session of the Seventeenth Meeting of the Board of Governors', 17 May 1976 (Washington, IDB).

Oxaal, I. et al. (eds.) 1975 *Beyond the Sociology of Development* (London, Routledge and Kegan Paul).

Pahl, R. E. 1965 *Urbs in Rure: The Metropolitan Fringe in Hertfordshire* (London

School of Economics, Geographical Papers No. 2).
1975 *Whose City?* (London, Penguin).
Pan American Union 1959 *Plantation Systems of the New World* (Washington, DC).
Peach, C. 1968 *West Indian Migration to Britain* (London, Oxford University Press).
Peréz, L. A. 1973–74 'Aspects of Underdevelopment: Tourism in the West Indies'. *Science and Society.* 37(4): 473–81.
Puerto Rico 1970 *1970 Census of Population* (US Department of Commerce, Bureau of the Census).
Redfield, R. 1947 'The Folk Society'. *The American Journal of Sociology.* 52(4): 293–308.
Ribeiro, D. 1970 'The Culture-historical Configurations of the American Peoples'. *Current Anthropology.* 11: 403–34.
Roberts, G. W. 1968 'Demographic Aspects of Rural Development'. *Social and Economic Studies.* 17(3): 276–82.
Roberts, G. & Sinclair, S. A. 1977 *Family and Reproduction in Jamaica* (unpublished ms.).
Rodman, H. 1971 *Lower Class Families: The culture of Poverty in Negro Trinidad* (New York, OUP).
Rodriguez, J. 1965 'El Caribe en Cifras' in Andic, F. M. and Matthews, T. G. (eds.) *The Caribbean in Transition* (Rio Piedras, Institute of Caribbean Studies): 326–45.
Ryan, S. D. 1972 *Race and Nationalism in Trinidad and Tobago: A Study of Decolonization in a Multiracial Society* (Toronto, University of Toronto Press).
Safa, H. I. 1974 *The Urban Poor of Puerto Rico* (New York, Holt, Rinehart and Winston).
Sardinha, D. 1976 *The Poetry of Nicolás Guillén: an Introduction* (London, New Beacon Books).
Schlesinger, B. 1962 'Family Patterns in Jamaica: Review and Commentary'. *Journal of Marriage and the Family.* 30(1): 137–48.
Seers, D. 1969 'A Step towards a Political Economy of Development'. *Social and Economic Studies.* 18(3): 218–53.
Segal, A. (ed.) 1975 *Population Policies in the Caribbean* (Lexington, Mass., D. C. Heath and Co.).
Segal, A. & Earnhardt, K. C. 1969 *Politics and Population in the Caribbean* (Rio Piedras, University of Puerto Rico), Special Study No. 7.
Simpson, G. E. 1955 'Political Cultism in West Kingston, Jamaica'. *Social and Economic Studies.* 4(2): 133–49.
1970 *Religious Cults of the Caribbean: Trinidad, Jamaica, Haiti* (Rio Piedras: Institute of Caribbean Studies).
Simpson, J. 1973 *Internal Migration in Trinidad and Tobago* (Mona, Jamaica, ISER).
Sinclair, S. A. 1974a 'A fertility analysis of Jamaica: Recent Trends with Reference to the Parish of St. Ann'. *Social and Economic Studies.* 23(4): 588–636.
1974b 'Fertility' in Roberts, G. W. (ed.) *Recent Population Movements in Jamaica* (Mona, CICRED): 124–68.
Sinclair, S. & Boland, B. 1974 'Characteristics of the Population' in Roberts, G. (ed.) *Recent Population Movements in the Caribbean* (Jamaica, CICRED): 11–23.

Smith, M. G. 1962 *West Indian Family Structure* (Seattle, University of Washington Press).
  1965 *The Plural Society in the British West Indies* (California, University of California Press).
  1966 'Introduction' to Clarke, E. *My Mother who Fathered Me* (London, Allen and Unwin): i–xliv.
  1974 *Corporations & Society* (London, Duckworth).
Smith, R. T. 1956 *The Negro Family in British Guiana* (London, Routledge and Kegan Paul).
  1957 'Economic Aspects of Rice Production in an East Indian Community'. *Social and Economic Studies.* **6**(4): 502–22.
  1963 'Culture and Social Structure in the Caribbean: Some Recent work on Family and Kinship Studies'. *Comparative Studies in Society and History.* **6**(1): 24–46.
  1970 'Social Stratification in the Caribbean' in Plotnicov and Tudin (eds.) *Comparative Social Stratification* (Pittsburgh, Pittsburgh University Press): 43–76.
Soja, E. W. and Weaver, C. E. 1976 'Urbanization and Underdevelopment in East Africa', in Berry, B. J. L. (ed.) *Urbanization and Counterurbanization* (California, Sage): 233–66.
Solien, N. L. 1960 'Household and Family in the Caribbean'. *Social and Economic Studies.* **9**(1): 101–6.
Stone, C. 1973 *Class, Race and Political Behaviour in Urban Jamaica* (Mona, Jamaica, ISER).
Stycos, J. M. & Back, K. W. 1964 *The Control of Human Fertility in Jamaica* (Ithaca, NY, Cornell University Press).
Talbot, N. 1974–75 'A Note on Tourism in the West Indies'. *Science and Society.* **38**: 347–9.
Tannenbaum, F. 1947 *Slave and Citizens: The Negro in the Americas* (New York, Knopf).
Thomas, H. 1971 *Cuba or The Pursuit of Freedom* (London, Eyre and Spottiswoode).
Thompson, E. T. 1959 'The Plantations as a Social System'. Pan American Union, *Plantation Systems of the New World* (Washington, DC): 26–41.
Tilly, C. 1967 'The State of Urbanization'. *Comparative Studies in Society and History.* **10**(1): 100–13.
Trinidad and Tobago 1972 *Manpower Report. Vol. 1., No. 1* (Port of Spain, Central Statistical Office).
  1974a *Household Budgetary Survey*, HBS 1–2 (Port of Spain, Central Statistical Office).
  1974b *Estimated Internal Migration* Bulletin 1 (Central Statistical Office, CSSP Round 16).
  1974c *Manpower Income Report* (Industry). Vol. 1., No. 4 (Port of Spain, Central Statistical Office).
United Nations 1974 *Carifta/Caricom Countries: Overview of Economic Activities 1973* (Port of Spain, Economic Commission for Latin America).
Valdés, N. P. 1971 'Health and Revolution in Cuba'. *Science and Society.* **35**: 311–35.
Wagley, C. 1960 'Plantation America: A Cultural Sphere' in Rubin, V. (ed.) *Caribbean Studies: A Symposium* (Seattle, University of Washington Press): 3–13.
Walton, J. 1975 'Internal Colonialism: Problems of Definition and Measurement'

in Cornelius and Trueblood (eds.) *Latin American Urban Research*. Vol. 5 – *Urbanization and Inequality* (California, Sage): 29–50.

Weber, M. 1958 *The City* (Glencoe, Ill., The Free Press).

West India Royal Commission 1945 *Report*. Cmd 6607 (London, HMSO).

Williams, E. 1951 *Education in the British West Indies* (Port of Spain, Teachers' Economic and Cultural Association).

1964a *Capitalism and Slavery* (London, André Deutsch).

1964b *History of the People of Trinidad and Tobago* (London, André Deutsch).

1970 *From Columbus to Castro: The History of the Caribbean 1492–1969* (London: André Deutsch).

Wilson, P. J. 1973 *Crab Antics* (New Haven, Yale University Press).

Wirth, L. 1938 'Urbanism as a Way of Life'. *American Journal of Sociology*. **44**(1): 1–24.

Wolf, E. R. and Mintz, S. W. 1957 'Haciendas and Plantations in Middle America and the Antilles'. *Social and Economic Studies*. **6**(3): 380–412.

Wood, D. 1968 *Trinidad in Transition: The Years After Slavery* (London, OUP).

World Bank 1975 *World Bank Atlas* (Washington, World Bank).

Index